i told my soul to sing

i told my soul to sing

finding God with
EMILY DICKINSON

KRISTIN LeMAY

PARACLETE PRESS
BREWSTER, MASSACHUSETTS

2013 First Printing

I Told My Soul to Sing: Finding God with Emily Dickinson

Copyright © 2013 by Kristin LeMay

ISBN 978-1-61261-163-1

Scripture quotations are taken from the King James Version of the Bible.

Library of Congress Cataloging-in-Publication Data

LeMay, Kristin.
  I told my soul to sing : finding God with Emily Dickinson / Kristin
LeMay.
      p. cm.
  ISBN 978-1-61261-163-1 (pb french flaps)
  1. Dickinson, Emily, 1830-1886—Criticism and interpretation. 2.
Dickinson, Emily, 1830-1886—Religion. 3. God in literature. 4. Belief
and doubt in literature. I. Title.
  PS1541.Z5L3765 2012
  811'.4—dc23   2012024523

10 9 8 7 6 5 4 3 2 1

Published by Paraclete Press
Brewster, Massachusetts
www.paracletepress.com
Printed in the United States of America

Prove it me
That He — loved Men —
As I — love thee —

CONTENTS

Let Emily sing for you
because she cannot pray . . .

—Emily Dickinson to
Louisa and Frances Norcross, 1863

EMILY DICKINSON was a rebel in matters of religion. She gleefully would have added "infidel," "gypsy," and "rogue." She bragged that she was "one of the lingering *bad* ones," often "surly – and muggy – and cross," "quite vain," "*wicked*," occasionally "a Pagan," "one of those brands almost consumed," and long since "past 'Correction in Righteousness.'" Evidently, she also possessed a sly taste for self-deprecation and irony. On loftier days she'd go so far as to name herself "Eve, alias Mrs. Adam," "Simon Peter," even "Barabbas."

Now, you've probably seen that famous picture of Emily Dickinson that stares out from the cover of nearly every book relating to her, including this one: Emily the waif, slim and pale, looking about as bold as a limp piece of lace. Forget that sepia color scheme. She was a redhead. Forget too whatever rumors you might have heard about her broken heart, her melancholy, her obsession with death. While we're at it, please purge from your memory those polite lines of her poetry that get reprinted on magnets and coffee mugs, foremost among them: "I'm Nobody! Who are you?" and "If I can stop one Heart from breaking / I shall not live in vain," as well as "'Hope' is the thing with feathers –" and "This is my letter to the World / That never wrote to Me –." Return to sender. We need to start fresh.

Let's start, as the biographies do, with her family tree. If we were to trace Emily Dickinson's spiritual lineage along the Tree of Knowledge, we'd find her forefathers and mothers poised on the craggy limbs, where the crows stand and—let's be fair—where the songbirds build their nests. There'd be Saul, persecutor turned proselytizer, high in the upper branches, and skeptic Thomas would balance on a wobbly, low bough. Jacob, who sparred with angels and tricked everyone he could, would grip the trunk of this family tree. At its root we'd find Eve, reputed another redhead, who hid from God once her rebellious tastes had blossomed. And it's possible that Lucifer— brightest star in the firmament, first rebel against God—might flicker an instant over the scene, before disappearing with the dawn. Emily asks, "was not temptation the first zest?" To this crowd of doubters, fighters, and faithful infidels Emily Dickinson belongs.

This is not the family in which most scholars or biographers would place the poet they call "Dickinson"—but this book is neither scholarly study nor biography. Although I build gratefully upon such work, I take a more personal tack. In these pages, I call her Emily, because this book tells of two intertwining lives, Emily's and mine, and shares how her poems have led me toward the God she both jabbed at and sought. Through her very struggles with religion, Emily has become for me a sort of unlikely patron saint, and we don't call the saints by their last names.

I am also a redhead. While not much of a rebel, I do struggle with religion. If I were to chart my spiritual path over the last decade, it would look more like an EKG than a slow and steady climb toward grace. Grace Emily dismisses with a shrug as "*unmerited* remembrance – 'Grace' – the saints would call it. Careless girls like me, cannot testify." I'm careless, too, and sympathize. Take, for instance, my spotty record with church:

I've floated in and out of Methodist, Congregational, Lutheran, nondenominational Christian, and Episcopal congregations, but the only church I haven't left is, typically enough, the single one that I can never truly join: a community of monks. Given these spiritual shortcomings, I've come to love Emily for exactly those qualities that might appear to disqualify her for sainthood: impiety, inconsistency, irreverence. Saint Emily, patron of all who wrestle with God.

While much of Emily's life, and a bit of mine, will unfold across these pages and through her poems, let me sketch here the broad brushstrokes to offer some context for what will follow. One of the struggles we face in reading Emily is how the myths and rumors—the reductive biographies that stare from the tags of Emily Dickinson plush dolls—can obscure the genius we meet in her poetry. We'll tackle the cultural perception as we go, debunking myths, piercing misconceptions. But first, here's the short version of the story: rumors, myths, and all.

Emily was born to the prominent Dickinson family on December 10, 1830, in Amherst, Massachusetts, which her own family would help to turn into a university town through the creation of Amherst College. She was well educated for a woman of the time, but this is not surprising, since her grandfather championed female education. Yet after one year at Mount Holyoke Female Seminary, she left—some say because of illness, others, homesickness, neurosis, or simply the need (either on her part or theirs) to be with her family.

Once she returned home, Emily never again left the family she simultaneously adored and resisted: her stern father, Edward, and her domestic, fussy mother (another Emily). Her older brother, Austin, was her close confidant in youth, then married and moved next door. Emily's relationship to Sue, Austin's wife, yields differing views: she's variously called Emily's closest friend, her beloved, her muse, her key reader and editor, as well as something of a manipulative bully. Last, there was Emily's sister, Lavinia, who managed the house as their mother had once their mother no longer could, though Vinnie added more catty impressions of the neighbors and more cats. None of the three Dickinson children ever moved away. With the exception of a few trips to Boston, Philadelphia, Washington, DC, and two lengthy stays in Cambridge to treat an eye ailment, Emily never traveled.

She also never married, though many readers and biographers speculate about a significant and ultimately failed love that left her wrenched in her late twenties and early thirties—right around the same time she became quite serious about writing poetry, copying hundreds of poems into the hand-sewn books she made to record them. She never published her poems, though ten did appear in print in her lifetime. It's not clear whether they were published with her consent. Before she turned forty, she stopped going much beyond the fenced-in yard. (She'd stopped going to church in the decade before.) Around this time she also took up the habit of wearing only white and refusing to receive visitors. Within the limits of the yard, orchard, and meadows, Emily tended a vast garden and cultivated exotic plants in her greenhouse, having a passion for botany and a skill for horticulture that had endured since her early education. She also, famously, baked.

When she died at fifty-five, her family had little idea of the legacy she'd left behind. Lavinia found nearly eight hundred poems secreted inside a rosewood box and nestled in the bottom drawer of the cherry dresser in Emily's upper-story room of the family Homestead. When you lift the lid, the box tinkles a tune. Seeing this wealth of poems, Lavinia undertook to publish them. She enlisted Sue (and whether Sue gave help or hindrance depends on whom you ask), as well as Austin's mistress, Mabel Loomis Todd, and Emily's longtime correspondent, the important man of American letters Thomas Wentworth Higginson. The first volume came out in 1890, the second in 1891, the third in 1896. As letters and poems were collected, the count would climb to nearly eighteen hundred poems and over a thousand letters. As Emily herself said of such unanticipated boons: "The Heaven – unexpected come, / To Lives that thought the Worshipping / A too presumptuous Psalm –."

Such are the broad outlines of Emily's life and early afterlife. Notice how the poetry is tucked in there amid the neurosis, the family dramas, the broken heart, the baking, and the blooms? You'd almost miss it, except that *it* is the reason we care anything about the rest. It wasn't until 1955, when the first complete, nonbowdlerized edition of the poems was printed, that the world realized what it had in Emily Dickinson. In the earlier editions, editors corrected rhymes, adjusted imagery, smoothed syntax, and tidied her punctuation, stanza size, and line breaks. In the decades since the whole of her writing emerged, we've tried to parse what is true about Emily, as well as what is actually on the page.

So, in these pages, I try to figure out what was true about Emily's religious life, what her poems and letters suggest. Oh, and on that topic, here's one more telling fact: Emily insisted that she could not pray.

"Because she cannot pray"

As I've admitted, Emily is an unlikely patron saint for anyone to choose. In her lifetime, the state of her soul was called into question when she staunchly refused to give the public profession of faith that marked conversion, and it was further suspected when she stopped attending church altogether. In the hundred-plus years since her poetry was published, her soul has increasingly been the subject of debate. Was she a Christian? Did she believe in God? If so, how so? If not, why not? And what did her belief consist of—if belief it was—at thirty, at forty, at fifty?

The answers readers give to these questions couldn't be more varied. If you read around at the library or online, you'll find a range of readers assigning Emily to every possible spot on the spiritual spectrum: reluctant Christian, ardent mystic, atheist, agnostic, Buddhist.

Emily's spiritual life inspires so many diverse answers because her poems and letters offer such tricky evidence. Obviously, she's not around to answer our questions, and the record we do have is both sparse and inconsistent. By turns and by moods, Emily challenges, cajoles, cudgels, and coos at the God she dubs "the Foreigner," "that Bold Person, God," "Itself," "the imperceptible," "Tyranny," "a Mastiff," "Old Suitor Heaven," "Vagabond," "Sorcerer from Genesis," and "the Mysterious Bard," among other more generic names, such as "the Sky," "Might," "Deity," and "Omnipotence." And this is not to mention her broad use of those more traditional names for God: Lord, Savior, Maker, Jehovah, Sovereign, Creator, Redeemer, and Almighty. *God* is the thirty-ninth most frequently occurring word in all her poems. As the presence of these names attests, she wrote amply on the subject, alternately irreverent and pious, sometimes in a single poem, even a single verse. Take the poem with the first lines "Papa above! / Regard a mouse." It's a prayer of sorts, spoken to the "Papa above," but the tongue-in-cheek diction of *papa* and *mouse* keeps it from feeling particularly devout. Is she pointing out the childishness of faith through this mousy charade? Or might her playful tone hint at a true intimacy with her divine "Papa," the way biblical scholars say Jesus' intimacy with God is shown by his use of the Aramaic word *abba*, which translates more closely as "dad," even "daddy," than the formal "Father"? You could argue the matter many ways, in this poem and many others. The letters, too, leave the most significant questions up for debate: when she wrote, "Home is the definition of God," does she reveal that God is her home, or the reverse, that an earthly home is god enough for her, no other deity required? *Home* was also a common word she used to refer to heaven, following Jesus, who promised that in his Father's house there would be many rooms. Emily whispered, a year before she died, "Foxes have Tenements, and remember, the Speaker was a Carpenter –." Beautiful words, but can we lean on them to know where her home was or who she believed had built it for her?

Since Emily did not publish, she was the primary, often the sole reader she imagined for the majority of her writings, and consequently she had no need to explain her shifting moods or cryptic stances to herself. Besides, even in the case of published authors, short lyric poems are not held to the same standards of consistency and continuity as longer epic works. Whereas John Milton aimed to make a "great Argument" across the many books of *Paradise Lost*, to "assert Eternal Providence / And justifie the wayes of God to men," and whereas John

Calvin erected an edifice in his *Institutes of the Christian Religion*, John Donne wrote lyric poems that were lusty and devout without striving for consistency. Short lyric poems intend only to capture the intensity of a lyric moment. If those moments lasted, there would be no need to preserve them in verse.

Emily's correspondence isn't much clearer when it comes to revealing her soul. Though mostly in prose (verses do creep in between the lines and amid the pages) and written for specific recipients, the letters obscure as much as they reveal. Depending on the person she addresses, Emily can sound angry, indifferent, hopeful, scornful, skeptical, teasing, or full of trust about faith. Sometimes, she'll sound many of these ways in a single letter. In this Emily appears every bit as complex and self-contradicting as the rest of us. None of us writes our personal correspondence as a *summa theologica*, a coherent system of belief, in which we develop a logical, ordered position. And then, of course, time tromps on, bringing changes, fluctuations, shifts. Across her life, Emily returned to older works and revised them— sometimes after a significant gap. It seems that her poems lived for her long past the moment of composition. In her correspondence with the publisher Thomas Niles, from Roberts Brothers in Boston (who later was impressed enough to ask for "a M.S. collection of your poems"), she reached back twenty years to select a poem she was willing to share. Whatever one poem or letter might reveal of Emily's thoughts at the moment of its composition, we have no guarantee that she still thought so after one year, not to mention thirty years. We also have no guarantee that she didn't.

Finally, in case this scenario is not complicated enough, we have to account for the likelihood that, in any given poem,

Emily is using irony or impersonation, both of which she loved. She cautioned one of her most important readers—Thomas Wentworth Higginson, who would eventually help publish her poems after her death—not to draw a one-to-one parallel between the voice that speaks in the poems and the author who wrote them: "When I state myself, as Representative of the Verse – it does not mean – me – but a supposed person." While she may simply hope to protect herself from any aspersions (some poems get pretty risqué), Emily also wanted to be clear: that seemingly transparent letter, *I*, does not necessarily point to her, the poet, at all.

This challenge doesn't discourage me. Rather I'm buoyed up by Emily's inconsistency on the page. When I read tales of martyrs or tomes of the Church Fathers, the firm assurance of those voices makes me realize how I waver between the poles of belief and doubt. So I find Emily's mutability consoling. For her, as for me, Christ is one day "the Stranger," then the next, "the Savior." She pillories God one moment as "Judgment," prays to God the next as "Love," and in a third mood announces: "That Hand is amputated now / And God cannot be found –." And so it goes with me.

Despite her wavering, I do make some confident claims here about Emily's interior life. While we will never be able to itemize, year by year, Emily's deep-held religious beliefs, no reader of her poetry and letters can deny certain shifting trends in her views across her lifetime. Some ideas, like a childhood view of heaven (marble gates, shiny white-robed men and women), slip away. Other ideas grow in conviction. That the self is eternal Emily became increasingly sure. While there is room for doubt about some of the spiritual stances I claim for Emily in this book, there is also evidence that they are true.

In the pages that follow, I don't aim to present a scholarly account of Emily Dickinson's religious life—there are already several quite wonderful studies, such as Roger Lundin's *Emily Dickinson and the Art of Belief* and James McIntosh's *Nimble Believing: Dickinson and the Unknown*—but rather to tell how reading Emily's poetry and letters has infused and enriched my beliefs. As she has informed my religious struggles, so my struggles have illuminated aspects of her writings and life different from those the scholarly accounts stress. The portrait I etch here is intuitive as well as analytic. It comes from sensing how her images and tone shift across forty years of writing, and from watching how her poems have challenged and deepened my spiritual life, my beliefs and doubts. She proposes that "God seems much more friendly through a hearty Lens," and for a decade she's been my lens. Her language has inflected my spiritual landscape, and so, as I read, I reflect those images back onto the page. Our stories have intertwined through these poems, and so they do in these pages.

For certain readers, like myself, knowing what Emily believed is not solely a question of biographical interest, or a historical mystery, attractive for its uncertainty. For me, to know the resolution of Emily's long, tumultuous relationship with God seems to promise some hope or help in my similar struggles. She knew, as I do, that "Narcotics cannot still the Tooth / That nibbles at the soul –." If I could solve how (or if) Emily answered the all-important questions that troubled her, maybe it would help me to settle mine. "It comforts an instinct if another have felt it too."

For over ten years, I have turned to her poems as others have to Scripture: for joy, for hope or peace in distress. I've read her poetry the way others go to Bible study, in order to challenge what I know and to know better what challenges me. I've even prayed her poems when I had no words of my own to offer. (That practice started by accident on a turbulent autumn day—but I'll tell that story later.) Most importantly, I have returned again and again to Emily's poems simply to meet anew their fellow feeling and experience their beauty. Thus I've accepted the invitation that Emily extends in a letter to her cousins, "Let Emily sing for you because she cannot pray," because I, too, cannot pray and because I love her songs. Like her favorite biblical character, Jacob, Emily wrestled with God and insisted, "I will not let thee go, except thou bless me." Her poems are witness to the struggle. They also show how many blessings she received. I won't let her go until she blesses me.

"Let Emily sing for you"

In what follows, I hope to share the blessing of Emily's songs with you. From nearly eighteen hundred poems, I've chosen twenty-five to explore in detail, some for their fresh take on old spiritual problems, some for their playfulness toward established Christianity: "Our Old Neighbor – God –" can certainly stand a tease. I picked poems that illuminate a key facet of Emily's religious life or that speak to mine. I selected poems with a rare image, depth of insight, a stilling phrase—though in Emily's work, there's no shortage of these. I hope these poems will guide readers beyond the repetitive, limited set printed in anthologies and on bookmarks, beyond the cloying stereotype of the "belle of Amherst" and the myths and misperceptions that obscure Emily's genius, in and aside from her religious thought.

There are many quite wonderful poems about religion that I have omitted here, in part because they are readily available elsewhere: poems such as "This World is not conclusion" and "Some keep the Sabbath going to Church," as well as "The Bible is an antique Volume" and "My period had come for Prayer." These are powerful poems, widely known. "I hesitate which word to take," Emily sums up my problem perfectly, "as I can take but few and each must be the chiefest." I chose for "chiefest" the poems you might not otherwise encounter, the ones that open a window onto Emily's life and thought that might otherwise have remained shut. Here we'll look at her less familiar work, perhaps in a less familiar way.

This book is made up of meditations, each one rooted in a single poem. The poems are the origin and end of this book, and so my hope is that, when you end this book, you will head back into her writing on your own. I approach the poems as texts for reflection, much as a preacher might pick a verse or two from the Bible, then spin a sermon to untangle it. The meditations weave together theology, history, biography, Emily's writings, and my own experiences in an attempt to illuminate each poem's unique wealth. Each meditation aims to offer the occasion to engage deeply with that poem, to read and reread it, to encounter its insight and beauty.

So the chief thing I would ask is this: spend time with the poems. Read them. And read them again. I confess I sometimes skip or skim long quotes when I'm reading in a hurry. But Emily proposed, "A Book is only the Heart's Portrait – every

Page a Pulse –," and she guarded her heart, on and off the page. Her poems are challenging, and they take time to yield their meanings. When I teach Emily's poetry, I notice that students either find it laughably simple or bafflingly obscure. Both responses can be an excuse to shut the book and walk away, since in the first case it's not worth the time and, in the second, it takes too much time. There are plenty of other poets who offer tidy imagery and ideas, pre-chewed and digested. Emily's poems are more like a bird in flight. If you want to see how the bird sees, then you'll have to find a way to join it in the sky. To say the same thing in a different way: while Emily's poems pulse with amazing life, we have to slow down and hunker close enough to see it, as we would the minute but lively activity in a tidal pool. A page of my own volume of Emily's poems might suggest just how much slowness the poems require, as well as how much life such slowness can discover:

Her poems are alive and give life. But first, they ask the reader to lend her own lively attention to the enterprise.

This might not be a book to devour in a single sitting, any more than you could comfortably or enjoyably read a volume of Emily's poems cover to cover. Each poem is dense with so much life that it needs space and time to breathe. Have you ever seen an antique stereoscope? A precursor to the movie camera, it would hold a postcard photograph—of Niagara Falls, say, or the 1860 visit of the Japanese ambassadors to Boston—in a stand affixed by a slide to a pair of viewing goggles. Through a trick of curved glass and the adjustable distance of the slide, the two photographic images side by side on the postcard fuse when you look through the lenses, creating a single three-dimensional image. I suppose that, for the Victorians, it was pretty exciting. The Dickinsons owned one. The point of the analogy is that you could only look at a single scene at a time. So you'd visit Niagara Falls for a while, then slip in the next card, adjust the perspective, and be in the jungles of Peru. This is how I hope you'll travel through this book. The reward for your slow progress will be that these twenty-five poems become rich and familiar landscapes, and Emily herself will travel as your companion. Then, should you choose, the vast wilds of her eighteen hundred poems await your further exploration.

Finally, I hope that you might come away from this encounter with Emily and her poetry as I have, with a kindlier, even jauntier view of the God to whom the poems—in reverence and irreverence—point. This is a book about God, but less the God thundered from pulpits, graven in doctrine, or projected onto PowerPoint with rock band accompaniment than the one that Emily perceived and has helped me to glimpse—the God met in poetry, love, and birdsong. Though Emily insists she "cannot pray," she has abundant wisdom to share about God and the spiritual life. I hope you'll try not praying with Emily Dickinson and me.

BELIEF

I could not find my "Yes" —

CONVERSION

I shall keep singing!
Birds will pass me
On their way to Yellower Climes –
Each – with a Robin's expectation –
I – with my Redbreast –
And my Rhymes –

Late – when I take my place in summer –
But – I shall bring a fuller tune –
Vespers – are sweeter than matins – Signor –
Morning – only the seed – of noon –

NEARLY CHRISTMAS, it's cold in the assembly hall of the northeastern girls' boarding school, Mount Holyoke. The name suggests something of the school's tenor: Holy Yoke. At the front of the room stands the woman who holds the yoke. Nothing in her stern, lined appearance reveals that she is aflame with a mission to convert her young charges to God. When the girls first arrived at the school, trunks in tow, Miss Lyon (these names are worthy of a Dickens novel) had interviewed and classed each one according to her standing in the Book of Life. Looking down the rows now, does she register each girl's state? *Christian*: the word rings a halo around a blond head. *Hoper*:

a face glowing fresh with the promise of faith almost lit. And then her gaze stumbles on a knotty patch, a briar: *No-hoper*. The grooves beside her wide frog-mouth deepen. Time to weed that out.

Miss Lyon begins her address on the sacredness of Christmas and the birth of our Lord, the dangerous trend of levity and decking the halls with evergreens, the need for the girls to apply themselves earnestly to the work of salvation. Warming to her point, Miss Lyon launches her demand into the room: all those girls willing to spend Christmas Day in fasting and prayer should stand as a sign of their consent. The room rises, save for a few entrenched No-hopers who remain in their seats.

"They thought it queer I didn't rise," Emily later quipped. "I thought a lie would be queerer."

Narrowing her eyes, Miss Lyon increases the stakes. All who wish to be Christians should sit. (Her logic is good: how much easier for the rebels, already seated, to simply remain sitting.) The student body sinks onto the long benches, which sigh with the weight of the girls' collective will, and just as Miss Lyon lets out her held breath, a single redhead—narrow shoulders, nipped waist, bell skirt—rises from amid the seated crowd.

If Emily showed her resistance to becoming Christian so boldly in public (and in retrospective boasting about this event), she agonized in private over the question. In the 1840s and 1850s, her formative years, conversion raged through Amherst, Massachusetts, and the surrounding country, conquering as fully as a flood. A small awakening, seen by historical eyes, it did not feel minor to those in its thrall. Main Street in Amherst might as well have been the road to Damascus, for each day new souls walked abroad blinded by the light of conviction.

The bells seemed to speak more brilliantly, the preachers more heatedly, and women wept and men cried out during daily revival meetings. Even the stones and trees might be said to have yielded up and become Christian, since the very air seemed to preach to the unrepentant their need to convert. "Christ is calling everyone here," Emily confided to her school friend Jane Humphrey, one of the few to whom she spoke about spiritual matters. "In the day time it seems like Sundays, and I wait for the bell to ring, and at evening a great deal stranger, the 'still small voice' grows earnest and rings, and returns, and lingers, and the faces of good men shine, and bright halos come around them; and the eyes of the disobedient look down, and become ashamed." The air was thick with it. Those not taken in the first wave, arriving when Emily was eight, surely ceded under one of nine revivals that flooded Amherst from 1840 to 1862. Later swells claimed her father, sister, brother, and dear friend and sister-in-law, Sue. Her mother was already a convert. One by one, the whole rest of the family turned afresh to God, imbued with conviction, like little islands sinking into the sea. A lone island remained.

"I am standing alone in rebellion," Emily reported in 1850, at nineteen. (This was three years after the scene in which she'd actually *stood* in rebellion before Miss Lyon, as if to literalize the metaphor.) Now another revival was underway. For the previous four years, Emily had watched her neighbors and acquaintances "melt"—her word—in the fires of awakening. She was cautious and had decided to avoid the revival meetings that moved others swiftly to faith. "I felt that I was so easily excited," she explained, "that I might again be deceived and I dared not trust myself." It was not the conversion she dreaded, but rather its cause. She didn't fear a profession of faith; she feared that she might be "deceived" into a false profession simply because of the excitement in the air. Sociologists call this "mob mentality," when individual will is subsumed by the collective impulse.

In the thick, tight atmosphere of Mount Holyoke in 1847, there was a strong collective impulse for Emily to resist. Records show that Miss Lyon placed Emily not with the group of solid "Christians," nor within that wistful group of "Hopers," who might be hoped to convert soon, but rather with the "No-hopers." This status made Emily the project of the school's pious majority, who strove by private counsel and prayer meetings and exhortations to convert her.

Emily did not remain internally unmoved by the religious fervor around her. Clusters of letters from 1846 through 1850 revolve restlessly around questions of faith, conversion, and the afterlife. Emily was neither insensible to her lone position nor free from the desire to join the others in the joy of belief. In a letter to a friend, Abiah Root, who was struggling with the same questions, Emily confessed, "I continually hear Christ saying to me Daughter give me thine heart." Christ was not the only one exhorting and beseeching her. "Many conversed with me seriously and affectionately," she writes, "and I was almost inclined to yield to the claims of He who is greater than I." The prayer groups' tactics were working.

Yet if this letter hints at a softening of Emily's resistance—she's "almost inclined to yield"—her word choice also reveals her distrust of that inclination. Whenever she speaks to Abiah and Jane about conversion, Emily frames the matter in a consistent vocabulary, in terms of yielding and giving up:

January 31, 1846: "I hope the golden opportunity is not far
hence when my heart will willingly *yield* itself to Christ."
March 28, 1846: "I know that I ought now to *give myself
away* to God."
September 8, 1846: "I do not feel that I could *give up* all
for Christ."
January 17, 1848: "I have not yet *given up* to the claims of
Christ."

This consistent diction reveals one source of Emily's hesitation
to become a Christian: she saw conversion as surrender, a
yielding. Conversion meant loss, perhaps even of that most
precious sense of self that, from fifteen to nineteen, she was
strongly beginning to form. This coming-of-age and claiming
of identity is a struggle that most adolescents experience.
For some, religion offers an answer to this need. For others,
perhaps for Emily, resistance to religion can fill that role. If
Emily felt that conversion required that she "give herself away"
to God, it's no wonder she did not want to yield.

Reading through these letters, full as they are of her very
real and uncomfortable struggle, I find myself feeling glad,
even grateful, that Emily resisted. Emily's early letters to Abiah
are so drenched in the language of the Bible, the lugubrious
urgings of the preachers, the sentimental rhetoric of revival,
that her own voice gets submerged. Reading these letters, it
seems quite possible that if Emily had yielded then to faith,
with its strong language of belief and damnation, folds and
flocks and fiery pits, Emily *would* have given herself up. Had
she yielded to Christ as she longed to at fifteen, she might have
been happier, but she might never have written poems at all,

certainly not the individual, utterly personal poems for which we celebrate her now. Without the lifelong spiritual struggle that fed her writings, would she be able to feed so many now?

Of course, Emily did not have the benefit of this perspective and, once the season of fervor had passed with her still unconverted, she looked back over her resistance with regret: "I may never, never again pass through such a season as was granted us last winter. . . . I regret that last term, when that golden opportunity was mine, that I did not give up and become a Christian." Two years later, she regretted still the loss of that "golden opportunity" and urged Abiah and Jane to pray for her conversion: "You must pray when the rest are sleeping, that the hand may be held to me, and I may be led away."

We know from these letters that Emily did not, at fifteen or seventeen or nineteen, take the hand and become a Christian. Yet the question still bubbles up: did it ever happen? Did she ever convert? Emily does speak retrospectively of a brief, rosy season of belief that came, dazzled, and left: "The few short moments in which I loved my Saviour I would not now exchange for a thousand worlds like this." And so we know from her own lips that she did love God once, even called him her *Savior*. This knowledge leads only to more questions: Why did the "few short moments" end? Did the love ever return? Was the memory of that short time enough to define or inform her identity in the decades that followed?

If only within the trove of poems and drafts found in the upstairs bureau drawer she'd left a note like the one they found in her father's pocketbook at his end, "I hereby give myself to God," then we could stop wondering. Edward Dickinson even dated his promissory note to God, for the shift he had experienced was that certain and abrupt. One day, April 30, 1873, he was his own free agent, a lawyer, a man of reason. The next day, May 1, he belonged to another: "I hereby give myself to God."

Conversions do not always come with a date-and-time stamp. And of course, even when they do, there's no guarantee that a return to doubt and denial might not follow the momentous instant. Emily admits that "This timid life of Evidence / Keeps pleading – 'I dont know' –." Sometimes the certainty of conversion just doesn't stick. How fast the thing we knew becomes again, "I just don't know . . . " Perhaps this is why the wise tend to speak of conversion not as a once-and-forever event but rather as a way of life. Conversion does not happen once, they say; it must happen constantly. The very fluctuations and inconsistencies of human nature demand it. We do not feed the body once and have done with it; why then would we with the soul?

Conversion is continual, as long as life. No one knows this better than those men and women monastics, monks and nuns, who have given their lives over to its inner work. Their mode of life dates back before the sixth century, when St. Benedict of Nursia built upon centuries of desert fathers and mothers and carved out rules for the monastery in a document that we now call *The Rule of St. Benedict*. He dictated how monastic men and women should live to experience a continual conversion of habit and character: "See how the Lord in his love shows us the way of life," he pronounces, as he sets down the markers on the path. Fourteen hundred years later, his system is still in use. I've encountered it firsthand at an Episcopal monastery that has become my spiritual home, the Society of Saint John the Evangelist in Cambridge, Massachusetts. The Brothers there, along with other monastics around the world, continue to rework and rethink Benedict's legacy as they live out their own rule of life. Systems of living, like those rules followed in monasteries throughout the ages, would not be necessary if one could simply convert and be set forever. Instead, Benedict and other leaders throughout the history of the church have aimed at creating, in themselves and for others, conversion of life: they know that we must tend to the matter of our conversion every day, for the rest of our days.

What, then, does conversion look like? Perhaps not, as Miss Lyon thought, looking to those snarly No-hopers in the pews at Mount Holyoke, like a single moment of deep revelation that changes everything forever. Rather, Benedict and other monastics offer a different model: conversion comes through the daily work, study, prayer, and relationships that, across the slow tramp of years, change our matter from what we are to what we would become. So Benedict proposes to create "a school for the Lord's service." He explains, "The Lord waits for us daily to translate into action, as we should, his holy teachings." Conversion, in this school of thought, looks less like an exam, in which we study, answer all the questions properly, and pass (this example is not as silly as it might seem: think of the catechism, used for the conversion of souls within the Catholic Church for centuries). Instead, conversion looks more like training for a marathon, in which you work and eat and train toward a single purpose, until your very self is transformed. "Let us run with patience," St. Paul exhorts new converts, "the race that is set before us." So too Benedict: "We shall run on the path of God's commandments." As Paul and Benedict knew, conversion isn't a race you finish; it's life.

This, I think, is the kind of conversion Emily finally did experience: no sudden yielding in fervor, but rather a deliberate, painstaking, struggle-filled molding of the self to an ideal. And where some people turn to service and others to prayer as the means for their conversion, Emily turned to poetry.

Let me say that again: Emily used her poetry as a means for her own conversion. *Conversion*, after all, comes from the Latin *convertere* and only means "to turn." How fitting that the word *verse* shares the same root. In verse, Emily never stopped converting, which is to say turning and turning around those questions of life and death, Christ and God, eternity and the grave, that kept her from the profession of faith her friends and family sought. To borrow the traditional language of the church, poetry was Emily's means for working out her salvation. Where a priest might work out his salvation in the celebration of the Eucharist, a Franciscan in the practice of poverty, a Carmelite in silent prayer, Emily wrote poetry. "I work to drive the awe away," Emily explained, "yet awe impels the work."

Emily's conversion by poetry, like all conversions, was a circular process: work to drive away awe, awe impels work, work drives awe impels work drives awe. She could loop on like this forever. The same is true for the mystic or monastic. Awe of the Lord is never satisfied in prayer; otherwise, why stay in the monastery? For the monk too, there is an endless loop, in which awe impels prayer inspires awe impels prayer. He can't get rid of awe; he can't have done with prayer; no more could Emily with poetry. So Emily, as a poet, offers us another example of a life spent in conversion.

What might a poet's conversion look like? Imagine Emily walking at dusk. She sees a tree illuminated against the fading sky. The sight makes an impression so powerful Emily has to write a poem to explain it, to comprehend the feeling. "I work to drive the awe away." Instead of dulling the feeling, however, her work on the poem actually heightens it, since the poem reveals all the facets and depth of emotion the sight created. In fact, writing that poem could even increase Emily's sensitivity to such beauty, for the next time she sees a tree shadowed against a fading sky, all the emotions and reflections will rush back through her words. In the flush of second exposure, she may want to revise the poem or write a new one. The sky holds many poems; the mind holds more. "Yet awe impels the work."

No wonder, given this constant circuit from awe to poetic work back to awe, that Emily so often classed her poetry under that lofty term, *circumference*. "My Business is Circumference," she exulted. "*My* business is to *sing*." Emily's song was circumference because in it she traced the circuit of her experience, her hopes and fears, bending around and encompassing those greatest questions a human life can raise and, sometimes, answer. You might call Emily the most enthused *convert* of all, for she never ceased returning in her poetry to those questions about God and life and death that others around her settled sooner, with a speedy "Yes" in the pews.

While Emily did not give God her "Yes" at age fifteen, she also—at forty or fifty—never let "No" be the final answer. "I feel that I shall never be happy without I love Christ," she had declared at fifteen. So she took the matter of her conversion into her own hands, through her pen. "I shall keep singing!" she pronounced in a poem written in 1861. And that is precisely what she did for the next twenty-five years.

I shall keep singing!
Birds will pass me
On their way to Yellower Climes –
Each – with a Robin's expectation –
I – with my Redbreast –
And my Rhymes –

Late – when I take my place in summer –
But – I shall bring a fuller tune –
Vespers – are sweeter than matins – Signor –
Morning – only the seed – of noon –

As she watched others during the years of awakening fly
straight to "Yellower Climes" with their quick conviction and
their "Robin's expectation" of a summery future in heaven,
she toiled slowly at her songs, "with my Redbreast – / And
my Rhymes –." This poem reveals Emily's trust that such a
delay will yield rewards. The bird who is "Late" to summer
has a richer song to offer: "I shall bring a fuller tune –." Her
songs, she knew, were fitting her for summer, perhaps even
for heaven. They were converting her, rhyme by rhyme. The
songs were also, in the meantime, their own delight.

I picture Emily reciting this poem, with its anthem-like
quality, at the rising and setting of the sun, a kind of Matins and
Vespers prayer, like those she names in the second-to-last line,
and which monastics pray each day. Daily monastic prayer is
both an expression of faith and a means for sustaining it. "Lord,
open our lips. And our mouth shall proclaim your praise," the
service of Matins begins. That line returns every single morning,
in the darkness long before the sun rises. "Lord, open our lips.
And our mouth shall proclaim your praise," are among the first

words spoken since silence took hold the evening before when the "Greater Silence" began after Compline, the final office of each day. It's a beautiful prayer because it *is* the praise it asks the Lord to supply. While Emily may pronounce in her poem that "Vespers – are sweeter than matins – Signor –," I find Matins the sweetest of all the daily offices. The fact that the Brothers are willing to come every morning and sing those words, voices hoarse with sleep and disuse, is itself the proof of faith and praise that the prayer requests. "Lord, open our lips," they pray with open lips. And so conversion cycles around, another day of converting: "I work to drive the awe away, yet awe impels the work."

Emily also rose in the dark—to write poetry at the small writing desk in her room, just as the monk kneels at the prayer bench before dawn. This was her Matins: a breaking of the silence into verse. No wonder then that this poem contains something of a profession of faith, could be a creed, is almost a vow. In it Emily declares her strong belief that she will take her "place in summer," that her struggles will be rewarded with "a fuller tune." And for proof of these beliefs, she cites the abundant natural fact, reiterated every single day, that "Morning" is "only the seed – of noon –." From the limited light of the present moment, Emily knew her noon would come; just as she knew, sitting in the dark of her upper-story room, that morning would come. Until the metaphoric "noon" of faith rose within her, she would keep singing, trusting that the song itself would coax light from the darkness, as birdsong seems to do at dawn. Emily's song—like the monk's prayer at Matins—is the means for the conversion it promises, just as its melody is itself the promise of the "fuller tune" she foretells in the final lines. Emily sits down in the dark at her writing desk, the monk kneels before his prayer bench, and so conversion cycles around another day.

"I am alone before my little writing desk," Emily wrote at fifteen, "I am alone with God." For over forty years, Emily's writing desk was the site of her soul's continuous conversion. I've seen her desk, on display in the Houghton Library at Harvard. My husband and I had flown in from Chicago, cabbed to Cambridge, then walked up Harvard Street to the Yard, only to arrive at the library—bright-cheeked and breathless— and learn that the "Emily Dickinson Room" is only open on Fridays. It was Tuesday. We must have looked crestfallen, for the otherwise bristly security guard offered to ask the curator if something might be arranged. When we came back at two, as arranged, the guard pretended not to recall that he had helped us before and barked instructions. No coats! No pens! No loose papers! You need quarters for the locker! Cerberus at the gate of heaven.

We followed the curator up a winding white staircase, under a chandelier, down a banistered hall, and into a carpeted room on the left. And there it was. Her writing desk. The actual one. You simply would not believe how slight a space it carves out in the world. The glossy wood table is just big enough for a small leaf of paper and an inkwell, maybe. The table's companion, a low weather-beaten chair, has faint flowers on the seat. Even under the dim, artificial lights of the room, the wood shines warm with sunlight. Here, I think, standing before it, here she shook her fist at God. Here she turned and turned again. And here, as "Morning" is "only the seed – of noon –," she found.

I shall keep singing!
Birds will pass me
On their way to Yellower Climes –
Each – with a Robin's expectation –
I – with my Redbreast –
And my Rhymes –

Late – when I take my place in summer –
But – I shall bring a fuller tune –
Vespers – are sweeter than matins – Signor –
Morning – only the seed – of noon –

SCRIPTURE

WITH MARBLED BOARDS and a gilt cover lavishly embossed with arabesques and garlands around the name "Emily E. Dickinson," her Bible was a gift from her father in 1844, when she was thirteen. He wrote her name inside the front fly leaf, the *k* of *Dickinson* looping up so high it looks like a capital *R*: upright, erect, like *EdwaRd* himself.

The family's faith, like the Bibles he bestowed on each of his children, sheltered under Edward's authoritative presence. "Father is reading the Bible," Emily reported to Austin one Sabbath, "and Father's prayers for you at our morning devotions are enough to break one's heart." Most people reserve the capital *F* for the Father above, but Emily uses it for both her earthly and heavenly fathers, perhaps because for her they'd long since entwined, her father voicing the words of the Father to whom he prayed on their behalf. The association between her father and the Scriptures was strong enough that Emily could report on something as trivial as the arrival of a new servant: "Father calls him 'Timothy' and the Barn sounds like the Bible."

Much later, after her father had died, who took over leading the family's daily devotions? Not Emily, I feel sure, though with him gone, she did adopt his commanding scriptural tones to explain her drastic sense of loss: "All grows strangely emphatic," she wrote her dear friend Elizabeth Holland, "and I think if I should see you again, I sh'd begin every sentence with 'I say unto you –.'" Her father gone, she begins to speak like the Son. But lest she sound too orthodox, the next sentence qualifies her own relation toward that book: "The Bible dealt with the Centre, not with the Circumference –." Here we see her metaphor of the circle once again. This time she uses it to suggest how, in the context of daily life, the Bible misses things: it has depth, but not breadth; it treats what philosophers might call the essence of things, but misses the accidents of everyday life. This circle metaphor—center and circumference—also offers a revealing spatial logic for parsing Emily's relation to those Scriptures she terms "a tremendous Book." After all, the circumference is the circle's outer edge—neither inside nor outside, it is both at once. Such was Emily's way with Scripture: she rode the edge of an orbit a long way out from center, yet the Bible remained the axis from which she strayed.

My first Bible was a borrowed one. In Colorado Springs, on the night of my conversion, I went to bed with my friend's Bible clasped tight in my arms. For a very long time, I couldn't fall asleep for smiling.

A few weeks later, I ran as fast as I could through the streets of a beach town. While my family browsed souvenir shops, I made up a story and slipped away, to run to the far end of town, where I remembered once having spotted a religious bookstore. I hadn't told them yet that I'd become a Christian. Brand new and the only one in the family, I expected disapproval. Heady with my evasion, the smell of the store, and all the Holy Bibles arrayed before me, I was nearly trembling as I picked and purchased a teal volume, removed its shrink-wrap, and hid it in the backpack I had brought to secret it away. I kept thinking someone would come up behind me, clamp a hand on my shoulder, and ask: "What are you doing here?" Later that night, I hid the precious book beneath my pillow before I slept.

Back at home, three months later, I replaced the teal volume with an NIV *New Student Bible* that had better notes and bigger margins. This volume I devotedly annotated in color-coded pencils. Emily marked her books with pencil lines in the margin: a horizontal notch to point to a line of text; a faint wavering vertical to signal a passage. For me, the red pencil underlined historical facts to remember, blue shaded God's teachings and life lessons, and purple was for inspirational messages. The purple quotes I meant to memorize. I circled in purple the amazing words, "With God all things are possible," shaded them in, and then, becoming sleepy, tucked the volume back in its spot, just under the edge of my bed. I was one year older than Emily was when she received her Bible from her father. This was eighteen years ago.

> I held a Jewel in my fingers —
> And went to sleep —
> The day was warm, and winds were prosy —
> I said "'Twill keep" —
>
> I woke — and chid my honest fingers,
> The Gem was gone —
> And now, an Amethyst remembrance
> Is all I own —

Eighteen years later, "an Amethyst remembrance / Is all I own —." How many Bibles have I bought since then? With a reach of my arm today, I can touch at least seven: antique,

Vulgate, Oxford Study, pocket, NRSV, Tyndale, KJV. Those are just the ones within reach; I have more. I order them online, pick them up at garage sales, accept free copies bound in green plastic at the entrance to the subway. "Don't tell . . . ," Emily cajoled, "but wicked as I am, I read my Bible sometimes." Don't tell that, wicked as I am, I rarely do.

Emily would later call the book "your throbbing Scripture," as if disclaiming her own connection to it. Don't believe her. When Thomas Wentworth Higginson finally visited her in 1870, after eight years of correspondence, he reported back to his wife, among other things, about Emily's relationship to the Bible: "Her father was not severe I should think but remote. He did not wish them to read anything but the Bible." However true the report was—and Emily did tend to exaggerate for effect with Higginson—her father's insistence evidently worked, for the Scriptures are as constitutive of Emily's language as grammar and syntax. As we'll see in these pages, she weaves biblical imagery and diction into her writings as if she were moving around parts of speech: a familiar phrase crops up as an adjective would, to give color; like a verb, to give force. Mostly she thrills to apply a well-worn passage against the grain, pushing it far from the center into the circumference, where it jostles against the reader's expectation: "whom shall I accuse?" she queries when her aunt falls ill, "The enemy, 'eternal, invisible, and full of glory' – but He declares himself a friend!" The phrase "eternal, invisible, and full of glory" spins off the familiar string of praise given to God in 1 Timothy, "Now unto the King eternal, immortal, invisible, the only wise God, be honour and glory for ever and ever." Emily gives this rhapsody not to God but to "the enemy." A second twist: the enemy she's referring to is God. Feel how it jostles?

I had no center to stray from after my conversion, no family tradition of Scripture reading, so the Bible was for me the wild edge of possibility. Suddenly in the fold, I felt like a rebel. I remember sneaking away from the dinner table all that first week of faith just to touch my Bible's pages. Each word I read felt like a secret coronation. Every story was for me: its Savior, mine; its promises, mine. "Mine – by the Right of the White Election! / Mine – by the Royal Seal!" Emily exults in a stunning poem about being chosen (perhaps by God). I didn't know the poem then, but if I had, I would have chimed in with her in the new fervor of faith, "Titled – Confirmed – / Delirious Charter! / Mine – long as Ages steal!"

My deliriousness didn't last "long as Ages steal." And the Scriptures don't "throb" for me now. All those Bibles stack up on the shelves, largely unread. Sometimes, the memory of those early days of faith makes the present feel poor in contrast. I call it up to reproach myself. "I had rambled too far to return," Emily admits, "& ever since my heart has been growing harder & more distant from the truth & now I have bitterly to lament my folly – & also my own indifferent state at the present time." I could have written this letter years ago, if I'd been as honest with myself as she was.

Other times, when I recall those first, hallowed days, I don't feel the need to feel that way now. Why can't that memory resonate as other memories of childhood do: sufficient joy for having happened? My childhood made me and so it remains, though I will never be a child again. So too, I think that I will likely never again possess that zeal I knew at fourteen. Would I want to? "When I was a child," says St. Paul, "I spake as a child, I understood as a child, I thought as a child: but when

I became a man, I put away childish things. For now we see through a glass, darkly."

The darkened glass might be better, for now, than the gem. Today let the "Amethyst remembrance" be jewel enough for me.

DOUBT

Though the great Waters sleep,
That they are still the Deep,
We cannot doubt.
No vacillating God
Ignited this Abode
To put it out.

I WANT TO FALL ASLEEP inside this poem. My favorite of
Emily's poems feels like this: I want to float between the lines,
lulled by their rhythms into the mood they create. So I long
to take a dip inside this poem's assurance and cool my mind.
"What a Comrade is Human Thought!" Emily writes; "*all* are
friends, upon a Spar." Yes, if only I could prop myself upon this
poem's central line, "We cannot doubt," as on a spar, and drift.

The simplest of lines on anyone else's pen, these are four
astonishing syllables coming from Emily. "We cannot doubt."
Where's the rest? Knowing something of her character, I expect
an ironic reversal to follow, such as *We cannot doubt / Except
it all*, but no irony or reversal follows. I count on my fingers,
searching for the syllables that will make the line complete
Emily's well-loved rhythmic pattern of six- and eight-syllable
lines. Where's the denial?—the turn?—the complication that
will trouble this certainty with her characteristic doubt? I look

again, only to find that the extra beats do not come; nor does any doubt.

Instead the rhythm sweeps by with the sure pulse of the tide, stretching through the long, slow approach of the first two lines, "Though the great Waters sleep, / That they are still the Deep," to release, with the short relay of the third line, "We cannot doubt." Lines four through six follow the same shape: long, long, short. The rhymes, too, mimic this tidal pattern: they land twice upon the mind (*sleep / Deep, God / Abode*), like little wavelets, to then recoil across the third and sixth lines with a new rhyme, *doubt / out*. This third rhyme echoes across the poem's distance like the repeated sound of the waves' return.

As for the doubt I awaited, apparently doubt is one thing this tide will not bring in. For the poem sounds only with strong assurances. It declaims on the nature of God: God does not vacillate. It pronounces on the continuance of the self after death: it's still itself. And in that surprising middle line, it proclaims that there can be no question about these points: "We cannot doubt." In this turn toward certainty, even the characteristic dash that Emily so often uses cedes to the stauncher period. Each of the poem's phrases ends on a firm, unwavering point. Moored to its central denial of denial, rocked in the unerring rhythm of the tide, bound tight by returning rhymes, and sealed with certain punctuation, the poem takes on the assurance of a force of nature. Faced with a flood of "great Waters," there is little room for quibbling. What can you do but let yourself be borne along?

How many times have I floated down this particular poem? Poetry, like mantra, has power to inform reality, even shape it, simply through repetition. So Emily explained one way she understood her poetry to Thomas Wentworth Higginson: "I sing, as the Boy does by the Burying Ground – because I am afraid –." She compared herself to the widowed poet Robert Browning, singing "off charnel steps," that is, singing in the graveyard of all she's lost. I'm only mourning my lost childhood faith, but how many times has this poem bolstered me.

Yet, for all its assurance, this poem also rankles me. When not in duress, I try to swim against its tide. I don't understand how Emily has waded here into waters she so often denied. "We cannot doubt." What happened to Emily the subtle ironist, laughing into her sleeve at those who trust the assurances of faith? "We dignify our Faith, when we can cross the ocean with it," she smiles in one letter, then she smirks, "though most prefer ships." Emily not only preferred ships, but, to follow her metaphor, she made it clear that she was going nowhere near the waters of eternity without being certain of her vessel. From the time of Miss Lyon onward, she tossed and turned the promises of faith, examining them from every side, to see if she wanted to come aboard. "The shore is safer, Abiah," she admitted to her confidant, "but I love to buffet the sea –." Sixteen years later, she remarked to Higginson, "I was told that the Bank was the safest place for a Finless Mind." At thirty-five, she evidently still denied that she had the strong rudder, the "fin" of faith, to direct her course in the sea.

Such expressions of doubt and skepticism are dominant and persuasive enough that many readers call her an atheist or believe her when she speaks of herself as "a Pagan" and "one of the lingering *bad* ones." Readers, for instance, tend to take her at her word when she says, in a letter to Higginson (who, in addition to being a literary light, was also an ordained minister), "You have experienced sanctity. It is to me untried."

It's no surprise readers take her at her word since in the next line the letter sways into verse that hardly clarifies her own religious involvement: "Of Life to own – / From Life to draw – / But never touch the Reservoir –." In cases like these, we hear the "never" and stop there. We can miss that she's also calling God "the Reservoir."

At the least, skeptical readers would have to admit that "Though the great Waters sleep" was a favorite of sorts with its poet, since there come down to us five copies of it, all in Emily's own hand, written in the last three years of her life. Two more copies, known to have been sent, are now lost. Emily tucked this poem into letters, sent it to friends, and secured it among those pages she kept close by her at home.

> Though the great Waters sleep,
> That they are still the Deep,
> We cannot doubt.
> No vacillating God
> Ignited this Abode
> To put it out.

Just think, Emily sat at her writing desk penning these lines at least seven times, probably more. What did she think as she traced again, for the seventh time, its words of assurance?

Did she keep writing the poem because she believed its message so fully? Knowing the truth, this argument would run, she kept sending the poem out because she wished to convince others of the same. It's possible. But I doubt this is the reason, since other writings from this same period brim over with assertions of skepticism and spiritual unresolve. As those she loved died one after another, suddenly and too soon,

Emily begged from others confirmation of what she did *not* know about faith's promise of a life to come: "Are you certain there is another life?" she asked a trusted correspondent. "When overwhelmed to know, I fear that few are sure." Emily was not sure. Rather, she judged that, in this life, we are at best "Moving on in the Dark like Loaded Boats at Night," that is to say, charged vessels on uncertain waters: "though there is no Course, there is Boundlessness –." That boundlessness that waits at the end of our "Course" of life threatened her most. "One guess at the Waters, and we are plunged beneath!" It's evident that the "great Waters" she evokes so calmly in this poem just as often drowned her with fear. "Fathoms are sudden Neighbors."

Yet this period, dark as it was with uncertainty and suffering, also gave birth to this poem—*seven* copies of it. Amid her trouble, Emily clearly had another voice, the one we encounter here, calm with assurance. She could pronounce with conviction, "Death – so – the Hyphen of the Sea –," as if death were but a pause, a bit of punctuation barely worth noticing in the great phrase of life; she could pronounce this even while she thrashed and kicked to keep the fear of that "Hyphen" from lodging in her throat and choking her. We might well ask how a poem, born out of unrest, can be so restful for those who read it. How can it make me want to drift into the peace it promises, if its poet knew no peace? For all her doubts, Emily looks in this poem's faithful lines toward "that Great Water in the West – / Termed Immortality –" and shows a surprising amount of trust in the promises of faith. It shines forth in that middle line: "We cannot doubt."

The coexistence of this peaceful poem with letters of such turmoil suggests to me something true about the relationship between belief and doubt: they coexist. This idea sounds obvious, when stated outright, but I think we instinctively distrust it, in our own experience and in the writings of others. Doubt seems to negate belief, like two columns of a giant scorecard, in which every notch on one side renders void the parallel notch on the other. I know as I repeat the Apostles' Creed, the central expression of the Christian faith, my mind is racing between the two sides. What can I affirm and what do I say while mentally crossing my fingers? How might Emily have ticked through the lines? Here's my guess at her answer:

Believe It	Doubt It
One God, the Father the Almighty	
Creator of Heaven and Earth	
One Lord, Jesus Christ, only son of God	
	He was conceived by the Holy Spirit
	and born of the Virgin Mary
He suffered under Pontius Pilate	
was crucified, died, and was buried	
He descended to the dead	
	On the third day he rose again
	He ascended into heaven
	and is seated at right hand of the Father
	He will come again to judge living & dead
Holy Spirit	
	Holy Catholic Church
Communion of Saints	
	Forgiveness of Sins
	Resurrection of the Body
Life Everlasting	

Her hypothetical score? A tie: nine for each side. My own score is equally divided (though we'd differ on which side some of the beliefs fall). I fear that, one day, a clause from my own "Believe it" column will migrate over to "Doubt it," and then, like those medieval images of souls being weighed, the scales will tip and my faith will be lost to doubt. Emily philosophizes rightly, "It is the speck that makes the cloud that wrecks the vessel, children, yet no one fears a speck." I now fear a speck, because doubt seems to work in a powerful, exponential illogic. Two becomes four becomes sixteen, until the whole system threatens to topple in doubt.

Given that it's hard to credit the coexistence of doubt and belief in our own experience, it's not surprising that we tend to deny that complexity for others. When we encounter expressions of belief and doubt side by side in a writer's body of work, we sift them, looking for evidence of which one was more true for the writer. Belief, especially in the centuries before ours, strikes us more as a custom unconsciously embraced than as a choice or personal conviction. Christian themes are so pervasive— for centuries they dominated art and music, morality and metaphor—that belief seems simply assumed. It's the status quo from which an individual can diverge. Emily could not escape her Christian upbringing or the awakenings that swept by her with heightened religious rhetoric. Nor could she change the fact that, for her generation, the Bible was the axis around which all other writings, her own included, turned. So, we nod, the presence of some residue of Christianity in her poetry probably doesn't prove anything about the state of her soul. It's more like lead poisoning, a residual environmental effect. Take a comment like "That the Divine has been human is at first an unheeded solace, but it shelters without our consent –." Will you read this as testament that she found "shelter" and "solace" in the Incarnation of Christ? Or will you hear the gall that might hide in those words "unheeded" and "without our consent"?

Many readers have taken the latter tack in reading Emily. If belief strikes us as received, and thus rote, we tend to view doubt as a proof of the individual, free mind really working and thinking. In short, doubt seems more devastating to belief than belief triumphant over doubt. So in a case like Emily's, where doubt and belief clearly coexist, we often grant doubt the stronger claim. The doubtful poems, not the faithful poems, seem to express the true position of Emily's soul. And in her letters, when she shows evidence of belief, we assume it was just a social nicety, written more for the recipient's sake than the writer's. Listen again: "I believe we shall in some manner be cherished by our Maker – that the One who gave us this remarkable earth has the power still farther to surprise that which He has caused. Beyond that all is silence." Do you hear the stridency of "I believe we shall" and her confident view of God as "our Maker"? Or do you hone in on her hesitancy, "in some manner," and the rejection of doctrinal explanations about the afterlife, "Beyond that all is silence"? When you weigh those lines in the scale, which rises: doubt or belief?

This is the wrong question. Doubt and belief, Emily would be the first to say, are not necessarily in opposition. Emily judged that doubt enhances belief, since doubt's uncertainty keeps us hunting after God: "The Risks of Immortality are perhaps its' charm – A secure Delight suffers in enchantment –." Her insight stretches deep into human nature, within and beyond religion. Not only do sureties bore us after a time, but the reverse also is true: we yearn most for what we cannot have, long for the thing that we lack. So Emily observes, "Remoteness is the founder of sweetness," or, to quote one of her poems' opening lines, "Water, is taught by thirst." I could quote a hundred ways she says this, for the observation formed one of the key laws of her universe.

She saw that this law of lack was nowhere more true than in relation to God. Absent the doubt from a life of faith and you're left with comfort, conviction, a cool untroubled pool of certainty. But still ponds stagnate and breed disease; perhaps still faiths do too. Doubt, on the other hand, like a rapid, a riptide, keeps the waters of faith churned up and on the move. It certainly keeps things engaging for the swimmer. "How Human Nature dotes / On what it cant detect —."

As an experiment to test this theory, just think: What if the whole universe, seen and unseen, human and divine, were provable and knowable in a scientific, rational system that left no room for doubt? What if we could study God as an objective fact? Emily toys with the notion: "A Diagram — of Rapture! / A sixpence at a show — / With Holy Ghosts in Cages!" Would you go to church? Read books like this one? Would you seek God, if God sat, keeping weekly sessions like Lucy in the Charlie Brown cartoons? Speaking from my own vantage, I can say if that were the case, the whole Christian system likely would become as uninteresting to me as the mechanics of a car or the proof of water on Mars. These scientific knowns, game changers though they may be, do not exactly keep me up at night. As often as I wish for a doubt-free faith, I have to admit that doubt does keep things interesting. Perhaps that's why Emily could pronounce, "Sermons on unbelief ever did

attract me." The unknown is more thrilling than the known;
the doubter more compelling than the convert. At least I know
that doubt keeps *me* interested. "The unknown is the largest
need of the intellect," Emily observed, "though for it, no one
thinks to thank God." I certainly never have. What a prayer
that would be: *thank you, God, for the doubts that make me
wonder if you exist.*

Well, Emily's joke about diagramming rapture and putting the
Holy Ghost in a sideshow cage has a real target. She watched the
theologians of her day attempt to create theological science to
fight the doubts that Darwin had interjected into the Christian
faith—doubts about the age of the universe and the origin of
humanity: "we thought Darwin had thrown 'the Redeemer'
away," she quipped, though for many of her contemporaries,
the quip would have launched the very barb that had pierced
them. Her conclusion was that theologians did not need more
or better proofs for faith, but rather that "Too much of Proof
affronts Belief." For her, doubt doesn't sap belief. Proof does.

If "Proof affronts Belief" for Emily, doubt was its boon. In a
letter to Sue from 1884, she states the matter as clearly as she
ever did: "To believe the final line of the Card would foreclose
Faith – Faith is <u>Doubt</u>." She's strident about the point. She even
underlines the word "<u>Doubt</u>" in her letter. Her stridency shows
how important it was to her to assert that doubt does not oppose
faith but is itself a form of faith. Without doubt, faith becomes
knowledge, and knowledge, to put it simply, is not faith; it's
fact. So Emily can reference "the Balm of that Religion / That
doubts – as fervently as it believes –." Doubt, in her hands,
becomes not an aloof stance of disengagement but a fervent
wrestling. Doubt can be a "Balm," even a boon to faith, since

at its most secure, faith can claim only an "uncertain certainty." This phrase of hers, "uncertain certainty," is a contradiction, a paradox, yet is no mere cleverness or sly sophistry. The phrase's contradiction reflects Emily's experience of faith as one of perpetual paradox: "We both believe, and disbelieve a hundred times an Hour, which keeps Believing nimble." Doubt keeps believing nimble.

"Though the great Waters sleep" gives proof of her nimbleness in navigating between belief and doubt. Even as she herself struggled to believe that the self does not die, that death is not the end, Emily kept working through poetry to turn her doubts into belief. This poem suggests one specific way she might have practiced the poetic conversion of her soul: Emily didn't write only what she already believed, she also wrote what she wished to believe. She wrote poems about eternity, God, and immortality not from a belief in these ideas, but rather, in order to believe them. She took those doubts about death and eternity that her letters reveal and turned them into this poem, full of a calm assurance she did not yet feel.

This behavior is not as unusual as it might at first seem. It's similar to how we talk ourselves into a sunnier view of a bleak situation. *It's not that bad; things could be worse; tomorrow will be better; just keep trying; something good will happen.* Whether the issue is dating, disease, or doubt, we often tell ourselves a truth we only half believe, even as we hope that saying *this too shall pass* or *things are looking up* will make things, in fact, pass or look up. We often believe, despite ourselves, in the power of language to shape our will and, through that will, our reality.

Believers of all sorts do the same. Consider the couple exchanging vows of love at the altar. They don't speak their vows because they know with certainty that they will love each other "until death do us part." Divorce rates make such assurance unlikely. Instead they voice that vow because it expresses their deepest wish to share such love and because they hope that speaking the vow will help make it true. Some might call this kind of profession hypocrisy. You might also call it prayer. I know I often speak the words of the liturgy I hope to believe, whispering behind them in the silence of my mind, *Amen, amen,* may it be so, let it be true, thus praying that, somehow, saying the words will make the belief true for me.

The use of language to convert the soul has a long history, one that goes back a lot further than 1884, when Emily wrote this poem. In fact, such a belief in the power of words rests at the root of repetitive prayer, a practice developed over centuries by monastics in the East. The strict Hesychasts, following a prayer tradition in the Eastern church that dates back to the fourth century, speak only the Jesus Prayer, "Lord Jesus Christ, Son of the living God, have mercy on me, a sinner." Other contemplatives choose to repeat the name "Jesus Christ," or a verse from the Psalms. As they speak the chosen words in constant repetition, they interpret that scriptural instruction to bind God's words upon the arm, between the fingers, about the head, to "write them upon the table of thine heart." This familiar instruction made its way to Emily's fingers in 1845, when she embroidered a sampler ending in the prayer to Jesus: "And write thy name thyself upon her heart." Repetitive prayer practice aims to create stillness of mind, much as wordless meditation does. It also hopes to weave the repeated words themselves into the fabric of the soul. The idea is that through this repetition, the words—and the God to which they point—will cease to be a hoped-for belief, to become instead intrinsic to the one who speaks and respeaks them.

So Emily rewrote this poem, not because she knew of her lost friends "That they are still the Deep," but because she wished to know it. She wished to believe, beyond a doubt, that her own self would not dissolve when she entered into the "great Waters," when she too was plunged beneath "the recallless Sea." From the depths of her desire, she wrote this poem; then she rewrote it and she copied it, and I do not doubt that she spoke it to herself in the still watches of the night. Her cousin Louisa Norcross, whom Emily called "Loo," relates the memory of peeping into the pantry and watching Emily recite her poetry "while she skimmed the milk"—a homely image that could come straight from the manuals of the Hesychasts and other monastics who blend work and prayer and words into a single experience aimed to make the recited prayer as instinctive as breath. So I think that Emily rocked herself upon this poem's rhythm, using it to sound within her its promises of faith, much as water spins whorls into the sand beneath the waves.

Now Emily has gone into the "Deep" about which she wondered; she has become a part of the "drift called 'the infinite.'" Three years before she went there she wrote, "I cannot tell how Eternity seems. It sweeps around me like a sea." Now she is in the sea. She who marveled, "I wonder how long we shall wonder; how early we shall *know*," she knows or, at least, wonders no more.

I—still in wonder—take up these lines. I bind them to my arm and set them in watch over my heart, speaking her words again, so that I might believe.

Perhaps, sometime, this poem could be your companion. It's a good one to have. You could recite it when you do whatever homely work you do: cooking, waiting at the photocopier, mowing the lawn. Perhaps you will find a way—and if you do, please let me know—to fall asleep inside its peace. And then Emily will teach us how we too can come to say, as surely as the waves return, "We cannot doubt."

> Though the great Waters sleep,
> That they are still the Deep,
> We cannot doubt.
> No vacillating God
> Ignited this Abode
> To put it out.

BELIEF

❧

"WE CANNOT BELIEVE FOR EACH OTHER –," Emily observed, "thought is too sacred a despot." Centuries of evangelists, apologists, theologians, and preachers might disagree, as they've devoted their lives to helping others believe. In the seventeenth century, the French philosopher and mathematician Blaise Pascal set out to write the ultimate defense of Christianity. He never finished it, but he did leave behind a fragmentary collection of notes we now call the *Pensées*. Therein, Pascal famously defines faith as a wager. He reasons: since God is distanced from us by an unimaginable gulf, God's existence can never be proven by human reason; yet God either exists or doesn't, and we simply have to choose which way to believe. It's a gamble, a wager: "*Oui, mais il faut parier. Cela n'est pas volontaire, vous êtes embarqué.*" The game was set in place before we got here; we're in it now; no choice but to choose a side. Pascal urges us to cast our bets for God by believing. If God exists, we'll gain all for having believed. If not, we've lost nothing in the gamble. For many of us, Pascal's wager might not strike a comforting chord. As Emily notes in a stark poem about loss of faith, "The Crash of nothing, yet of all – / How similar appears –." Imagine God does not exist: to lose the *nothing* we thought God was would be to lose *all*.

Emily takes up the metaphor of the wager in a waggish, early poem, asking herself, "Soul, Wilt thou toss again?" She too ponders the benefit of such a dicey gamble: "Hundreds have lost indeed, / But tens have won an all –." In her scenario, the betting goes both ways. While the sinner gambles on heaven, heaven also gambles on the sinner: "Imps in eager caucus / Raffle for my soul!" When Higginson chose this poem in 1890 to be among the fourteen published in *The Christian Union*, the earliest posthumous publication of Emily's poetry, he titled it "Rouge et Noir," after the colors on the roulette wheel. He asks, almost in caption to the poem, "Was ever the concentrated contest of a lifetime, the very issue between good and evil, put into fewer words?" Place your bets, ladies and gentlemen: *rien ne va plus.*

Decision theorists have parsed and visualized Pascal's logical argument for the gamble of believing in God by equating his argument's terms with variables:

	God exists	God does not exist
Wager for God	∞	f1
Wager against God	f2	f3

They then calculate the two sides of the argument, with E standing in for the "expected utility of the wager": E(wager for God) $= \infty * p + f1 * (1 - p) = \infty$. On the other side: E(wager against God) $= f2 * p + f3 * (1 - p)$. Ah, yes, clearly. Here then, we spot an extreme version of what results when reason makes the case for believing in God. Am I alone in thinking that assent to such a rational proposition is not quite belief or faith?

"Do you wish to understand?" St. Augustine asked his listeners in the fourth century. You can almost see them nodding on the page. He offers them a one-word solution, "Believe." He goes on to explain, "Understanding is the reward of faith. Therefore do not seek to understand in order to believe, but believe that you may understand." According to Augustine, understanding in matters of Christian belief is not a product of reason but of faith. A millennium later, Anselm of Canterbury brought Augustine's formula from the second to the first person: "For I do not seek to understand that I may believe, but I believe in order to understand. For this also I believe, that unless I believed, I should not understand." So Anselm speaks of *fides quaerens intellectum*—faith seeking understanding. The two theologians agree that reason seeking understanding will fail; only faith can give understanding about the matters of belief. And how do you have faith? Simple: believe.

But what if you seek belief? This question is starting to feel like one of those unsolvable algebraic equations in which you cannot pin a value on any variable, and so none of the other variables can be solved. How do you begin with belief if you don't have it, or if it's become shaky? In one of her most cynical poems on the topic, Emily declares: "we believe / But once – entirely – / Belief, it does not fit so well / When altered frequently –." I hope she's wrong; I fear she's right. My own slide from fierce conviction to fumbling doubt has certainly made my belief not "fit so well" as it once did, in that first surge of certainty. Emily felt strongly about this point, also perhaps from her own experience, as she writes movingly about the loss of faith. Comparing it to "the loss of an Estate –," she explains that both faith and estate are "Inherited with Life –," a point particularly true in the centuries before ours, when religious instruction was simply a given of education. But loss of faith is the worse of the two scenarios, according to Emily, because "Estates can be / Replenished – faith cannot –." What follows sounds like a warning: "Belief – but once – can be – / Annihilate a single clause – / And Being's – Beggary –." The vehemence of her feeling rises through the diction: *annihilate* and *beggary*. These are strong words to describe strong loss.

Perhaps Emily's assertions about the loss of belief sting me so sharply because, in them, Pascal's logic of the wager surfaces again. Emily depicts a scenario in which all is lost upon a single throw, from riches to rags. "Annihilate a single clause" of belief, and it's over. This threat resembles the scorecard I'd fretted over earlier, worrying that if a single clause of the Creed migrated from belief toward doubt, my whole system of faith would tip into loss. Can Emily possibly be right, that faith can't be "replenished"? Can belief truly hinge on "a single clause"? Even my reason rebels against this model. Belief simply cannot be as fickle as the roulette wheel the croupier spins. Whatever our gamble of belief entails, God does not come to us by chance, leave by luck. Belief must be more substantial and lasting than a contract voided by a single "No."

One possible path away from the gambler's and rationalist's view of belief lies in the word *belief* itself. Etymology reveals that belief, at its core, is not about reason, understanding, luck, or fate. Belief, at its core, is about love. The two words share the same root: *lief*. And *lief* does not lift, like branches, into the lofty regions of the mind, but rather, like roots, tunnels down into the heart, into the realm of desire, love, and cherishing. The same is true for *credere*, the Latin verb "to believe" that Augustine uses in that famous formula, *crede ut intelligas*, "believe that you may understand." There, *cor* ("heart") and *dare* ("to give") combine into one verb, *credere*, which means, literally, "to give the heart." "Peter, do you love me?" Jesus asked him, three times in a row. In the King James Version Emily read so deeply, this verse is translated, "Simon, son of Jonas, lovest thou me?" He does not ask for Peter's rational understanding of the facts of his resurrection. He does not even ask for his belief; he asks for Peter's love, expressed to others in the command he gives him next: "Feed my sheep." Belief should not be an assent of the mind, but a gift of the heart.

How funny, because that is the very thing Emily reports to her friend Abiah. Remember? "I continually hear Christ saying to me Daughter give me thine heart." Christ only asked her to believe. And while she later remarked that "'Give me thine Heart' is too peremptory a Courtship for Earth," she deemed it "irresistible in Heaven —." Watch how:

> He showed me Hights I never saw —
> "Would'st climb" — He said?
> I said, "Not so" —
> "With me —" He said — "With me"?
>
> He showed me secrets — Morning's Nest —
> The Rope the Nights were put across —
> "And now, Would'st have me for a Guest"?
> I could not find my "Yes" —
>
> And then — He brake His Life — And lo,
> A light for me, did solemn glow —
> The larger, as my face withdrew —
> And could I further "No"?

"And lo," Emily makes it sound so easy. She turns to leave, and the light starts to glow, "The larger, as my face withdrew –." She's walking away, playing hard to get, and yet (in this poem at least) God comes chasing after her. Until the turning point at the final stanza, "And then – He brake His Life," the poem could easily be about an earthly courtship. It records a series of escalating invitations, spoken with great intimacy. (In another version of these lines, sent next door, Emily wooed Sue, "I showed her Hights she never saw –," and the reversal of roles shows further the intense, personal tone of the dialogue.) But the final stanza's mention of that broken life reveals that the subject could also be Christ. And Emily does name God elsewhere "a distant – stately Lover –" who woos us "by His Son – / Verily, a Vicarious Courtship –." So all those hints about love tinge toward belief— which, as we saw, means the same thing anyway: to give the heart.

Christ simply breaks his life, and her "No" becomes a "Yes." How does this happen? While Emily may declare, "'No' is the wildest word we consign to Language," we all know that "Yes" can be far wilder. *No* is refusal, renunciation, the wall built around the self to keep the world out. *Yes* is the open door, the locks on the dam let go. So Emily wrote to Sue, in her final years, "Remember, Dear, an unfaltering *Yes* is my only reply to your utmost question –." This is how love speaks: "an unfaltering *Yes*." Love does not say about the "utmost question," *maybe, might we renegotiate, let's think this through, given the odds.* Love says, "an unfaltering *Yes*." Could this have been what Augustine meant when he said, "Do you wish to understand? Believe." Say "Yes."

Emily doesn't offer much help here on how to move from "No" to "Yes." While she never actually utters the final "Yes" in the poem—that would be too simple—she implies it in the closing question: "And could I further 'No'"? That question also holds within it the other "know" that's been troubling me in my drive to seek rational understanding, since *no* and *know* are homonyms. Could I further *know*? The implied answer is "No" (another no!), by which, of course, she means to move toward a greater, more encompassing "Yes." In life, unlike in logic, two No's don't make a Yes, any more than two wrongs make a right, any more than Pascal's logical wager could lead a doubter to belief, but perhaps it's time to put the logical puzzles, the rational gambles, the moral equations aside. Perhaps the wheel spins round?

I think it did for Emily. She recounts how she literally ran away from God when she was a girl, much like she does in this poem: "When a Child and fleeing from Sacrament I could hear the Clergyman saying 'All who loved the Lord Jesus Christ – were asked to remain –' My flight kept time to the Words." She was running not to the altar but out the door. After that, she started finding excuses to stay home from Sabbath meetings, long before she wrote those famous lines, "Some keep the Sabbath going to Church – / I keep it, staying at Home –." The weather, an indisposition, a note that simply had to be finished. "The bells are ringing," she reports to Sue in one such unapologetic letter, "and the people who love God, are expecting to go to meeting. . . . They will all go but me, to the usual meetinghouse, to hear the usual sermon; the inclemency of the storm so kindly detaining me." She makes use of the stolen time to invite Sue to join her instead at "the church within our hearts," where love is preaching. Later, in her thirties, Emily left the church, never to return. When her brother, Austin, supervised the building of a new church, just down the road from the family Homestead, Emily sneaked out in the dark to see it, but did not go inside. And yet this poem hints, miraculously, that the further away she got, the larger the light shone, calling her back. "Daughter give me thine heart." Or as Augustine says, "Believe."

Even Emily urged the same to others. She wrote to Higginson, in mourning for his wife: "let Redemption find you –, as it certainly will – Love is it's own rescue, for we – at our supremest, are but it's trembling Emblems –." Love can rescue us, she believed, from anything life throws at us—even death. So perhaps, even doubt. A triumphal poem chants the credo of this ultimate belief in love: "Love is like Life – merely longer / Love is like Death, during the Grave / Love is the Fellow of the Resurrection / Scooping up the Dust and chanting 'Live'!" In Emily's hands, love takes on the attributes of the whole Trinity: Father, creator of "Life," the Son "during the Grave," and the Spirit who breathes life into our "Dust."

So how does this view of love link back to my dilemma, to belief? Well, it turns out that, for Emily, love and belief were even closer than her dictionary knew. In an earlier draft of these lines, Emily placed the word *Faith* at the head of each of the claims: faith is like life; faith is like death; faith is the fellow of the resurrection. Halfway down the page, a little hatch mark in the margin beside *Faith* signals an alternate word choice— *Love*—squeezed in above the line.

So faith, in the first draft, became love, in the second, because for Emily the two were one. Love/Faith is its own rescue. "Daughter give me thine heart."

> 89-6
>
> While "it" is alive —
> Until Death — touches it —
> While "it" and I. lap
> one. Air —
> Dwell in one Blood —
> Under one +Firmament — + Sacrament
> Show one +Division + Can -Could
> split — or pass! + Love
> +Faith" — is like —Life —
> +Only, the longer — + merely
> Faith — is like the —Death
> During — the Grave —
> Faith — is the Fellow of
> the Resurrection,
> Scooping up the Dust —
> And chanting — "Live"!

I am inclined to believe her, even without quite understanding how, perhaps because those I've loved on earth teach me that a heart can be a simple thing to give. I give my heart, quite freely, to close friends, my family, to my beloved. If to them, why not to God? *Credo ut intelligam.* Or as the father prayed to Jesus in Mark's Gospel, out of his love for his suffering child, "Lord, I believe; help thou mine unbelief."

PROOF

That I did always love
I bring thee Proof
That till I loved
I never lived – Enough –

That I shall love alway –
I argue thee
That love is life –
And life hath Immortality –

This – dost thou doubt – Sweet –
Then have I
Nothing to show
But Calvary –

EMILY NEVER MARRIED, but that she gave her heart, at least once, seems clear to most readers. She called him "Master" and wrote to him some of the most beautiful letters ever penned in English, called by scholars the "Master letters." These three letters are so singular they've been published separately from the rest of her correspondence in a special edition. The slim volume comes with an envelope tucked inside, filled with photographic reproductions of the handwritten letters. Opening the envelope and pulling out the loose pages feels like discovery, as if the stunning words are the first clue in a mystery that you will solve. Emily's hieroglyphic handwriting adds to the feeling of archaeology. The earliest letter, from 1858, flaunts her more floral swooping script:

By the third letter, in 1861, her pen moves faster, and the page look less ceremonial as the words spill and scrawl in urgency.

Those who first entered the Egyptian tombs surely did not feel more thrilled than I did the first time I ventured into the twisting lines of the Master letters' poetic prose.

For all I've learned about Emily, I've never solved the mystery of who "Master" is. No one has or probably ever will. I lean to two contenders. Runner up: Samuel Bowles, the charismatic editor of the *Springfield Daily Republican*, in whom Emily confided more fully than anyone else we know. And, on very scanty evidence, my favorite choice: the Reverend Charles Wadsworth, whom she termed after his death, "My closest earthly friend," "my Shepherd from 'Little Girl'hood," "my Clergyman," "my dearest earthly friend," and "My Philadelphia," after the town where he'd dwelled. There is almost no proof of the "intimacy of many years with the beloved Clergyman" as she names it, beyond the lining up of dates and places, but the tiny clues seep romance: Emily's trip to Philadelphia, where he drew crowds with his emotive preaching; a single letter he sent her years later, though it's rather impersonal (he even misspells her name, "Dickenson"); the fact that, decades later, she still had new copies of his sermons on hand to share with friends; and his two visits to her house in Amherst, in 1860 and 1880. At twenty years' remove, he came back to see her again after his wife died. What happened in between? She narrates these visits—and rhapsodizes over Wadsworth—in the strikingly tender correspondence she began with two of his friends after his death:

> He rang one summer evening to my glad surprise – "Why did you not tell me you were coming, so I could have it to hope for," I said – "Because I did not know it myself. I stepped from my Pulpit to the Train," was his quiet reply.

It's some of the most immediate writing of her whole œuvre. We glimpse her as the person, not the oracle, can even envision her in real-life situations. We get dialogue—breathless phrases—and we're left to imagine the rest:

> I knew him a "Man of sorrow," and once when he seemed almost overpowered by a spasm of gloom, I said "You are troubled." Shivering as he spoke, "My Life is full of dark secrets," he said. He never spoke of himself, and encroachment I know would have slain him. . . . He was a Dusk Gem, born of troubled Waters, astray in any Crest below. Heaven might give him Peace, it could not give him Grandeur, for that he carried with himself to whatever scene –

Perhaps *because* there is so little evidence, and so rich, the imagination runs wild.

Who exactly Master was we'll probably never know for sure. In fact, while I assume this mysterious figure was "he," a group of readers would fault me for presuming even the minimal knowledge of that pronoun. They consider that Master may rather have been mistress of Emily's heart, and they point to her dear Sue, the sister-in-law who lived next door, to whom Emily addressed ecstatic letters and sent a wealth of poems, far more than to any other person. Then there are other readers, more figuratively inclined, who proclaim that Master was neither he, nor she, but He, the bridegroom of humanity, the Master who loved the world so well He made Himself a slave. Still other readers argue that Master was no one, human or divine, but rather all of these and none of these, just the imagined creation of an intensely imaginative mind. They say that Emily, some dull afternoon, created for herself this liberating prompt: Emily made up the figure, Master, to make poems *with* it, and then away with it she flew, "No Bird – yet rode in Ether."

While it is difficult to prove that Emily's Master letters and poems are pure pose, it is infinitely harder to prove that they are not. How do you, at one hundred and fifty years' remove, prove love? Then again, how do you prove it at all? Someone inclined to doubt your love will never be convinced, whatever proof you give. Shakespeare made a masterpiece of the fact in *Othello*.

"One drop more from the gash that stains your Daisy's bosom," Emily begins one of the Master letters, "then would you *believe*?" Whether or not Master believed her—and many readers hypothesize that he never had the chance, that the letters were never sent—Emily obviously loved to enumerate love's proofs, for she expounded her love in poem after poem.

In "That I did always love," she convenes her own court of
love, arguing her ardor through a series of advancing claims,
just as a lawyer might prove a case.

> That I did always love
> I bring thee Proof
> That till I loved
> I never lived – Enough –
>
> That I shall love alway –
> I argue thee
> That love is life –
> And life hath Immortality –
>
> This – dost thou doubt – Sweet –
> Then have I
> Nothing to show
> But Calvary –

She swears in the opening line to the completeness of this love
in the past. And at the start of the second stanza, she gives
assurance for the continuance of this love in the future, "That
I shall love alway –." Even in this legalistic mode, Emily suits
the form of her message to its content: the word *alway*, with its
missing *s*, remains forever unfinished, echoing the unfinishable
eternity for which she vows to love him.

Since she promises eternal love, she musters all time as a proof
of this love. She conjugates her love throughout the verses,
like a verb—*That I did love, that I loved, that I love, that I shall
love*—to prove how she, in all tenses, belongs to her beloved.
And more important than these promises of pluperfect, simple
past, and future love is her testimony to the power of this love

in the present. The poem's final claim pronounces that, in the here and now, as well as in eternity, this "love *is* life." Her love is all and alway, the very breath of life to her who lives by it and through it, life unimaginable without it.

Her words are beautiful. And yet, does the poem offer the proof it promises? Although Emily promises at its start, "That I did always love / I bring thee Proof," the "proof" never really appears. She brings forth no evidence to substantiate her claims. She doesn't recall a shared moment of intimate history, a conversation, a gesture that would prove her early and constant love. Instead, her own assurance actually seems to dwindle: she starts out claiming to prove but, by the second stanza, the authoritative *prove* has yielded to a weaker verb, "I argue thee." Even this solid argument becomes, by the final stanza, only an inconclusive *showing*: "Then have I / Nothing to show / But Calvary –." Though Emily begins with the intent to prove her love, she leaves off by pointing to Christ as an example.

Of course, Christ is not exactly paltry evidence of love. Christ's coming is said to be a proof of God's love for humanity, Christ's dying a proof of his own love—as he shares our all, both burden and bliss—and his rising a proof of love's power, even over the mortal force Emily names the "supple Suitor." For someone who wishes to prove her love by example, Christ is pretty much the best example around. Christ exemplifies how far love will go (to the grave), how long love will last (past the grave), and how triumphant is love's reach (even into all our graves). To prove his own love for humanity, as Emily writes in another poem, "Our Lord – thought no / Extravagance / To pay – a Cross –." So, Emily swears by association, will she.

Yet, still I have my doubts, obstinate as that may seem. Even Christ's death, as proof of love, cannot be proven—not in the way a jealous lover or a doubting soul might require. The evidence of the cross was "paid" two thousand years ago, and some of the proof might seem to have worn off the transaction in the meantime. After all, the proof of the cross has been challenged by factors such as science, religious pluralism, and, oh, the Enlightenment. These troubling facts muddied faith in Emily's day just as much as in ours. Faith has to keep finding fresh answers to address new challenges as they arise. So Emily names "Faith – The Experiment of Our Lord –," because the conclusion is not assured. And while countless numbers still manage to believe, Emily returns repeatedly to the metaphor of experiment to talk about faith: "'Faith' is a fine invention / For Gentlemen who *see*! / But Microscopes are prudent / In an Emergency!" Clearly, Emily is one of those who would prefer the microscope. She tells how faith "plucks at a twig of Evidence –," in its search for substantial answers. What are we looking for through the microscope? From the twig? Proof.

As proof, the cross is not particularly successful, since our need for proof of faith, God's love, and eternal life has never ceased. "Experiment escorts us last –," Emily reasons, and whether we go toward that last moment with faith or fact in hand, it's an experiment for us all. In fact, so far from proving anything, the cross has become just one more thing that needs proving. This was true even two thousand years ago, when it first happened: the man his disciples and the crowds claimed was the Lord had died in shame and infamy; he was buried; it was over. That the Crucifixion was glory, not shame, had to be proven by the resurrection; it wasn't, in fact, glory until the resurrection made it so. The truth of the resurrection, in turn, had to be proven by Christ's resurrection appearances. And these appearances had to be proven, to some of the less credulous disciples, by yet more tangible proof. So the final chapters of the Gospels are full of disciples running back and forth between the tomb and the twelve, trying to figure out, against the odds, what is happening. Thomas, the most skeptical proof-seeker of all, demanded to put his finger straight into Christ's wounds before he would believe that this living being before him was the same Jesus who had died on the cross. He wanted a microscope too: "Except I shall see in his hands the print of the nails, and put my finger into the print of the nails, and thrust my hand into his side, I will not believe." As Emily jabs in one of the Master letters, "Thomas' faith in Anatomy, was stronger than his faith in faith." Who could blame him?

The problem with proofs is that they can pile up ever so high, but they often carry little lasting effect. Faith is not a science. No evidence will convince a doubter. The soul inclined to doubt will doubt again, even after a proof that seemed, in the moment, incontrovertible has come and gone. A few months after Thomas's dramatic experience, when Christ had once again departed from the scene, Thomas may well have felt anew a halting need for some proof.

At least this is how it goes with me. I've had more proof than anyone has the right to hope, yet each time, the quick assurance fades too quickly into doubt. A few summers ago, I kissed what was famed to be the crown of thorns and stood an arm's length from a nail purported to be used in the Passion. I'm ashamed to say "famed" and "purported" now, since standing there in Notre-Dame de Paris, I did not feel there was anything famed or purported about those artifacts. No, I felt like Thomas, that I had seen the wounds and touched the hands and shared the bread with one supposed to be dead but miraculously living, there, in front of me.

I'd gone into Notre-Dame that morning, like the thousands of other tourists and lookers-on, just to see. I certainly did not think that the *couronne d'épines* on display was *the* crown of thorns. I knew better. Sainte-Chapelle was built by one of the Kings Louis, to house relics brought back from the Crusades. Chief among these relics was the crown of thorns, miraculously preserved for nine centuries and available for purchase right there at the moment when the crusading Europeans passed through. Every so often, Sainte-Chapelle lets the crown out on display. This time it was at Notre-Dame, so in I went. How many chances do you get to see the crown of thorns, even if it is a fake?

The procession passed down the aisle of the darkened church, the organ rumbling somewhere very far away. I couldn't fix my eyes on what they were carrying—just a dim sense of a Plexiglas box with a circlet of extremely large thorns inside. The thorns looked overemphasized, gaudy. I wanted to call in the props department and suggest that next time they use something a bit more subtle. Then another group walked past, lifting high—I craned to look around my neighbor—a nail. No, a spike. It was so huge you could have used it to secure railroad ties. It took me a moment to realize what I was seeing, and suddenly I felt dizzy and almost scared. "I could not see to see," Emily describes dying, and so that moment felt to me. I couldn't see, hear, or think anything. All I could do was feel my proximity to a presence so compelling it overpowered my rational objections. I knew that that spike was not one of the nails used in the actual Crucifixion. And yet, I felt in my veins, like electricity, that it was. My chin began to wobble and my knees—it's a cliché—shook. It wasn't the crown that convinced me, but rather the way I felt about the one who may or may not have worn it. It didn't matter. I believed.

How long before we slip back down the slope from faith to doubt? Before the truth we sealed, like wax with hot fire, begins to crack in cold reason? As the old questions rise to my lips—the same lips that kissed the crown that day—I think of Judas's kiss in the garden.

Yet in the wake of that experience, this poem of Emily's has taken on new resonances. I'd long cherished it for its expressions of absolute earthly love. Now the most poignant line is the one at the last stanza's start: "This – dost thou doubt – Sweet –." For the only thing I know for certain now is that I will always doubt. *That I shall doubt alway – / I argue thee.* And however much Emily may underline, "Faith is <u>Doubt</u>," the two don't feel the same. I could, like Thomas, place my finger in the wounds of Christ's hands and I would still doubt. Then again, the only one who could pronounce without a single doubt "That love is life – / And life hath Immortality –" is Christ, who can, indeed, point to "Calvary" for proof. For the rest of us, there must always be some doubt.

So even as my doubts return, and they "alway" do, I also know that I am changed by that quick-fire moment of proof and the conviction it lent me. See, I no longer hear this poem only as one that Emily wrote to an earthly beloved. I also hear it as one that Christ speaks in proof of his love.

He points to the cross with those nail-marked hands. He says to us:

> That I did always love
> I bring thee Proof
> That till I loved
> I never lived – Enough –
>
> That I shall love alway –
> I argue thee
> That love is life –
> And life hath Immortality –
>
> This – dost thou doubt – Sweet –
> Then have I
> Nothing to show
> But Calvary –

PRAYER

Prayer is the little implement

HYMN

THREE AND A HALF INCHES TALL by two and a half inches
wide, and very fat, the hymnal fits in my palm. Even opened, it
doesn't span the hand. The deep hide of the binding, crackled
like topography, carries a faint impress of gold on its spine,
announcing in one word the book's contents: Watts. In 1828,
the year of its printing, that would have been enough. Everyone
would have known who "Watts" was.

Inside—open it gently, the spine must not be forced—the
pages don't shine like modern white stock. They don't have the
elegant linen-like texture of paper from more expensive books
of the period. These pages feel almost damp, less like paper
than flannel or cambric, soft and sturdy fabrics. This is a paper,
like those fabrics, that lets you work. I wrap my hand around
the book. Holding it, I feel held.

For generations of Protestants, Isaac Watts's words were
central to the experience of faith. His hymns entered into
the American tradition of hymnody that started with the *Bay
Psalm Book*—metrical paraphrases of the Psalms to be sung in
Christian worship—the very first book printed in the colonies
that would become the United States. Watts innovated on this
and earlier books of hymnody by composing his own hymns to
be printed alongside the more conventional translations of the
Psalms sung in worship. With this innovation, Watts opened

up the possibility of penning sacred songs not based solely on biblical texts. Perhaps this is one reason why Isaac Watts was one of Emily's chief tutors in poetry.

The Dickinson library had an 1810 copy of Watts's translation of the Psalms "carefully suited to the Christian worship," as the title page proclaims, and two editions, 1817 and 1834, of Watts's *Hymns, Psalms, and Spiritual Songs*, both inscribed with Edward Dickinson's name. And those are just the copies that we know about. The family library was much vaster than the 565 books that have been reconstituted in the Houghton Library's collection today. Retracing the books Emily might have read from that evidence is like trying to imagine the appearance of a living creature from the fossil it leaves behind: you get a sense of general structure, but much of the detail, texture, and color is lost. Even in the now-truncated collection of Dickinson books, Watts shows a significant presence.

He also shows a significant presence in Emily's poems. Watts's hymns were as pervasive in nineteenth-century New England as the Bible, and Emily imbibed them just as deeply as she did that larger tome. In 1853, she chided her brother Austin, away at Harvard Law School, "Trust you enjoy your closet, and meditate profoundly upon the Daily Food! I shall send you Village Hymns, by earliest opportunity." The hymns were understood to be as much a part of the "Daily Food" of spiritual sustenance as Scripture, and so Emily nudges her equally disobedient brother in something of a shared joke about the volume used to impress upon them proper Sabbath behavior. Five years later, still in the youth of her writing, Emily played directly with one of Watts's hymns, "There Is a Land of Pure Delight." The final stanza of one of her poems opens with two lines (slightly misquoted) from that hymn: "'Oh could we climb where Moses stood, / And view the Landscape o'er.'" But where Watts goes on to conclude with traditional biblical imagery, "Not Jordan's stream, nor death's cold flood / Should fright us from the shore," Emily tweaks his tone to sound a more contemporary gong: "Not Father's bells – nor Factories – / Could scare us any more!" Her use of Watts suggests both his influence on her developing ear and the playful engagement with hymns that characterizes her poetry. While she borrowed content from the Bible—characters, imagery, clusters of powerful language—she took from Watts the form and sound.

From Watts's hymns, Emily learned a wealth of rhythms that she went on to spin into her poems: Common Meter (8.6.8.6), Psalm Meter (8.7.8.7), Short Meter (6.6.8.6), Long Meter (8.8.8.8.), Sevens, Sixes and Sevens, Twelves. Doubled and particular meters allowed for longer stanzas, cyclical patterns. These hymn meters provide the basic templates—line length, syllable count, stanza structure—for Emily's nearly eighteen hundred poems. Now, since Watts's hymns were songs, not poems, each hymn text could be matched to an array of tunes that worked with that arrangement of syllables. Emily would have heard hymn tunes, from earliest age, played on the double bass that the First Church in Amherst used to accompany the congregation. The bass's deep vibrations must have rumbled these rhythms right into her bones. "I dont wonder," Emily wrote at nineteen, "that good angels weep – and bad ones sing songs." A "bad one" in her own estimation, she joined their choir. When she stopped singing hymns in church, she went on to weave those same metrical patterns into her own sort of hymns. *Hymn* is not my word for her writing. It's Emily's.

> I rose – because He sank –
> I thought it would be opposite –
> But when his power dropped –
> My Soul grew straight.
>
> I cheered my fainting Prince –
> I sang firm – even – Chants –
> I helped his Film – with Hymn –
>
> And when the Dews drew off
> That held his Forehead stiff –
> I met him –
> Balm to Balm –
>
> I told him Best – must pass
> Through this low Arch of Flesh –
> No Casque so brave
> It spurn the Grave –
>
> I told him Worlds I knew
> Where Emperors grew –
> Who recollected us
> If we were true –
>
> And so with Thews of Hymn –
> And Sinew from within –
> And ways I knew not that I knew – till then –
> I lifted Him –

The story of this poem—dramatic and romantic—happened in less poetic ways throughout her life. Emily endlessly offered solace "with Hymn –," as she sent out her poems to those in distress. Sending a stanza to Loo, she named it "a little hymn." She remarked on another occasion, "I have promised three Hymns to a charity." As in the poem printed above, she helped her loved ones through song: "I sang firm – even – Chants – / I helped his Film – with Hymn – ." Emily did not sit by the bedside chanting Watts's familiar hymns, "O God Our Help in Ages Past" or "When I Survey that Wondrous Cross." After all, she said she offered "Thews of Hymn – / And Sinew from *within* –." The hymns within her were her own, as much a part of her as the "Thews" of muscle, tendon, and sinew that made up her hand as she penned them. Church may have supplied the meters (those "firm – even – Chants" the poem names), but the texts were her own. So when Emily invited Fanny and Loo, "Let Emily sing for you because she cannot pray," she wasn't being metaphorical; she was literally offering her poems to them as song.

Her poems are songs, in the same way that Watts's hymns are, because you can sing them. Many of Emily's poems follow a hymn meter so closely you can actually sing them to hymn tunes. For instance, all the poems written in Common Meter, with alternating lines of eight syllables and six syllables, can be sung to the familiar tune "New Britain," which we now associate with the song "Amazing Grace." That text and that tune were paired for the first time in *The Southern Harmony*, printed in 1835, which went on to become the most popular hymnal of the nineteenth century.

You might just as easily pair the tune with Emily's poem: "God is indeed a jealous God – / He cannot bear to see / That we had rather not with Him / But with each other play." Try singing it:

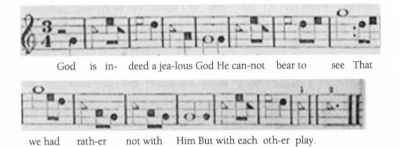

Buoyed on the strains of that well-known tune, this quatrain becomes, as Emily predicted, "a little hymn," if rather a naughty one. (After all, "bad ones sing songs.") Pairing words to tunes like this would have been natural for Emily, who grew up doing so in church. Today's hymnals tend to print the melody's score with a hymn's words directly underneath the music. Nineteenth-century hymnals often did not. Throughout Emily's childhood, a given text could be matched, from one time to the next, with different tunes. Tunes and texts were interchangeable. In printing words and music together, *The Southern Harmony*

suggests the beginnings of a trend in printing that continues into our time. But even before this trend began, some pairings of tunes and words could become standard simply through repetition and congregational practice: in fact, before the "New Britain" tune was paired with the words to "Amazing Grace," it was common to pair it with Watts's hymn "There Is a Land of Pure Delight," the very hymn we watched Emily playing with earlier. Just think: Emily may have been imagining her alternate lines, "Not Father's Bells . . ." while humming the tune we now know as "Amazing Grace." And not just this poem; not just this tune. Emily easily could have summoned many tunes to match the varied meters she used. For her, the matching itself might have been a kind of musical game, just as it's natural now for us to make up spoofs of popular songs by supplying new words. We know that Emily did so during her early years in church. She wrote to Sue, recently converted in the latest revival, "Susie, when they sang . . . I made up words and kept singing how I loved you, and you had gone, while all the rest of the choir were singing Hallelujahs."

Once she'd stopped attending church, Emily could have continued to play with the hymn tunes she knew, even making up her own impromptu tunes. She was an accomplished musician, legendary among houseguests at the Homestead for rising to play haunting melodies of her own composition in the middle of the night. Her father particularly loved to listen to her play. Emily reported that on the day before he died (though she did not know then that it would be the final time), she played hymns for him: "Almost the last tune that he heard was, 'Rest from thy loved employ.'" Standing in front of her ornate piano in the Houghton Library at Harvard, I picture her slim fingers easily tripping along in the pattern of the familiar tunes, her mind turning over new words for them.

If it's exciting to be able to sing so many of Emily's poems, it's equally exciting to discover how many you can't sing. Good luck matching the poem printed above, "I rose – because He sank –," to any hymn tune. The meter is simply too irregular; no tune could follow it: 6.8.6.4 / 6.6.6 / 6.6.3.3. / 6.6.4.4 / 6.4.6.4 / 6.6.10.4. A jazz musician might be able to play this poem, but it would be mostly riffing, with no clear melodic line. The stanzas don't even have a regular number of lines.

In fact, this willed irregularity in her meter was likely one factor that made Emily hesitate to publish, for her freedom was neither expected, nor much accepted, by readers of her day. When, in 1862, she boldly sent a handful of poems to Higginson for his appraisal, he evidently criticized her meter, since her reply to his letter is tart on precisely this point. She quoted him back to him: "You think my gait 'spasmodic.'" Looking back at the outline of syllables in each line that I've sketched above, you may also find their "gait spasmodic." Indeed, it is. The lines lurch and trip at different speeds. And yet the meter is spasmodic as modern dance is, with a purpose. Emily employs meter too adeptly for us to presume her rhythms and breaks in rhythm are anything but knowing and intentional. Here she uses the uneven meter just as she uses the evenness of meter in other poems: to enhance meaning.

Look, for example, at the last stanza. From a couplet of six-syllable lines (a pattern she's used already several times in the poem), she breaks from anything we've encountered so far, to introduce a grand ten-syllable line. It's perfect iambic pentameter, the standard, most powerful form in English poetry from the Renaissance onward:

And so with Thews of Hymn –
And Sinew from within –
And ways I knew not that I knew – till then –
I lifted Him –

The stanza's third line swells to ten syllables just as Emily speaks of finding unknown resources. So the unexpected abundance of her strength, discovered in song, is mimicked by the unexpected abundance of syllables in the line, which swells beyond all expectation. Form matches content in a meaningful and energizing way. And then, after that plentitude, the next lines suddenly drops to a short four syllables: "I lifted Him –." There's a bold contrast between the long stretch of the ten-syllable line and the short clap of the four-syllable close, "I lifted Him –." This contrast emphasizes the simplicity and strength of that unexpected act of lifting. In context, the final line feels like the sturdy landing of a gymnast after a complicated airborne combination, when flips and turns and twists end on solid ground. The meter in this poem may not be even, but Emily knows how to work the unevenness she creates for effect.

When I hold the 1828 Watts hymnal, printed two years before Emily was born, I can easily envision her as a girl holding her own small volume in church, learning the meters she later would come to weave into her songs. As a child in my own family of five, we shared the three hymnals arrayed in the white pew rack in front of us at Stanley Congregational Church, where my dad had attended as a kid and then played the organ. My mom would hold one hymnal. My dad, another. I shared his, hearing over my shoulder his rich voice, suited for Irish ballads. And then my brothers would take the third, which they'd use as a desk to scribble notes, writing new words for the hymns—just as Emily did. Of course, Emily's songs were not just adolescent rebellion, the play of an idle hour; they gave way to the practice of a lifetime and some of the greatest art ever created by an American poet.

As she perfected this art, Emily worked with standard hymn patterns when she wanted and broke them when she wanted, just as she finally broke the pattern of attending church, so she could make her own kind of hymn. On Sundays, when the rest of her family is in the family pew at the First Church of Amherst, singing Watts's hymns to the sound of the double bass, she's upstairs in her room, holding one of the small paper books she sewed to hold her hymns: "Humming – for promise – when alone – / Humming – until my faint Rehearsal – / Drop into tune – around the Throne –."

PRAYER

Prayer is the little implement
Through which Men reach
Where Presence – is denied them –
They fling their Speech

By means of it – in God's Ear –
If then He hear –
This sums the Apparatus
Comprised in Prayer –

IF EMILY ADMITTED TO MAKING HYMNS, she rarely admitted to prayer. When she asks her cousins, "Let Emily sing for you because she cannot pray," the keyword is *because*. Song is a substitute, a compensation that she offers *because* of her inability to pray. Nor is Emily's profession in this letter an isolated incident. Emily was downright adamant, and persistently so, that she did not pray. She traces the roots of her inability in a letter to Higginson, stating that she was "not reared to prayer" and, to Samuel Bowles, "we did not learn to pray." To an injured friend nursing a broken foot, she excuses herself with a boast: "Knew I how to pray, to intercede for your Foot were intuitive – but I am but a Pagan."

Her letters not only pronounce her inability to pray on her own, they also testify to how often she bowed out of common prayer. On Sundays, when the family was off at church, she grinned to be home writing letters, "It is Sunday – now – John – and all have gone to church . . . and I have come out in the new grass to listen to the anthems." Again song—even the songs of the crickets and birds—stands in for prayer. Of the family's daily morning prayer, her reports indicate her mental distance: "They are religious – except me – and address an Eclipse, every morning – whom they call their 'Father.'" The third person plural "They" tells us that she (though present) doesn't include herself; Emily was otherwise engaged. Even when she was attentive, her attention turned past the prayers toward the pray-ers. She describes her father's manner at prayer with great precision: "'I say unto you,' Father would read at Prayers, with a militant Accent that would startle one." In the face of his militancy, it seems Emily beat a hasty retreat, leaving prayer behind on the field.

This protestation continues in Emily's poems. "I prayed, at first, a little Girl," she explains in one iconic poem, "Because they told me to – / But stopped . . . " Prayer doesn't make it past the third line. And even when Emily admits to attempting prayer as a last-ditch effort, "My period had come for Prayer – / No other Art – would do –," she concludes her attempt with the equivocal announcement, "I worshipped – did not 'pray' –." She puts *pray* between scare quotes, which gives the line an ironic tone: this so-called prayer that other people supposedly "pray." She, obviously, cannot attest.

To be sure, some of this denial is just grandstanding. As we've seen, Emily relished presenting herself as a sort of renegade, especially about great matters like religion. (Think back to how she stood up to Miss Lyon at Mount Holyoke.) She clearly took pride in standing apart from the flock and smiling at the sheep that followed blithely along. We only know about Emily's small rebellions against the norm because she liked to retell these very stories. She brags: "Austin and I were talking the other Night about the Extension of Consciousness, after Death and Mother told Vinnie, afterward, she thought it was 'very improper.' She forgets that we are past 'Correction in Righteousness' –." Emily evidently preferred more to be "past Correction" than correct.

And yet, her denials about prayer must also be more than just grandstanding. She pronounces that she does not, cannot, will not pray in such frequent and diverse ways; it seems likely that she's also telling the truth and that this truth mattered to her. However flip her tone can be, Emily seems to have had real reservations about prayer.

Scanning her most straightforward poem on prayer, we might not wonder at Emily's resistance.

> Prayer is the little implement
> Through which Men reach
> Where Presence – is denied them –
> They fling their Speech
>
> By means of it – in God's Ear –
> If then He hear –
> This sums the Apparatus
> Comprised in Prayer –

I want no part of this sort of prayer either. Emily presents prayer as a complicated scientific experiment. Where did she dig up this unusual language of "implement" and "Apparatus"? It makes me feel as if I might need safety goggles. At the very least, her scientific diction makes me fear that prayer will require me to regulate variables and maintain a control case.

In truth, this fear is not far off, for Emily's poem does describe an experiment with multiple variables. There's a deficiency of "Presence," which the experiment means to use the "implement," prayer, to correct. There's the variable of the "Speech" that men "fling"—a haphazard way of moving rather like the scatter effect, I imagine. They fling this variable, "Speech," across an unknown distance, to attain an object they can't perceive, "God's Ear." Now, even if they reach this ear, they cannot be assured of getting the desired reaction, namely, that God, the experiment's second independent variable, will hear. If, however, the whole prayer apparatus functions as it should, and if the appropriate speech is flung on the proper arc with the correct velocity in the desired direction, and if it strikes the ear in the wanted manner at the necessary moment, and if, above all else, the ultimate variable, God, is inclined to hear, then—*poof*—the complex chemical reaction called prayer will have occurred. The odds don't seem good. There are too many variables.

Emily embeds her skepticism about prayer in her manner of narrating it. First, she shows men "flinging" their speech, a word that injects randomness and disdain into the process, for one cannot control words merely flung into the ether. It's fair to assume that a poet, who crafts her words and phrases with exquisite care and then revises them multiple times, might not embrace any linguistic business that requires *flinging*. Moreover, Emily shows that this random word-flinging arises from a preliminary deficit:

a person only attempts prayer because the greater good, God's "Presence," actively "is denied them –." Not a propitious start. The one who prays begins already at a disadvantage, addressing an absent God. Furthermore, the poem does not seem optimistic that this absent God will suddenly be inclined to listen, since it acquaints us from the start with God as a figure who "denies." So God's initial denial of "Presence" seems prone to become a second denial, this time of our attempts at prayer.

Finally, in case these unfavorable conditions didn't put you off sufficiently, Emily breaks the poem into two stanzas at a crucial point. Between the "Speech" men fling and "God's Ear," which might or might not hear, Emily opens the wide expanse of a stanza break. Although she could have composed an eight-line poem—nothing simpler—she chooses to split the poem into two distinct halves, the men half and the God half. Between the two, her poem makes clear, there stands a sizeable gulf.

Oh yes, it's a pert little poem, thoroughly deprecating in tone. Just how deprecating becomes fully apparent only when you set it beside other poems on prayer by more pious poets. George Herbert's warm and wondrous poem "Prayer (I)," for example, offers an excellent counterpoint. We know that Emily read Herbert in the poetry pages of the *Springfield Republican*, as well as in *The Poetical Works of George Herbert*, a red-bound, illustrated book in Austin and Sue's library at the Evergreens, next door to the Dickinson Homestead. In an interesting twist of publishing history, two stanzas from Herbert's "Mattens" (another of his prayer poems) were misprinted as Emily's own work in the 1945 volume of her poems, *Bolts of Melody*. The poem's querying middle stanzas, "My God, what is a heart," passed easily for a poem by Emily, especially since they were found copied in Emily's hand, customary dashes and all, and left among her papers. Emily evidently felt that Herbert's poem slid naturally among her own, since she left his stanzas there with hers in the rosewood box. So I'll follow her lead here and slip "Prayer (I)" next to "Prayer is the little implement."

Listen, as Emily did, to Herbert's vastly different definition. Whereas Emily describes prayer through the metaphor of scientific variables, Herbert describes it using a sensuous variety of metaphors. Twenty-seven of them in fact:

> Prayer the Churches banquet, Angels age,
> Gods breath in man returning to his birth,
> The soul in paraphrase, heart in pilgrimage,
> The Christian plummet sounding heav'n and earth;
>
> Engine against th'Almightie, sinner's towre,
> Reversed thunder, Christ-side-piercing spear,
> The six daies world-transposing in an houre,
> A kinde of tune, which all things heare and fear;
>
> Softnesse, and peace, and joy, and love, and blisse,
> Exalted Manna, gladnesse of the best,
> Heaven in ordinarie, man well drest,
> The milkie way, the bird of Paradise,
>
> Church-bels beyond the stars heard, the souls bloud,
> The land of spices, something understood.

On and on Herbert goes, calling upon color and texture and taste and sound to craft his unspooling definition of prayer. The whole body exults in this ever-lifting, sumptuous flourish of language. Clearly, Herbert loves to pray. And who wouldn't, if prayer felt the way he describes? Prayer sounds positively delicious: "Church-bels beyond the stars heard, the souls bloud, / The land of spices." Herbert's poem makes my pulse accelerate. Now compare his vision with Emily's: "Prayer is the little implement / Through which Men reach / Where Presence – is denied them –." After Herbert's lushness, Emily's definition feels as inviting as a mouthful of gravel.

I wish I could pray as Herbert tells it, all spices and milkie way, but I'm afraid that I actually approach prayer much more in the way Emily describes. I begin as if I were coordinating a set of variables. If I can only go to the right place, I think. If I go to the chapel at the right time and in the right mood; if I bring my prayer beads and books; and if I hold my hands and feet, head and face, with the appropriate stillness; if I can speak good words with a true intention; and if, above all, I can keep distraction and doubt at bay, then all these variables might just add up to sum "the Apparatus / Comprised in Prayer –." People set out on the Oregon Trail with less preparation than I make to pray.

Yet shouldn't prayer do more than just happen? Isn't prayer meant to "comprise" something else, like communion or communication or, to borrow the final words of Herbert's poem, "something understood"? Perhaps Emily's poem feels so stifling because it merely draws a stationary circle around itself, from first word, *Prayer*, to last word, *Prayer*. Even the last two lines just keep circling around: since *sums* and *comprises* are synonyms of sorts—both loosely meaning "to be"—you might translate the closing lines, "Prayer is prayer is prayer." It's almost nonsensical. The poem's key terms, *implement* and *qpparatus*, close this contained prayer-circuit yet further. For *apparatus* comes from a Latin word meaning "to make ready, to prepare" and *implement* from one meaning "to fulfill." In naming prayer "implement" and "Apparatus," Emily makes prayer both the preparation and the fulfillment of the preparation, the origin and end, the first word and the last word. No wonder her prayer doesn't work. Isn't God supposed to be the origin and end of prayer?

For Herbert, God was both. "I cannot ope mine eyes," Herbert sings to God in the poem "Mattens," the very poem Emily copied for herself, "But thou art ready there to catch / My morning-soul and sacrifice." Herbert begins his poem with the trust that God is "ready there," *already* there, waiting by his pillow, to catch every drop of prayer. God is the origin of his offering. God is also its end. No vast gulf lurks in the middle of his poem, no capricious "If" about God's hearing. Herbert knows that God will hear because he knows that God inspires the very breath that, waking, becomes the prayer God cannot wait to hear. From its first word, *I*, to last word, *thee*, Herbert's "Mattens" works as prayer should, binding our I with God's thee.

For all her posturing and skepticism about prayer, Emily knew this kind of communion. "It was then my greatest pleasure," she speaks of her teenage experience of faith, "to commune alone with the great God & to feel that he would listen to my prayers." After she'd grown up and out of this experience, she still could not entirely shake it. She would write of moments of communion: "A Grant of the Divine – / That Certain as it Comes – / Withdraws – and leaves the dazzled Soul / In her unfurnished Rooms –." Even her scornful "Prayer is the little implement" hints at such dazzling contact. While she scoffingly goes on about implements, apparatuses, and men flinging speech across wide stanza breaks, Emily nevertheless hides some optimism in the rhymes. Two perfect rhyme pairs chime out through the irony, one in each stanza: *Speech / reach* and *Ear / hear*. In each case, the sound pattern binds together a noun and a verb. Through these perfect rhymes, Emily intimates that each action is so harmonious with each actor, completion is guaranteed. Our Speech reaches; God's Ear hears. The rhymes tell us that they know no other way. For all she scoffs, she also marvels: "God it is said replies in Person / When the Cry is meant."

I don't know exactly how God replies, whether prayers can be answered with action, but still, I find comfort in the simple, hidden testament to Emily's hope, even her knowledge, of prayer's success, tucked into rhyme. Just as our ears register the first rhyme, *Speech / reach*, we hop across the stanza break and find that the second rhyme comes a line sooner than anticipated, forming an early couplet, *Ear / hear*. God's ear, a line sooner than we expected and with no delay at all, hears. The second rhyme hastens forward to show that, before we've even begun to hope for it, God's Ear hears.

The Brothers I know from the Society of Saint John the Evangelist teach something similar about prayer. They suggest that prayer is actually a response on our side, not an instigation. When we pray, we're not reaching up to God to get God's attention, we're responding to God, who's always already reaching for us. God begins prayer—has always already begun prayer—all we have to do is answer. To say it another way, God's Ear hears, always, because God is always listening for us to speak. The other words in the short sixth line, "If then," reinforce this impression. We'd been weighing possibilities before, much in the way that logicians craft If-then statements: *if* the variables of folded hands, listening ear, and spoken words line up, *then* prayer will happen. But Emily removes all those intervening words: "If then," it's already happened, and the rhyme rushes forward, *Ear / hear*, to confirm it. Her skeptical poem intimates a happy end to prayer. "Prayer –," she sighs at the close of another poem, "The Only Raiment I should need –."

If she could wrap herself in prayer, why did Emily so commonly swear that she never learned to pray? This poem offers a hint to the reason for her resistance. The prayer Emily forswears may be the very mode she mocks here, the prayer of "implement" and "Apparatus." Through her odd language of scientific variables, she pillories that particular mode of prayer that demands specific conditions, such as folded hands and a bowed head. "And shape my Hands – / Petition's way," she glosses such prayer. And its self-referential definition—prayer is prayer is prayer—might further deride the occasionally self-serving aims of prayer. Don't some modes of prayer make God into little more than a universal errand boy, hastening to fulfill our requests? "Of Course – I prayed –," Emily gestures toward this, "And did God Care? / He cared as much as on the Air / A Bird – had stamped her foot – / And cried 'Give Me' –." Disdaining such modes of prayer, Emily would not participate in them. "I threw my Prayer away –," she sulks when it does not yield the desired effect. I think she threw away only the kind of prayer that asks God for a desired effect.

Yet how many varied and delightful ways can the soul pray! Herbert's "Prayer (I)" unfolds a litany of options beyond implements and apparatuses. It also shows us twenty-seven ways that we might spot prayer in Emily's poems aside from the recognized verbal forms that begin, "Oh Lord," and "Our Father." Herbert's definitions suggest that prayer can be as simple as a mood, "Softnesse, and peace," or as lofty as a meditation on the cross, "Christ-side-piercing spear." You might say that his poem shows us that prayer comes in as many modes as there are people to practice it. The Brothers know this and teach this: walking can be prayer; breathing can be prayer; the whole of life can be prayer. Prayer is not about the words spoken, but about a disposition of the soul toward God.

So where in Emily's life might we spot the sort of prayer that Herbert shows in his poem? "The soul in paraphrase, heart in pilgrimage": Emily wrote innumerable poems with just those dimensions, from "I dwell in Possibility –" and "Dare you see a Soul at the 'White Heat'" to "I dreaded that first Robin, so," and "I felt a Funeral, in my Brain." Each of these poems tells a different "paraphrase" of the soul. As for "pilgrimage," sometimes Emily quite literally told the pilgrimage of others, as in her writings on the martyrs, "Through the Straight Pass of Suffering" and "Unto like Story – Trouble has enticed me –." More often, she told versions of her own journey to other realms: "I shall keep singing!" which we looked at earlier, and "I heard, as if I had no Ear," which we'll see later. The most frequently occurring word in all her work—*I*, appearing 1,682 times—suggests just how often she narrated her "heart in pilgrimage." While not every journey she described went toward God, she seems to have known, as Herbert did, that reflecting on the heart's pilgrimage, wherever it is headed, is a form of worthwhile attentiveness that some would call *prayer*.

And how many wry comments show Emily hefting her trusty "Engine against th'Almightie," as Herbert names a more aggressive kind of communication with the divine, like that Job practiced? Her faux prayers come to mind, "'Heavenly Father' – take to thee / The supreme iniquity / Fashioned by thy candid Hand / In a moment contraband –," but also the scalding inquiry of poems such as "If pain for peace prepares" and "Of God we ask one favor, that we may be forgiven –." "Oh God" she cries out in a prayer poem, "Why give if Thou must take away / The Loved?" The engine has been launched.

And what about the prayer contained in joyous admiration of the natural world, the kind Herbert terms "The six daies world transposing in an hour"? Emily could not have stopped that prayer if she'd tried. "My chancel – all the plain / Today," she sings her prayer far away from any altar. There must be many kinds of churches, as there are many kinds of prayer, since even Herbert made his *Temple* out of poems. And all of Emily's poems on ecstasy and awe, wonder, joy, and eternity reveal how she discovered in the quotidian that very prayerful joy that Herbert terms "Exalted Manna, gladnesse of the best, / Heaven in ordinarie, man well drest." No wonder she pronounced that she never learned to pray. Emily could not be taught these forms of prayer; she lived them every day in her way. There can be no question that she knew "Heaven in ordinarie."

Emily's poems are full of such experiences and so they are full of prayer, just not the kind of prayer we envision when we seek it through formulas, implements, and apparatus. By tucking the tiny, realized prayer of *Speech / reach* and *Ear / hear* within the otherwise dismissive "Prayer is the little implement,"

Emily not only reveals that she prays, she also reveals how. She doesn't wrap her prayer in discourse as a philosopher might. Nor does she express it through theology, as a preacher would. A poet, she prayed in the mode that mattered most to her and tucked her prayer in a hopeful rhyme, hymn meter, the careful crafting of a beautiful phrase. Attending persistently in her poetry to "Church-bels beyond the stars heard, the souls bloud / The land of spices," it's no wonder that Emily had little time left for prayer.

> Prayer is the little implement
> Through which Men reach
> Where Presence – is denied them –
> They fling their Speech
>
> By means of it – in God's Ear –
> If then He hear –
> This sums the Apparatus
> Comprised in Prayer –

INTERCESSION

SOMETIMES WE PRAY BETTER for others than for ourselves. This seems to have been true for Emily. For all her protestations and reluctance to admit to prayer, there are exceptions, and most often these exceptions arise as intercessions, prayers for others. At twenty-three, if a friend is happy: "I kneel and thank God for it, before I go to sleep." Twenty-eight: "I ask God on my knees to send you much prosperity, few winter days, and long suns." At thirty-two, during the Civil War, she writes to Higginson, who was commanding the first regiment of freed slaves, "though not reared to prayer – when service is had in Church, for Our Arms, I include yourself." And at forty-seven, she offers for a friend's children "a wish that would almost be a Prayer, were Emily not a Pagan –." If she couldn't pray for herself, she would for them, at least occasionally. And in her adjusted style: "Our freckled bosom bears it's friends – in it's own way – to a simpler sky."

Yet if intercessory prayer can be a path to God, it can also be a deterrent. Emily certainly struggled as she watched those around her pray for healing or relief for themselves or loved ones to no avail. What happens when "long interceding lips / Perceive their prayer is vain"? Emily answers in a manner that lets us hear the sharp sting, "'Thou shalt not' is a kinder sword / Than from a disappointing God / 'Disciple, call

again.'" Any reply would be better than no reply. Far worse
than a God who denies us something we desire is a God who
simply doesn't answer. So even as Emily admits to practicing
a sort of intercession, she also shakes her head in dismay at
all those bowed heads around her: "Prayer has not an answer
and yet how many pray!" It's easy to criticize, in a collected
moment, the very practices we turn to in our need. For Emily,
it's also natural to jest about them. See how she tucks her very
real concern about whether God answers prayers into a wry
comment to a delinquent friend: "You are like God. We pray to
Him, and He answers 'No.' Then we pray to Him to rescind the
'no,' and He don't answer at all, yet 'Seek and ye shall find' is
the boon of faith." It's like a bad knock-knock joke, but in this
one, the God who invites us to knock runs away the moment
our hand reaches for the clapper. What happens when faith's
"boon" becomes its barrier?

Prayer blocks me now; I admit it. I went to divinity school, in
large part, to relearn how to pray, because I'd grown so uneasy
about it. *Why do we pray* became *how do we pray* became *to
whom do we pray?* "I fumble at my Childhood's Prayer –," Emily
mirrors my confusion. Well, I'd fumbled so long at prayer, I'd
finally lost the ball. In retrospect, I see that my educational
plan made as much sense as going to the demolition derby
to learn how to drive, but my intention, if misguided, was
good. Shortly into my time in school, I realized that studying
the history of theology and prayer practices wouldn't offer
me much help with my prayer problem, so I decided to go
someplace that would: a convent. I began taking weekend trips
to the Sisters of Saint Margaret in Roxbury, Massachusetts. The
community prays together in the chapel five times each day:

Morning Prayer, Eucharist, Noonday Prayer, Evening Prayer, Compline. The rest of the time the Sisters keep silence, to foster the primary work of prayer. In a convent, you're always praying: vacuuming, trimming candles, sorting sheet music, wiping down tables in the refectory—everything becomes prayer. Sometimes this can get comical, as when I once caught an older Sister (who was, to be honest, rather loopy) praying aloud: "Oh Lord, you in your wisdom did let Brother Spoon get dirty. Help me to clean him. Help me to wash his sins away." Truly.

Yet for all my time in the silent convent, I spoke more words to the Sisters than to God. I'm in the gatehouse, with Sr. Sarah, learning how she got started making rosaries. I'm in the kitchen, talking with Sr. Marie-Louise about baking. I drift to the gift shop and strike up a conversation with the cleaning crew. Is that someone in the main office, fixing the computers? Better stop by. The Mother Superior—she stands four feet tall and moves through the world like a trucker—would send me to my room with a chastisement and an assignment: pray. I'd go, but when I got there, I'd pick up a book, plunk into a chair, and think about God, which is almost like praying, right?

As the weekends wore on, the Mother Superior's commands became increasingly emphatic: "Now you stop gabbing and go *pray!*" I never did. I recited some Psalms. I made lists of intercessions and ran through the names in the silence of my head. But prayer, the spontaneous communication of my soul to God? Not really. I managed to spend two and a half days in a convent, twice a month, for several months, without consenting to a single drop of prayer. This takes a unique kind of talent.

My problem is not just reluctance or laziness alone; it feels more like inhibition or incapacity. Emily teases a very real problem for me when she flutters with false naiveté, "My Tactics missed a rudiment – / Creator – Was it you?" I've missed that rudiment lately, and the Creator, too. It's the oddest thing: when I try to pray, the stream of words within me just dries up. I try to begin, "Oh Christ," and it sounds like a curse. It might as well be, because nothing else comes. I should, as Emily does in one poem, leave it at "Please, Sir," because that's about as many words as I can manage before I become blocked. "Oh Jesus . . . Lord . . . Savior," I flail linguistically. "Oh Jesus – in the Air –," Emily mimics such perplexity, "I know not which thy chamber is – / I'm knocking – everywhere –." So too, I knock around in language, as if by starting with the right word, by some powerful incantation, more words will follow. But they don't. Because I found the words to every thought I ever had but God.

> I found the words to every thought
> I ever had – but One –
> And that – defies Me –
> As a Hand did try to chalk the Sun
>
> To Races – nurtured in the Dark –
> How would your Own – begin?
> Could Blaze be shown in Cochineal –
> Or Noon – in Mazarin?

For the great gift of language—and English sparkles with rich words like *cochineal* and *mazarin*—there are still emotions, experiences that no word can touch. Emily's contemporary

Herman Melville captures this issue instantly: "Wonderfullest things are ever the unmentionable; deep memories yield no epitaphs." Or as Emily puts it, "Abyss has no Biographer –." There are deep concepts words won't grasp.

For centuries, theologians have written about the problem of using words to describe God. One of the most influential theologians on the topic, Thomas Aquinas, speaks in terms of analogy, that everything we express in limited human language, from our limited human vantage, about an ultimate God must necessarily be understood analogically. When we say God is *Father*, we mean to illustrate God's nature by analogy to an earthly father. He's *like* a father. The same too with words like *nature* and *being*. Emily also understands this point. She depicts the problem in the poem above: "Races – nurtured in the Dark –" have no frame of reference by which to understand or even to imagine suns, so how could one "chalk the Sun," that is, sketch or describe it to them? By analogy. An earthly word like *cochineal*, the deep red dye made from scale beetles that live on cacti in the desert, points by its color and location to the heat of the sun. And *mazarin*, the rich blue of judicial robes, is saturated like the sky. These are vibrant words, yet Emily uses them to suggest the limitations of analogy: even such sumptuous colors cannot hold the blaze and blue of noon. Well, when it comes to words about God, theologians like Aquinas will tell you that we're the races nurtured in the dark trying to "chalk the Sun." Or, in this case, the Son. We can only speak about God, Father, Son, and Holy Spirit, by analogy to human things like fathers, sons, and spirits. It's something, but a very limited something, and so it's important for us to recognize language's limitations.

Other theologians, apophatic theologians, find this linguistic limitation so pressing that they commend the *via negativa*, the "negative way." Rather than parsing the things we *can* say about God, they suggest we take a different tack and enumerate what we *can't* say about God. Don't try to capture the truth of God; instead embrace the darkness of all we don't know. "I pray," writes Pseudo-Dionysius, "we could come to this darkness so far above light!" To do so, he commends that we follow a way of negation, unsaying all that we have said about God, to end up with God alone. The diction in which he argues for this practice is as thick and twisted as his logic, so don't worry if he loses you a bit: "as we climb from the last things up to the most primary we deny all things so that we may unhiddenly know that unknowing itself which is hidden from all those possessed of knowing amid all beings, so that we may see above being that darkness concealed from all the light among beings." His logic is utterly counterintuitive, and he articulates it confusingly. Boiled down, the instruction is this: know by unknowing. Look for the darkness concealed above the light. For all his syntactical twists and turns, Pseudo-Dionysius ensures that this approach works: "shedding all and freed from all, you will be uplifted to the ray of the divine shadow which is above everything that is."

While it is highly unlikely that Emily read Pseudo-Dionysius, she seems instinctively to have understood this apophatic approach to divine things. One of her poems, "You'll know it – as you know 'tis Noon – / By Glory –," takes up the way of unknowing. She argues against trying to label and define things that are bigger than language: "By intuition, Mightiest Things / Assert themselves – and not by terms – / 'I'm Midnight' – need the Midnight say –." You won't come to know midnight through terms but rather in the pure darkness of experiencing it. Stop theorizing about "Midnight" and stand in the pitch black. Emily has the same advice for the theologians as Pseudo-Dionysius does: lose the definitions; scrap the doctrines. "Omnipotence – had not a Tongue –."

My problem wasn't Omnipotence's tongue, but mine; not speech about God, but speech to God. I'd given up prayer, almost for good, resigned myself to an uncomfortable urging toward that Being I could not address, when a solution of sorts appeared. I had torn off to the monastery chapel, concerns pressing on me from every side. I was weighted with them, but especially weighted with concern for my beloved: job stress, family stress, life stress. I felt choked with it for him. I remember now that I sat in the side chapel, since I couldn't confront the crucifix—wordless before the Word. The seats there, wide and wicker, point toward an old, polychromed altarpiece that depicts golden saints gesturing around a stiff-faced God the Father. I'd always found it odd. But sitting before it that day, half staring at the central face, half stewing in the middle distance, another divine name suddenly rose in my mind. *Father.* It was the name I'd used most for prayer in the first flush of faith, yet now it felt wobbly and unsteady on my tongue, like riding a long-unused bicycle. And then, before I had a moment to impede what was happening, words followed: *Father, I bring thee not myself, that were the little load. I bring thee the imperial heart I had not strength to hold.* The words flowed from me, effortlessly, in that way I had wished for but not known how to summon. The words were a prayer, simple and felt; they simply weren't mine. They were Emily's.

Now that the poem-prayer had come, it seemed so obvious. That day, facing a golden Father, I discovered that I could pour my word-poor desire for prayer into Emily's poems, as in a mold, and let it settle there. "Father – I bring thee – not myself –" was just the first of many poems to serve me for a prayer. From none, I now have a whole round of prayers. One hundred and forty years later, Emily was interceding for me. Her poem was my prayer.

For now, it's enough to borrow words for prayer. To "Races – nurtured in the Dark," wishing to know the sun, even limited words like *cochineal* and *mazarin* can be a boon. I remember reading that missionaries to the Inuits could not explain the concept "Lamb of God" to their new flock. To races nurtured in the ice, it seems, the lamb is empty imagery. So the tenacious evangelists devised a solution: in that frozen clime, the faithful praise Jesus, Seal of God. Emily knew that "The Missionary to the Mole / Must prove there is a Sky." She tests out the convicting power of words to paint it: *mazarin, cochineal.*

Just as there are countless forms of prayer, intercession also comes in many modes: a prayer about someone else, a prayer on behalf of someone else, the words you write that become a prayer in the mouth of someone else, as Emily's did for me that day in the monastery. Emily interceded throughout her life in all these ways. When her dear friend Elizabeth Holland lost her husband, Emily comforted her: "After a while, dear, you will remember that there is a heaven – but you can't now. Jesus will excuse it. He will remember his shorn lamb." How could she promise this? Emily was able to offer this assurance because once, many years ago, the Hollands themselves had interceded for her: "I shall never forget the Doctor's prayer, my first morning with you – so simple, so believing. *That* God must be a friend – *that* was a different God – and I almost felt warmer myself, in the midst of a tie so sunshiny." Her light, too, was borrowed.

Sometimes when we are "in the Dark," we can let others be our light. I speak the borrowed words again in the darkness of my mind, *mazarin*, to dream of blue, *cochineal*, to pray for light. While the words alone can't heat me, as the sun would do, I think they hold within themselves the beginning of the "Blaze." Cochineal. Mazarin. Seal of God. Father. Emily prods anew: "How would your Own – begin?"

JESUS

Jesus! thy Crucifix
Enable thee to guess
The smaller size –

Jesus! thy *second* face
Mind thee – in Paradise –
Of Our's.

EMILY USES THE NAME *JESUS* twenty times in her poems.
Christ, ten. And *Jesus Christ*, one single time. It's not too
surprising that she avoids *Jesus Christ*, since the name conjures
up the impossible, paradoxical hope that faith alone claims,
that marriage of unmarriables: the fleshliness of Jesus and
the exaltation of Christ; earthly man and heavenly God;
the condemned and the Savior; the crucified and the risen
one. Faith proclaims that these two realities are one reality,
unsunderable in the single being who defies the laws of the
universe. "I am Jesus –," Emily has him say in one poem, "Late
of Judea – / Now – of Paradise."

There are various Jesuses that can be construed from the
Gospels: Jesus the teacher, the healer, the prophet, Jesus who
overturns rabbinical law, Jesus the fulfillment of rabbinical law,
Jesus liberator of the poor and oppressed, political upstart,

unjustly condemned man. I can eke these Jesuses out, give them a nod when they appear in a biblical verse or a pop-cultural reference. But the Jesus Christ of faith has become slipperier. That identity not grounded in the parameters of this world, not provable by any argument, has lost its personal reality for me. Obscured by an increasing rational haze, that Jesus has become a troubling concept. Jesus Christ, Son of God, Lamb of God, Word of God—God?

A while back, I stopped praying to him because I didn't quite know to whom I was praying. And now? Now I'm left with only Jesus, a mysterious sort-of-man, and Christ, an abstract sort-of-God. These days, it feels as if I squint at Jesus Christ down a long tunnel of ideas yet can no longer discern the face fading on the other side. I don't feel disillusionment, precisely, but a growing distance from my goal. The more the distance grows, the less capable I feel to bridge it. While I can narrate about Jesus or argue about Christ, I don't have much to say about Jesus Christ, whom only faith can know or address. I echo Emily's consternation, "And 'Jesus'! Where is *Jesus* gone?"

I turned to Emily for help, looking to see how she used that faith-filled name in her letters. I knew she used the name once in her poems, but her letters are broader and harder to plumb. Off I went to the Dickinson Electronic Archives, www .emilydickinson.org, to search her correspondence. The site's search page offered me a white screen and an empty box to fill with my search terms. Above the box perched the polite prompt: *What are you looking for?* My fingers keyed the name, J-e-s-u-s_C-h-r-i-s-t. I hit enter.

It was a revelation. Not the results of the search—turns out Emily uses the name but once in her letters too. The revelation was that what I'd typed was true. Only in that casual context, with the impersonal keyboard at my fingertips; only through the unexpected prompt of the screen, "What are you looking for," the very phrase that is the first word Jesus utters in the whole Gospel of John, to the men who will become his disciples; yes, only by this series of circumstances did I realize just how true an answer I had given. I'm looking for Jesus Christ. I've been looking for Jesus Christ for years. For years, I've been trying to glue my shoddy Jesus and tattered Christ back together again. And for glue, I'd recently turned to this:

> Jesus! thy Crucifix
> Enable thee to guess
> The smaller size –
>
> Jesus! thy *second* face
> Mind thee – in Paradise –
> Of Our's.

Twenty words in all, it makes a fine, tiny prayer. I'd noted it in my volume for the rarity of finding a sincere prayer amid Emily's poems. When they come, as I've said, they're often ironic or jab good-naturedly at some unsavory aspect of the divine: "Grant me, Oh Lord, a sunny mind – / Thy windy will to bear!" Or she'll pray for freedom from the very God who confines her: "God of the Manacle / As of the Free – / Take not my Liberty / Away from Me –." Prayers, yes. But not particularly pious ones.

Then I started praying these lines while I walked or waited in the chapel for services to start. It's a perfect size, just big enough for one inhale and one exhale. And the lilt of its syllables pleases, for it has a sort of rolling rhythm, like a coo: 6.6.4. / 6.6.2. The second stanza runs two syllables shorter than the first, and that gap gives the mind some space in which to whir, before starting over. Finally, of course, it talks to Jesus, to whom I'd stopped talking long ago. I suppose it seemed a good way to start back in.

Emily begins here with Jesus and his cross. It's where she often began with him. She saw Jesus as a sufferer, the one who trod before us (maybe for us) the way of grief and death. She considered that his knowledge of suffering is what draws people to Jesus: "When Jesus tells us about his Father, we distrust him. When he shows us his Home, we turn away, but when he confides to us that he is 'acquainted with Grief,' we listen, for that also is an Acquaintance of our own." Jesus is a sufferer, and to know Jesus' suffering we need only look to the cross, which is where Emily points us in the first line of this poem.

I always feel a bit sheepish in praying this opening stanza. What care could I bring that would measure up against those Jesus bore? Whatever my questions about his divine origin and eternal destination, I know that the man did suffer. Can I offer up the small worries of work stress or familial cares against the great injustices of the world? Gone are the days when I used to pray about everything, *Jesus, help me find my keys; pass the test; cook the dinner.* Emily shares my skepticism about the value (or validity) of such prayer. How would it really feel, she asks, "If I believed God looked around, / Each time my Childish eye / Fixed full, and steady, on his own"? Her question makes me picture God, seated before an array of bells, as in the old servants' quarters of fine houses—at the Evergreens where

Sue and Austin lived, the bells still hang as they did in Emily's day—having to pop up and jump into action every time the bell rings for the "Dickinson Homestead." Even if God doesn't mind the constant stream of demands, such petty prayer can seem an affront to those with more massive cares: *Jesus, let us eat tonight.* Seen in this light, the cross threatens to become only a symbol of how much more deeply other people have suffered, and thus how unworthy of notice is our "smaller size" of grief.

Yet Jesus' acquaintance with grief goes back before the cross, and in her writing Emily often attended to those earlier griefs, familiar to us in our less epic lives. "The loveliest sermon I ever heard," she reported, years after the fact, "was the disappointment of Jesus in Judas. It was told like a mortal story of intimate young men." The very earthly, human scenes of sadness in the Gospels drew her—Peter's denial of Jesus, Judas's betrayal in the garden—for they show that Jesus knew the mundane suffering our lives contain. She even finds in the promise of salvation a tragic mismatch of love like we sometimes suffer on earth: "Could Pathos compete with that simple statement 'Not that we loved him but that he loved us'?" God can't enjoy being rejected in love any more than we do. So Emily finds the smaller heartbreaks Jesus endured—the rejections, the betrayals—almost more devastating than the cross itself: "'They have not chosen me' – he said – / 'But I have chosen them'! / Brave – Broken hearted statement –." In meditating on such sorrows, Emily came to identify Jesus as a fellow sufferer to whom she could turn while she endured her "smaller size" of grief. I suppose my smaller size is also big enough. The Bible promises that even the fall of a sparrow won't go unnoticed by God. I hope "God keeps His Oath to Sparrows," as Emily quotes the endearing promise, and that every hair on our heads is counted.

So Emily prays to Jesus out of her suffering and in light of his: "Jesus! thy Crucifix / Enable thee to guess / The smaller size –." The prayer feels familiar; nothing in it jars the mind. After all, Jesus instructs his disciples to take up their cross and follow him, and Emily alludes here to her cross's "smaller size." But these brief, familiar-feeling lines actually reverse a fundamental teaching of the church, the *imitatio Christi*. The imitation of Christ: model your life on his. Given that a literal interpretation of this practice would end in death, commentators suggest that one way we imitate Christ is by learning to peer into our own sufferings to see the greater suffering of the Lord. Thomas à Kempis's famous fifteenth-century treatise *Of the Imitation of Christ* instructs: "The whole Life of Christ was a Cross and a Martyrdom, and do you seek rest and pleasure? You err, you err, if you seek anything else but to suffer tribulation; because the whole of this mortal life is full of miseries, and signed on all sides with crosses." Two copies of this book, 1857 and 1876, both inscribed with Emily's name in Sue's hand, have come down to us. The most marked chapter in the later edition? The chapter from which I've just quoted, "Of the Royal Way of the Holy Cross." As Thomas instructs here and throughout the volume, we must always look to the cross: "The cross, then, is always at hand, and everywhere awaits you. You cannot escape it, run where you will; for wherever you go, you take yourself with you, and you will always find yourself. Look above you, look below you, look without you and within you, and everywhere you will find the cross." Once you've found the cross, it acts as both a gauge and a guide. As a gauge, we learn by it to know that we have suffered nothing compared to Christ. As a guide, we learn, through the cross's example, to endure more suffering still, and gladly, for Christ's sake.

But this is not how Emily sees the cross, nor how she addresses the crucified Jesus in this poem. She does not pray, as Thomas would commend in the *imitatio Christi*, to gain understanding of Jesus' pain on the cross through her suffering. No, she asks the reverse: she prays that Jesus will use *his* cross to understand what *she* endures. "Jesus! thy Crucifix / Enable *thee* to guess / The smaller size –." In other words, she asks God to use his own cross as a gauge of her suffering.

It's a bold move. And yet she goads Christ with his cross as a friend might use a shared memory, to get him to give her the help she needs. This tactic feels reminiscent of the book of Psalms, where Israel sings the praises of the God who once brought them through the Red Sea in the hopes of jarring that same God into present action: "Awake, why sleepest thou O Lord? arise, cast us not off forever." Goading God has a long tradition—think of Job. And who would trade Emily's and Israel's boldness for some prayer more conventional in tone, more formal in reverence? "Say, Jesus Christ of Nazareth –," Emily calls out in her single poem to use that name, "Hast thou no arm for Me?" I try her informality on for size: "Hey, Jesus Christ, get over here. You're getting hard to see."

But I needn't make up a prayer to see Jesus' face. I can just continue on and pray the second part of this poem. So I do. "Jesus! thy *second* face / Mind thee – in Paradise – / Of Our's." After pointing in the first stanza to the cross, that sign of earthly agony, Emily points in the second stanza to Jesus' "*second* face," the proof of his heavenly exaltation. Although she names him anew by his simple earthly name, "Jesus," she addresses him in full glory, as Jesus Christ. She now places him in Paradise and notes the splendor of his "*second*," risen face.

In this second stanza, too, there's a twist. Emily again reverses one of the church's traditional teachings. This time she takes on the *imago Dei*, the idea that we are all made in God's image. "Let us make man in our image, after our likeness," God says in one creation story in Genesis. We're supposed to remember that we bear the image of God and act better for the remembrance. But Emily doesn't redress her forgetfulness of God in this poem; she addresses her fear that God will forget her. So she reverses the traditional order of the *imago Dei* by pointing Jesus to his own face for a necessary reminder of us. In Paradise, Jesus' second face must be at once human and divine. Bearing traces of his earthly suffering, Jesus' face now bears *our* image. Emily nudges Jesus with a stern reminder of his promises. "Remember our faces," she prays. Or, to say it more emphatically, "Don't forget us, Jesus Christ."

While this stanza reaches into Paradise, it also recalls the scene of the Crucifixion. It actually paraphrases the words of the thief who begged Jesus from the cross beside him, "Lord, remember me when thou comest into thy kingdom." Emily repeats the thief's plea: "Jesus! thy *second* face / Mind thee – in Paradise – / Of Our's," lest Jesus forget what he promised the repentant thief and neglect to take us to his side. The scene was one she often dramatized in her poems; "Remember me," in a simpler mood; in loftier tones, "Recollect the Face of me / When in thy Felicity." It was a signal scene for her.

In fact, Emily goes a step further than mere paraphrase. When the two stanzas are read together, they speak in the voice of one crucified alongside Jesus. Stanza one tells that she too bears the cross. Stanza two asks, from that cross (as the thief did), to be remembered by Jesus in Paradise. Praying as one of those crucified alongside Jesus on Calvary, Emily does well to pray for mercy. She knew only too well that while one of the thieves was saved, the other thief was lost. As frequently as her poems quote the thief's plea, "Lord, remember me," she also references in equal measure that terrible threat of Jesus: "Many will say to me in that day, Lord, Lord . . . And then will I profess unto them, I never knew you." This same threat is linked with the cross in that much-marked chapter in her copy of Thomas's *Of the Imitation of Christ*: "This seems a hard saying to many, 'Deny yourself, take up your cross, and follow Jesus.' But it will be much harder to hear that last sentence, 'Depart from Me, ye cursed, into everlasting fire.'"

We glimpse Emily's Calvinist roots in the emphasis she repeatedly places on this threat. While in later years she could laugh at the inheritance—writing, for instance, to a newly engaged friend, "I fear my congratulation, like repentance according to Calvin, is too late to be plausible"—her earlier works are not so sanguine. She often mentions her fear of being shut out of heaven, forgotten by the faithful, or excluded from the happy number who will share joy for eternity. "Christ – omitted – Me –": she boils the fear down to a few terse words. Indeed, the doctrine of predestination, for which Calvin is best known, was likely Emily's most detested Christian theme. "Mr. S. preached in our church last Sabbath upon 'predestination,'" she reports, "but I do not respect 'doctrines,' and did not listen to him." The doctrine was particularly unappealing for those not predestined for salvation, since Calvin claimed no recourse could be taken. You were born damned and would die damned, and not a damn thing you could do would change it. When Emily heard a visiting minister preach about "what would become of those, meaning Austin and me, who behaved improperly," Emily noted that her own response was quite different from that of the preacher: "somehow the sermon scared me." Telling the story to Elizabeth Holland, she confessed that while her father and Vinnie, both converts, watched and nodded, Emily was much troubled by "such an awful sermon." Perhaps most troubling of all was how the preacher's fire in describing the punishments of the lost could sound a lot like glee: "The subject of perdition seemed to please him, somehow. It seems very solemn to me." This emphasis on perdition and predestination did not please her, though it also clearly moved her. It ripples through her early writing and surfaces occasionally in later years. When someone pushed this doctrine too hard, too far, Emily shoved back. In a note written to Sue right around the time of the one to Elizabeth Holland, Emily bucks against the threat of exclusion that the revivalist preachers loved to raise: "though in that last day, the Jesus Christ you love, remark he does not know me – there is a darker spirit will not disown it's child." I'm not sure who the "darker spirit" is, but I do know that against that day, against that threat, I'll pray this poem: "Jesus! thy *second* face / Mind thee – in Paradise – / Of Our's."

These two brief stanzas hold within themselves the cross and Paradise, the hope of heaven and the threat of hell, God's love and his neglect, Jesus and Christ. It's a lot for twenty words to bear. In truth, Emily's manuscript shows signs of that strain. On the manuscript page, her script looks frantic, like two horses harnessed together but running at different speeds. It's almost as if her hand could not contain the paradoxes it penned, for a deep tension seems to ride within the letters, racing the words forward and jostling the lines. You can almost *see*, in the fierce movement of her hand across the page, the tensions this poem voices, the tension between hope and fear, faith and doubt, life and death.

Seeing that tension made visible in the manuscript, I suddenly remembered having seen it somewhere else before. And then, at once, I knew where: I saw it in the face of Jesus Christ. On Easter morning, the day that I was baptized.

Emily may never have been baptized, but she writes about the ritual as if she had, recalling "The name They dropped upon my face / With water, in the country church" in a poem about being called: "Baptized, before, without the choice, / But this time, consciously, Of Grace – / Unto supremest name." To what creed or identity this later baptism led her, no one can say for certain. It could have been the claiming of a renewed or altered sense of identity—as God's, as her own self, as a poet. Though my father likes to say he baptized my twin brother and me as infants, in the shower, I also chose "consciously, Of Grace," to be baptized on Easter several years ago.

We met in the dark, in the thick hours before dawn, the Brothers of the Society of Saint John the Evangelist and those of us lucky enough to join them. They built a fire in the guesthouse garden; the fire fed a candle, which then lit our thin tapers as we processed into the chapel, its darkness broken only by those many haloed lights. *The light of Christ.* For two hours we sat in the flickering dark as the Brothers chanted Psalms in beautifully dissonant polyphony, like grinding gears, and read the salvation history of Israel. Then the light started to climb through the stained-glass windows, making them faint hollows in the high stone wall. Birdsong began to pierce the dark.

The hour had come: *Do you desire to be baptized?* I stepped forward and said, "I do." And then I gave my word, three times, to God. I gave my word to God as many times as Peter denied him by the fire. *Do you turn to Jesus Christ and accept him as your Savior?* "I do." *Do you put your whole trust in his grace and love?* "I do." *Do you promise to follow and obey him as your Lord?* "I do." Water bound me to these promises and to the Lord I had just vowed, three times, to love. Then Br. Curtis wrote with oil a cross upon my forehead, formed one also on each cheek, and spoke to me the promise given to all the baptized: *Kristin, you are sealed by the Holy Spirit in Baptism and marked as Christ's own for ever.*

Moments later, in a shock of brightness and a burst of bells, all the lights sprang on, and the whole congregation pronounced the impossible claim of faith: *the Lord is risen!* I turned to share the triumph and, as I turned, I saw before me the face of Jesus Christ—not in a vision, but in an icon that the Brothers hang behind the altar on Easter.

This ancient image (shown on the following page) comes from St. Catherine's Monastery in the Sinai desert. It visually depicts the paradox of Jesus Christ: the left half of his face shows the exalted, transfigured *"second* face" of the risen Christ; the right half shows the hollowed agony of the crucified Jesus. Invisibly, the two sides merge to make a single face, just as the tensions of life and death, God and man, suffering and glory come together

in that single being whom faith calls Jesus Christ. That morning, with the water still dewing my hair, I saw this face in the icon for the very first time and knew him for Jesus Christ.

Seven years from that morning, I am in the dark again. With so much lost assurance since, I share Emily's concern, "No Verse in the Bible has frightened me so much from a Child

as 'from him that hath not, shall be taken even that he hath.'"
With Emily, I pray for help.

> Jesus! thy Crucifix
> Enable thee to guess
> The smaller size –
>
> Jesus! thy *second* face
> Mind thee – in Paradise –
> Of Our's.

GOD

No one can go where God is not. The Psalmist sings this belief with great beauty: "If I ascend up into heaven, thou art there: if I make my bed in hell, behold, thou art there. If I take the wings of the morning, and dwell in the uttermost parts of the sea; Even there shall thy right hand lead me, and thy right hand shall hold me." Even the uttermost parts of the sea, as Jonah knew, are not far enough to escape the hand of God. In this Psalm, happily, the hand of God reaches out not to strike but to hold. One of Emily's poems imagines how faith "bears the Soul as bold / As it were rocked in Steel / With Arms of steel at either side –." While steel might not be the softest of cradles or embraces, it is secure. Wherever you could fall, her image promises, God is solidly there, waiting to catch you. (Yet, I also can't help but think of Emily's witticism: "Grace – perhaps – is the only hight from which falling is fatal –.") God is everywhere, the church promises. *Until he isn't*, I hear the always mutable Emily qualify.

"God is everywhere" is a commonplace, of course, like "God is love." And the belief has perhaps become so familiar, so truly commonplace, that it no longer chimes meaningfully for many of us. Even the Psalmist's lyric thrumming about "the wings of the morning" does little to make the promise real in my day-to-day life. *If I take the 1 train to Times Square, if I descend to Penn*

Station, behold thou art there, that might seem more tangible, but
the truth is that I don't experience much of God in that particular
everywhere. Did Emily experience God as everywhere? She
once whispered to Mary Bowles, in mourning for the inimitable
Samuel, "Let the phantom love that enrolls the sparrow shield
you softer than a child." Is Emily's "phantom love" a play on
Holy Ghost? Both are invisible, immaterial, and hard to grasp.
Maybe. Only, I hear the pique in that word *phantom,* for the
tender, sparrow-shielding God is often a figment, mostly a
mirage, truly a ghost to me. God seems more accessible in the
abstract places the Psalmist conjures, the "uttermost parts of
the sea" and "wings of the morning," than in a daily coffee and
commute. Those sites cannot be located on a map; God either.

Emily pinpoints my problem in an instant: "They say that God
is everywhere, and yet we always think of Him as somewhat of
a recluse." The promised "everywhere" of God often feels so
far away from our here and now. So when we pray, we go off
in search of God, as if God were hiding. Emily highlights this
tendency when she notes ironically how "God grows above – so
those who pray / Horizons – must ascend –." Her irony is self-
directed, as she admits to joining in the skyward hunt: "And
so I stepped opon the North / To see this Curious Friend." She
too tries to "step North" to seek God, since, after all, God is *up
there* (near the "wings of the morning," presumably). Admit it:
have you never looked *up* during a moment of prayer, as if to
make eye contact, or sky contact? Emily knew this common
mannerism, and so she riffs on prayer as "My Business – with
the Cloud," as if prayer simply entailed jabbing a finger into the
air to get the sky's attention. Yet, since we must make contact
with God here on the ground, pilgrims go off to foreign lands,

tramping from site to site, seeking clues about God's presence.
We talk about "finding God" as if it were a treasure hunt. Is
God so lost that we must find him?

Emily puzzles out the problem in a spare four lines:

> The Infinite a sudden Guest
> Has been assumed to be –
> But how can that stupendous come
> Which never went away?

She notes our collective silliness: God can neither come nor go.
Yet we do treat God like a "sudden Guest," a sort of sought-after
celebrity whom we want to grace our gatherings. *Maranatha*, the
earliest recorded prayer of the fledgling Christian communities,
begs in Aramaic, "Come, Lord!" We try to coax God into our
weddings and funerals, prayer circles and hospital bedsides. "Be
with us Lord," we pray, hoping that God will consent to drop in.
But it's not God who's missing and must be found. Emily is right:
"that stupendous" never goes away.

What's missing is merely our awareness of God's continuous
presence. I suppose I'm not waiting for God, but rather for
the moment when the belief in God's constant presence will
become real to me. Not merely understood, but known, even
experienced. I'll look up from my work and say: *There you are,
God. Ah, but you were here all along.*

Emily's poem records precisely such a dawning of awareness.
The poem is actually crafted out of two distinct couplets, each
one penciled on a separate scrap of paper. The two scraps
become a poem only through the presence of a pin, which
literally holds the two thoughts together. The first pair of lines
contains a proposition, an observation on a common trend:

"The Infinite a sudden Guest / Has been assumed to be –." Read on their own, they mull over the behavior of God and those who seek God. They seem to challenge this "Infinite" to make an appearance. A gauntlet thrown down: let's imagine Emily standing at her upper-story window, pale curtains lit with winter's crisp light, looking toward the hemlock hedge and the meadows beyond, waiting for some proof, a sign of presence. *People say that God visits them; well, God, come on.* Then she'd pull a scrap of paper from her pocket, and the stub of pencil, tucked there to capture thoughts that came to her throughout the day. I see her scratching down this musing. Maybe even issuing it as a challenge to God, "The Infinite a sudden Guest / Has been assumed to be –" with a lift of one lofty brow. She may have carried those two lines around for a long time, before the second couplet came.

And then it came. Although the second half of the poem comes in question form, it answers the observation, perhaps even the challenge, of the earlier lines. The second couplet's question holds the dawning of realization: "But how can that stupendous come / Which never went away?" Emily pinned the poem together when she knew, at last, and for herself, that God cannot come because God never goes away.

MORTALITY

The tranquiller to die —

INCARNATION

⚜

THERE ARE MANY WAYS TO LOVE GOD, and you can tell
a lot about a person's relationship to him by the language she
uses. One believer might know God as a Savior and sing warm
strains of Messiah, salvation, and grace. To others he's rather
more of a buddy, so they call Jesus brother, lean on him in
chatty prayer, like a friend. Others still might honor God the
King with regal language—kingdom, power, glory. For Emily
these terms were not coequal, and she often singled out her
favorite of the three: "Cherish Power – dear –" she wrote to
the powerful Sue. "Remember that stands in the Bible between
the Kingdom and the Glory, because it is wilder than either of
them." On the whole, Emily preferred powerful words, which
is why she calls God names like "Adamant" and "God of Flint."
While flint can spark in flame, adamant does not budge. This is
not a particularly friendly vocabulary for God. One vocabulary
almost entirely missing from Emily's language for God is that
of the Trinity. "The Jehovahs – are no Babblers – / Unto God –"
is about as plural as she gets. Of the three-in-one, Christ gets
from her pen the most attention.

His Incarnation compelled her most. When she reflected
on how, in Jesus, God becomes human, Emily marveled at
his abasement, that one so high would come so low for us.
Sometimes she calls up the Incarnation in a jolly way, remarking

how "The Savior must have been / A docile Gentleman – / To come so far so cold a day / For little Fellow men –." But docility isn't the characteristic that most often strikes her in this unparalleled act. No, as she tries, across her life, to think her way inside the thick theological concept of the Incarnation, she keeps turning to the oddest word—not *gift*, not *grace*, not *salvation*, but *stoop*. She sings, "Ah, what a royal sake / To my nescessity – stooped down!" On three distinct occasions, it's for his "stooping" that she lauds God in Christ.

> Perhaps you think Me stooping
> I'm not ashamed of that
> Christ – stooped until He touched the Grave –
> Do those at Sacrament
>
> Commemorate Dishonor
> Or love annealed of love
> Until it bend as low as Death
> Redignified, above?

"Christ – stooped until He touched the Grave –," so Emily sums up his thirty-three years between stable birth and Crucifixion. God made one long stoop down to the grave.

About this stooping, Emily ponders the question other skeptics before her had asked: were the Incarnation and Crucifixion a source of honor or dishonor for God? The early Christians faced this objection to their belief, especially in regard to their odd practice of coming together to eat a dead man's body and drink his blood. Emily asks the objectors' question in the lines above: in the "Sacrament" of the Eucharist, do Christians "Commemorate Dishonor"?

Even leaving aside charges of cannibalism, early critics boggled at the very premise of the Incarnation, which forms the basis of the Christian faith: if this man Jesus was "God," how could God so dishonor Godself as not only to become human (bad), but also to die (preposterous), and even to submit to a criminal's death on the cross (impossible)? God has traditionally been understood to possess such qualities as immortality, omnipotence, omnipresence, and immateriality. God could never *stoop* so far as to enter a mortal body, not to mention die in one. They judged that if God did, God would not be God anymore.

Emily judges the other way. She considers that stooping is not an aberration but a fundamental aspect of God's nature: "'Tis true – that Deity to stoop / Inherently incline – / For nothing higher than Itself / Itself can rest opon –." Inherently, she argues, God must stoop, since God has nowhere to go but down. So she riffs on the lyric opening to the Gospel of John— where we hear tell of "the Word made flesh"—marveling, "Could condescension be / Like this consent of Language"? Jesus the Word made flesh becomes "This loved Philology," as if in Jesus, the Word *Love* condescended to become a human love among us. For us, the word *condescension* tends to come veiled with negative overtones, which might make us hear in these lines a certain haughty tendency in God. God from his great height consents to condescend to lowly us: now say thank you, young lady. Yet the Latin verb *condescendere* literally means "to descend together." Etymologically, Emily's view of God's "condescension" actually looks like a generous act, done of love. In fact, it looks a lot like the theological concept of *kenosis*, a Greek term that means "self-emptying." We glimpse this view of the Incarnation in the ancient hymn that comes down to us in Paul's Letter to the Philippians:

> Let this mind be in you, which was also in Christ Jesus: Who, being in the form of God, thought it not robbery to be equal with God: But made himself of no reputation, and took upon him the form of a servant, and was made in the likeness of men: And being found in fashion as a man, he humbled himself, and became obedient unto death, even the death of the cross. Wherefore God also hath highly exalted him, and given him a name which is above every name: That at the name of Jesus every knee should bow, of things in heaven, and things in earth, and things under the earth; And that every tongue should confess that Jesus Christ is Lord, to the glory of God the Father.

These lines are in the King James Version that Emily read, but modern translations render the key phrase "made himself of no reputation" as "he emptied himself." Emily employs the very same concept in the poem quoted above, through an equally powerful image: "Christ – stooped until He touched the Grave –."

To explain the *kenosis*, or condescension, or "stooping" of the Incarnation metaphorically (Emily is, after all, a poet, not a theologian), she takes her poem's decisive image of "love annealed of love" from metallurgy. Her imagery here is rich enough to repay a brief unpacking. Annealing is the process by which metal is subjected to heat to make it pliable and pure. Emily applies this metallurgic process to understand the abstract concept of the Incarnation. How did God become flesh and dwell among us? Imagine God becoming so hot in the furnace of his own love for humanity that God begins to grow soft, to bend. A drip flows down, the burning bush; another drip, a prophet. More love creates more heat, more heat leads to more bending, until finally, as Christ, God becomes human and stoops "as low as Death." Some might consider the divine state better than the human one because of that final clause of death, but Emily judged otherwise: "To be human is more than to be divine; for when Christ was divine, he was uncontented till he had been human." This is love annealed of love: a God so full of love for us he had to become us. "Could condescension be?" For Emily, there is no condescension better than this: Christ is God melted and brought as low as us in the fire of God's love.

When God seems to me too distant, cold and high, when the names *Savior* and *Lord* feel void, I remember this poem. And then I see Christ, a silver stream, melting down in one long swan dive from God's great height to me.

LEARNING TO DIE

⟡

Let down the Bars, Oh Death –
The tired Flocks come in
Whose bleating ceases to repeat
Whose wandering is done –

Thine is the stillest night
Thine the securest Fold
Too near Thou art for seeking Thee
Too tender, to be told –

IN NINETEENTH-CENTURY NEW ENGLAND, death dwelled
much nearer than it does for many of us in America today.
Mourning was an elaborate ritual that went on for years,
with its own coded sequence of proprieties and even attire.
Cemeteries began to be designed as landscaped parks where the
living would stroll among the dead. Mount Auburn Cemetery
in Cambridge, begun the year after Emily was born, in 1831,
lead the way to a whole range of beautiful burial grounds.
Emily visited Mount Auburn on a trip to Boston when she was
fifteen. She reported back with great enthusiasm about the
peacefulness of the spot and the success of the scheme.

The cemeteries filled up faster in Emily's day, too. Tuberculosis
was a silent stalker, taking rich and poor, threatening infection

in Amherst's murky town common. Some biographers even conjecture that it threatened Emily throughout her life and was a cause of her increasing seclusion. In the Civil War, which Emily watched from a distance—though no distance was sufficiently far to avoid it—a whole generation of men was cut down. Lieutenant Frazar Stearns, a friend of her brother Austin, was carried back to Amherst in a coffin. "Nobody here could look on Frazer – not even his father. The doctors would not allow it." While Austin suffered most, the whole Dickinson family was shaken, almost shattered, by the loss and its violence: "Austin is chilled – by Frazer's murder – He says – his Brain keeps saying over 'Frazer is killed' – 'Frazer is killed' . . . Two or three words of lead – that dropped so deep, they keep weighing –." In the year following Frazar's death, Emily sketched the battlefield in poetry, the evocative lines showing how much she still felt the weight:

> 'Tis populous with Bone and stain –
> And Men too straight to stoop again –
> And Piles of solid Moan –
> And Chips of Blank – in Boyish Eyes –
> And scraps of Prayer –
> And Death's surprise,
> Stamped visible – in stone –

Alongside the brutal cruelty of war, there was also death's unpredictability, its mystery. One day—January 21, 1874—her Uncle Sweetser simply disappeared. No trace. For Emily, death came earlier, oftener.

Nor was death an abstraction, since the dead were not removed from the family home nor left in hospitals to die, as they so often are today. People died at home, in bed, and the living were left to clean and dress their bodies, lay them out in parlors for visitors to see. When photography arrived, the living used it to take hold of their lost, posing the dead as if they were still alive, sometimes holding favorite books or playing with beloved toys. Babies lie, eyes closed, in cradles, rattles clasped in rigor mortised hands. There's one of these postmortem photographs in the Dickinson archives. It's a photograph of Judge Lord, the close friend of Emily's father who went on to become, in Emily's final years, her beloved. The oddest thing about this photograph is that no one who reprints it recognizes, in caption or footnote, that in it Judge Lord is dead. He sits in a chair in the garden, wearing his hat, with his cane leaned up against him. His eyes are closed; his head juts back as if he's lifting his face to the sun, but the angle is wrong. His hands rest on the chair arms unnaturally, too limp or too stiff or, somehow, both at once. I'd always found it a terrible photograph, unsettling in the extreme, because he looks so corpse-like in it. Then, one day I looked more closely and realized that he *is* a corpse in it. Emily had lost too many, too closely, touched their cold hands, to imagine that death dwelt at any distance from her door.

Try as I might to avoid the topic, it stalks me too, attacking in even the most peaceful of locations. I'm in the monastery chapel, where the wood-raftered roof forms an ark over my head. Solid stones and warm-scented air conspire toward snugness. As the liturgy moves from hymn to Psalm to sermon, the familiar pace lulls me into a happy peace. (Liturgy is salvation for those with no words of their own to pray.) The marble floor swirls with sea and foam; and in the rose window at the back, the outside world coheres into a blue-and-gold hint of joy in other realms. I sing, I sway, I can't resist when the organ plays. My eyes move again to the seventeenth-century Spanish crucifix, where Christ dies so gracefully, he seems less to suffer than to dance, and I half wait for him to lift up from the cross upon his outstretched arms, like wings. In this chapel, the incense rises, and so do I.

Then a Brother speaks the prayer that makes the whole scene cut to ice: "We pray for those who will die this day, suddenly and unprepared." My peace shudders away. It could be me.

It's odd this prayer shakes me as it does—and it always does—since I'm pretty constant in my worry about the places death might lie in wait for me throughout the day. With a self-defeating zeal, I note them all: a stumble out the open window, down the stairs, the swerving car, the gas left on, the mischewed bite. Then again, I might at any moment be diagnosed with a swift-acting disease. More pernicious still, each ache or twinge could be the first in the constellation of symptoms that, even now, begins my end.

Yet the words still take me by surprise. They say, "We pray for those who will die this day," and I feel suddenly unprepared. Today will be the day for someone, many someones. It could be the day for me. When death feels near like this, words from one of Emily's poems steal through my mind:

> The possibility – to pass
> Without a moment's Bell –
> Into Conjecture's presence
> Is like a Face of Steel –

> That suddenly looks into our's
> With a metallic grin –
> The Cordiality of Death –
> Who drills his Welcome in –

Oh, she gets the fear of death, suddenly dawning, perfectly right. Have you never met the "Face of Steel" in the chill of night and dreadful fear, when "Conjecture" feels suddenly quite close, and the thought of death assaults you, like a killer with a tinny grin glimpsed peeping through your windowpane? Death does have a horribly icy stare when, with a sudden chilling thought, he "drills his Welcome in –." I feel the drill just thinking about it.

If Emily can capture the awful face of fear, even noting the "metallic" sting of adrenaline in the mouth, she coaxes us in other poems away from fear and toward a different view of death's "Cordiality." Sometimes she jokes quite darkly about just how *cordial* Death is in extending the same welcome to everyone: "How cordial is the mystery! / The hospitable Pall / A 'this way' beckons spaciously – / A Miracle for all!" In its utter equality, death garners from Emily that greatest American praise: "Ah! democratic Death!" she exclaims, tongue firmly in cheek.

In "Let down the Bars, Oh Death –," Emily trades this sort of ironic glee for a mellower mood. Here she ushers us to pastures mild and a bucolic setting rather like Mount Auburn Cemetery or the landscape that opens the familiar Twenty-third Psalm. Yet we see that the Lord is not the shepherd of this peaceful landscape. Instead, Emily figures Death as the shepherd who will "Let down the Bars" on the eternal gate, holding us, the sheep, safely inside. She hymns to him:

Let down the Bars, Oh Death –
The tired Flocks come in
Whose bleating ceases to repeat
Whose wandering is done –

Thine is the stillest night
Thine the securest Fold
Too near Thou art for seeking Thee
Too tender, to be told –

It's an odd choice, figuring Death as a shepherd. Imagine how the Twenty-third Psalm would sound if Death were the shepherd there: *Death is my shepherd; I shall not want. He maketh me to lie down in green pastures; he leadeth me beside the still waters. He restoreth my soul.* The allusion is almost a bad pun. For of course Death does make us to lie down in green pastures—so Emily names death "the emerald recess"—but the reclining is not precisely restorative for those who experience or expect it. No, as Emily observes, "That *Bareheaded life* – under the grass – worries one like a Wasp." She underlined the word *bareheaded*, pointing baldly to the skull that every head will become. I know that the thought of that long, horizontal stretch under the grass stings me "like a Wasp," since no amount of grassy pasturing will restore the dead. Yea, for the flocks who enter the valley of the shadow of death, as this poem tells, "wandering is done –."

Perhaps I am not yet tired enough to value this rest; perhaps I haven't suffered enough, been battered sufficiently by the world, to want release from the toil and joy, the agitation and excitement of being alive. When Emily calls out, "Let down the Bars, Oh Death –," I cannot bring myself to see a sheep-pen closing to protect the flock nestled inside. Instead, each time I read the words, I hear the clang of prison bars locking down. The coffin nail. The first clump of sod. There's that "metallic grin" again. The shepherd's crook becomes a scythe, and I turn away, not willing to see what happens next.

Yet again Emily's poem goads me to take another look. Emily points here to Death as a friend who comes by invitation. "Let down the Bars," she summons Death, and you might almost think it's Christ she welcomes, for all the warmth of the tone. In fact, except for that most loaded of words, *Death*, this could easily be a poem about Christ. *Let down the Bars, Oh Lord*—there would be a hymn we'd recognize, one we might hum at funerals. After all, Christ is the one that faith calls the shepherd of the sheep: "I am the good shepherd, and know my sheep, and am known of mine," so Jesus promises in the Gospel of John. And Christians have taken him at his word, using the shepherd as an image for him ever since—from carvings on the earliest ossuaries, to devotional cards printed with a blue-eyed Christ bearing a lamb around his shoulders, the milky wool mingling with his perfectly waved locks. Were Christ but the one in charge of the bars, this poem could be the bearer of hope. The dying or the fearful could call out to Christ with confidence, in Emily's words: "Too near Thou art for seeking Thee / Too tender, to be told –." If God were so near and so tender, what could we care for Death and his drill? Death would have to go through God to get to us.

But this is a poem about Death, there's no debating it. And to read those final lines as lines about Death, rather than God, makes all that comfort *in potentia* dissolve into a bleak claustrophobia. I read the penultimate line again—"Too near

Thou art for seeking Thee"—and suddenly it seems that Death is stalking me up the stairs, down the hall, to my door, and there's nothing "tender" about my response to this proximity. Bad news: Death's stifling attention here is even worse than it at first appears. I've been cagey, you see; I've printed my preferred version of Emily's last line: "Too tender, to be told –." That closing line proposes there's tenderness behind Death's nearness. However, another ending exists. Emily left in her manuscript, as she often did, a variant choice for that line. A little hatch mark beside the word *tender* leads the reader to another final line, penned at the bottom of the page: "Too willing, to be called." Absent the tenderness; you're left with only a double reminder of just how at-your-heels Death lurks. So near and so "willing," you need not even lift your voice to call—Death's already there. Watching again at the window, while you sleep.

Emily wrote that variant final line, the un-tender version, because she knew that death was near. Life had taught her to know that. Yet, if death came near to her in this way, unbidden and claiming those she loved, Emily also chose to bring death near and nearer still, through her poetry. Let me explain: Emily didn't always feel so cordially toward death as this warm poem, "Let down the Bars, Oh Death –," seems to imply. She knew mortal terror, as every mortal must. You can hear Emily trembling in letters she wrote at fifteen: "I cannot imagine with the farthest stretch of my imagination my own death scene . . . I cannot realize that the grave will be my last home –." We all feel this way at one time or another (and another and another). We all wake at some point in a cold sweat, trying to guess what (if anything) comes *after*. Since death must come, will come—as Br. Kevin says, "We're none of us getting out of this alive"—Emily judged it better to be ready, in order that she would not be taken (as I so fear) "suddenly and unprepared."

Thus Emily confronted death head on, in the same way she confronted everything else in heaven and on earth: through the imaginative experience of poetry. If she could not imagine her death scene at fifteen, she could by thirty. She wrote it again and again. She imagines freezing to death: "First – Chill – then Stupor – then the letting go –." She imagines drowning to death: "Three times – the Billows threw me up – / Then caught me – like a Ball –." She imagines less dramatic deaths, too, chronicling the changes that overtake the figure in bed, which signal the great change to come: "The Forehead copied stone – / The Fingers grew too cold / To ache – and like a Skater's Brook – / The busy eyes – congealed –." Through poetry, Emily put herself on the bed, in the body of the dying, even beneath the mould. If, as she announced, "Looking at Death, is Dying –," then she died over and over again; "Just let go the Breath –," she counseled herself. And she did this with good reason: she was trying to prepare herself.

This courage seems to me to disprove the persistent rumor floating around: that Emily was morbid. You've probably seen cartoons of a ghoul-Emily in a graveyard, writing poetry; heard tell of how she was obsessed with death. These rumors have their basis in truth, since I literally cannot count the number of poems she wrote on the subject—on final sickness, death throes, the laying out of bodies, funeral processions, burial, mourning, the grave, and the afterlife. Some readers, encountering this mass of poems, conclude that Emily must have enjoyed thinking about death. They determine that she lived, depressively, with one eye on the grave. No one can deny that death was on her mind. A lot. But there is nothing depressive about the vast majority of her writings. Quite the contrary. I wager that readers would be hard-pressed to find elsewhere poems so full of life, joy, and delight. Immortality was her self-professed "Flood subject," the topic that kept flooding her thoughts, not death. So if Emily proposed, "Life is death we're lengthy at," which might sound morbid, this was not the end of the story for her, and the phrase goes on to call "death the hinge to life." No, I don't believe that Emily enjoyed thinking about death. She wanted to think about life, in all its dimensions, and knew that reckoning with death was a rather major part of it.

So the reason for her preoccupation is actually much simpler, more ordinary than the rumors would imply. Death became Emily's preoccupation because she knew she needed to make it so, in order to be most fully alive. The Christian tradition terms this awareness *ars moriendi*, "the art of dying," by which they mean learning to die well, by which they mean learning to live well. Today we find a focus on death morbid, but the artistic and religious traditions of the West have been far less squeamish than we tend to be. Now, we make up our corpses so they'll look as if they were still alive; previous generations surrounded themselves with representations of skulls, grim reapers, and skeletons to learn how to live in the short time before they, too, became bones. *Memento mori*, the skull on the philosopher's desk rattles, "Remember that you will die." By learning how to die—by remembering that we will die—we live as fully as we can, while we can. Emily calls this awareness "that Etherial Gain / One earns by measuring the Grave – /

Then – measuring the Sun –." The final darkness teaches us the beauty of light; the ticking clock reminds us to value this precious time.

I'll read Emily's poems about the grave, "Rafter of Satin and Roof of Stone –," but I can't step inside with her. Too cowardly to face that gruesome "metallic grin," I keep my distance from thinking about it. While Emily might promise that death is "as harmless as a Bee, except to those who run –," I fear the sting, so I am always running. The hospital stories, the funeral home, the sympathy cards in the grocery store—they always feel like an assault against the day's happiness, dousing my joy by reminding me that it all can be snatched away. I run.

Yet I do feel the desire to linger awhile beside Emily's sheep-pen. For, though I don't have Emily's nerve to stare down Death, I find I want to know better the shepherd she summons so gently here. He is Death, I know; the poem's first line makes that clear. But he's also God. This odd thing happens in much of Emily's writing, that God and Death merge so closely, they bear almost a single face. They are Alpha and Omega, beginning and end. They are the shepherd of the sheep. So when she mourns, "Now we have given our Mr Bowles – to the deep Stranger –," it's hard to know whether she thinks that Bowles has been handed up to God, whom she also named "the Stranger," or merely lowered down into the sod. Was death the ultimate end Emily expected; or did Emily believe that the Ultimate had ended death? It may be, paradoxically, that both were true at once. Take her characterization of Judge Lord after his death: "Neither fearing Extinction, nor prizing Redemption, he believed alone." With those three final words, she could mean "belief is all that sustained him," or "he believed all on his own." As is often the case, I think she means both at once. Perhaps one reason poetry so appeals to those who wrestle between doubt and belief, between yes and no, is how it can hold complexity. Belief *and* doubt, yes *and* no. I think this same complex view was true of her: Emily "believed alone."

Even this simple, hymn-like poem carries that complexity. You see, there's yet another variant reading I need to share. The opening of the second stanza, "Thine is the stillest night / Thine the securest Fold," can also read, "Thine is the stillest night / Thine the Paternal Fold." That one word, *paternal*, signaled with a hatch mark and lingering at the bottom of her manuscript page, changes the whole poem's meaning.

For with that one word, the identity of the shepherd expands beyond the pit, to ford the sky. Death has no Father, but Jesus, the good shepherd, does. When I ask what Emily believed, I hear again her own words circling back: "'So loved her that he died for her,' says the explaining Jesus." Emily must have known the good shepherd too, the shepherd who went as a lamb to death, to write those words, to write this poem of so much trust. Her confidence strides forward in repeated words, matched pairs, that start each of the last six lines. They ground the poem like tent pegs hammered into the mud: *Whose / Whose, Thine / Thine, Too / Too.* This poem knows what it knows, trusts whom it trusts. "The statement of the Lord / Is not a controvertible –," she assures us. "He told me, Death was dead –." Death is dead: now there's a repetition I can put my trust in. If she indeed bore that confidence, then her poem "Let down the Bars, Oh Death –" is not so different from one sung by another poet of the shepherd, the Twenty-third Psalm.

88-17

Let down the Bars,
Oh Death -
The tired Flocks
Come in
Whose bleating ceases
To repeat -
Whose wandering
is done.

Thine is the stillest
Night
Thine the securest
Fold
Too near Thou art -
for seeking Thee
Too tender, to be told.

+ Paternal + too willing,
to be called

Still waters, valley of death, but above all, a precious, final hope: "and I will dwell in the house of the Lord for ever."

> Let down the Bars, Oh Death —
> The tired Flocks come in
> Whose bleating ceases to repeat
> Whose wandering is done —
>
> Thine is the stillest night
> Thine the Paternal Fold
> Too near Thou art for seeking Thee
> Too tender, to be told —

MORTALITY

❧

ON THE TENTH DAY OF DECEMBER, the day Emily was born, I try to imagine her as a newborn. I know that she was brought into the world as we all are, with blood, much labor, the infant's first gasp and squall. But the scene I imagine always dissolves into murky generalities borrowed from period dramas. Try as I might, I can't envision a scene I believe. Emily seems to me somehow fixed and unchanging, as if she were always the Emily she became.

I try to imagine her in the grave she so often pictured. I've been there. She was laid between two parents and fenced in from the world. The oblong, upright stone reads *Emily Dickinson. Born Dec. 10, 1830. Called Back May 15, 1886.* "Called back" is the message on the final note we have from her, sent to Fanny and Loo. Visitors call on her now, bringing pens, pebbles, notes to place upon the stone. Her grave has become a site of pilgrimage. The day I visited, I sat in the rental car and watched a few birds flitting about the ironwork that surrounds the family plot. I'd brought poems to read, "Step lightly on this narrow Spot –," but now that felt all wrong—too cinematic, like the birth scene I kept trying to envision. August sun beat down on the roof of the car, and I needed suddenly to be in the fresh air and the shade. Emily wasn't there. She's too alive on the page for me to believe a grave can hold her. Her writings breathe and pulse, holding out the impression that she lives, whatever the dates prove or the gravestone confirms.

And yet I know they carried her out the back door, white coffin, white dress, lilies in hand, then the cortège processed to the cemetery across the fields she'd so long watched, all blazing with May's buttercups. She wrote once that she wanted buttercups to grow upon her grave. Nature indulged her early, it seems, and paved the way to it in gold—but I'm getting sappy again. Better to say I've seen the death certificate, her body become inanimate object, measured in inches for the coroner's record. I think about these things on May fifteenth, the day she died.

Yet this evidence of an ended life doesn't deter me. Even the saints die. What the saints continue to mean, in death, is what makes them saints. From death, the saints somehow hold out to us, undiminished, even strengthened, the promises of life. I owe to Emily the best definition of a saint I've ever read:

> That Such have died enable Us
> The tranquiller to die —
> That Such have lived,
> Certificate for Immortality.

She's a stranger to me, I know. She's more distant to me than my grandfather or a lost childhood friend. No church or institution will hand her a title or a halo (what she, redhead that she was, called "a Chapeau of fire"). But somehow Emily, with her chapeau of fire, of all people known and unknown, makes me feel easier about the grave that waits for me. She is the one who, by her death, makes me "The tranquiller to die —."

I was mostly joking when I called her, earlier, St. Emily. I wouldn't pray to her, as Catholics might to saints canonized and venerated by the church: St. Francis, St. Teresa, St. Jude. I know that Emily performed no miracles beyond those I blink at on the page. And yet I turn to her for companionship, for encouragement, in much the same way that others turn to saints, in and beyond the Catholic tradition: not for guidance from heaven, but for guidance about earth. We need spiritual companions as we approach those fundamental questions that leave us trembling. "Read – Sweet – how others – strove –," Emily urges in one poem, "Till we – are stouter –." She doesn't look to the saints for proof of their easy, effortless, faith-filled lives. What good would that do her? Instead, she values examples of striving and struggle, for that is what she knows and wrestles with. She seeks to hear "Clear strains of Hymn / The River could not drown –" so that she can go on singing in the riptide. She calls on "saints – with new – unsteady tongue –" to answer about the life after this one, preferring them, perhaps, to the more established Peters and Pauls, since her own tongue feels unsteady. In life she looked this way to George Eliot and Emily Brontë, figures that many readers call atheists. And so I turn to Emily. I read how Emily strove, and it encourages me to keep striving.

Emily offers tranquility through all her writings on the grave, even (perhaps especially) the turbulent ones. These we can muse over, muster courage on, assured that she faced the unknown as unknowingly as we will: "The bravest die / As ignorant of their resumption / As you or I –." We can take heart that she did not welcome death, but kicked against the very thought of it: "Oh how the sailor strains, when his boat is filling –. Oh how the dying tug, till the angel comes." And when those glimmers of assurance do break through, we can know that they were hard-won, and so keep striving alongside her. Listen: "I want to take hold of your Hand and tell you that Love lasts – though it grows unknown – in some dreadful instants – We are eternal – dear, which seems so worthless, now – but will be by and by, all we can remember –." How did she gain this surety? By the witness of all those whom she'd lost to death: "because it owns our own and must give them back –." Looking to those she'd loved and lost—not saints, but mere mortals like you and me—she found her evidence for heaven. Those loved ones were her "Certificate for Immortality."

And so she is mine. I think of her and feel more confident that there is another life after this one. I hear her toss aside with a wry look the question that most oppressed her, "Is Immortality a bane / That men are so oppressed?" Somehow in the quiet, sometimes in the roar, I sense her, "Beckoning – Etruscan invitation – / Toward Light –." Need a saint do more?

CRUCIFIXION

One Crucifixion is recorded – only –
How many be
Is not affirmed of Mathematics –
Or History –

One Calvary – exhibited to stranger –
As many be
As Persons – or Peninsulas –
Gethsemane –

Is but a Province – in the Being's Centre –
Judea –
For Journey – or Crusade's Achieving –
Too near –

Our Lord – indeed – made Compound Witness –
And yet –
There's newer – nearer Crucifixion
Than That –

IF THE PROMPT WERE PUT to Emily in what she called "the fair schoolroom of the sky –" to explain how the Crucifixion saves, I can't imagine what answer she would have given. Redemption. Salvation. Substitution. Justification. Sanctification. Propitiation.

Purification. Reconciliation. Sacrifice. Atonement. Ransom. So many syllables, yet not one term appears in her poems with any consistency. She doesn't use them to explain Christ's act upon the cross.

All of these theological (theologians would say "soteriological") terms share a common logic, presupposing: first, that humanity is fundamentally flawed and in need of saving; second, that Christ accomplished this saving through his death on the cross. Whether the particular term tells that Christ pays our debt (*redemption*), or cleanses our sin (*purification*), or rights us with God (*reconciliation*), each term assumes that, on the cross, Christ dies in our stead so that we, ultimately, might live, in this life and in the life to come.

The proper response to this act evidently is gratitude, even praise, but I, like Emily, am stuck wrestling with the premise: if God deemed that the death of one innocent man could save generations of guilty, reversing the original curse, why would God not simply say "Forgiven"? How can one more unjust death save anyone? Aren't there enough dead already? Emily goads me on, as she did not dodge hard questions. "Is God Love's Adversary?" she demanded to know, when another loved one died. Why would God be so adversarial as to create a world polluted with sin and make the penalty death, only to reverse the curse of Adam with Jesus, who also has to die? And if Jesus is truly God come down to us, the situation becomes only stranger: God sends God's "Son," who is also God and therefore cannot die, but who dies, as a human, yet goes to death as God, so that humans can live after death as gods . . . The more I try to grasp the knot to loosen it, the more the threads fray in my hands. This cross, promising salvation, becomes instead the crux of my problems. As I pore over the poems seeking Emily's answer to that question, "How does Christ save?" I hear only my own bafflement echoed back at me: *does Christ save?* Emily couldn't accept systematic answers like those found in doctrine and theology. She surely wouldn't have penned them.

She tells the story of an emblematic moment from childhood that sparked a lifetime of uncertainty: "When a few years old – I was taken to a Funeral which I now know was of peculiar distress, and the Clergyman asked 'Is the Arm of the Lord shortened that it cannot save?' He italicized the 'cannot.' I mistook the accent for a doubt of Immortality and not daring to ask, it besets me still." The funeral was for a suicide. And the very text from the Psalms that the preacher quoted in order to prove God's saving grace challenged it instead. Just a tremor in the voice, and Emily forever afterward heard in faith's promises that haunting *cannot.* Nothing was safe. She confessed how that dose of skepticism rippled outward, touching all. "Even in Our Lord's 'that they be with me where I am,' I taste interrogation."

I, too, carry a story from childhood; one that, like Emily's scene, "besets me still." It's one of my earliest memories. I was four, perhaps five, the same age Emily is in her story. I don't remember the trigger, I only remember that I was lying in bed, petrified by the thought of death. I went to find my mother in the den. I watched her, watching television, for a long time before stepping out of my hiding spot under the sideboard in the dark hallway, to ask her why we had to die and what happened when we did. My mom answered from her Catholic upbringing, about God and heaven and the life after this one. It was the first time I'd heard her mention these things. And then she said the words that echo still, "You don't think God would put us through all of this, do you, without giving us some kind of reward at the end?" By "all of this," she may well have meant only *all of this fear of death*, but, like Emily, I heard something else. I heard *all of this life*. The idea that life was something to be gotten through, which required recompense, troubled me more than the fear I'd hoped she would fix. To the sentence of death now there was added the penalty of life. Emily shivered with the same concern: "When we think of the lone effort to live, and its bleak reward, the mind turns to the myth 'for His mercy endureth forever,' with confiding revulsion." So at that bleak moment, I thought that this God must be terrible to "put us through" life only to kill us at the end. "His mercy endureth forever"? If God can make the life *after* this one good, why not just make this life the reward?

Like Emily, I carry around the bruise of that early misapprehension. And when I struggle to understand the Crucifixion today, I see renewing shimmers of the horrid God I glimpsed that night. Then I learned that God punishes us with life to justify the questionable reward of an afterlife. Now I worry that God condemns humanity for sin only to save us through an unjust and gruesome death. To whom do you turn when God is the trouble? "I suppose your friend – the Stranger – can comfort more than all of us –," Emily murmured to a more faithful friend, "but that is Dusk – to me –."

In her dusk, Emily did turn to the stranger on the cross—not for comfort, but for company. Although she avoids nearly all of those complex polysyllabic terms that interpret Christ's action on the cross, her poems often journey to Calvary. She names herself the "Queen of Calvary," even "Empress of Calvary." She calls out to a punishing God, "So Savior – Crucify –." And she places in her own mouth the rending cry, "Sabacthini," that Christ breathed in his final moment: "My God, my God, why hast thou forsaken me?" Though she received little comfort from the cross, Emily was no stranger to it. "See! I usurped *thy* crucifix," one poem calls out. And she usurps it here:

> One Crucifixion is recorded – only –
> How many be
> Is not affirmed of Mathematics –
> Or History –
>
> One Calvary – exhibited to stranger –
> As many be
> As Persons – or Peninsulas –
> Gethsemane –
>
> Is but a Province – in the Being's Centre –
> Judea –
> For Journey – or Crusade's Achieving –
> Too near –
>
> Our Lord – indeed – made Compound Witness –
> And yet –
> There's newer – nearer Crucifixion
> Than That –

Christ's crucifixion may get all the attention; Emily deems that the unsung others cannot be numbered even by "Mathematics." Christ "exhibited" his crucifixion, yet countless others occur unabated in silent rooms and piercing thoughts. The "newer – nearer Crucifixion" that the ending names is happening constantly and everywhere.

The meter Emily uses for this poem—her most explicit poem on the event of the cross—is very uneven. The first stanza's syllable pattern runs 11.4.9.4, the second, 11.4.8.4. The verses are so erratic, they land choppily on ear and eye. Stanzas three and four are odder still: 11.2.9.2 and 9.2.9.2. I've often wondered if the foreshortened length of the second and fourth lines in each stanza mimics in sound the insufficiency many find in faith's answers: against the great injustices and sufferings of the world (suggested sonorously in the elongated lines of eleven and nine syllables), faith chirps to cheer up since "Christ saves." The answer, like those truncated second and fourth lines in each stanza, just doesn't measure up. In the poem's last two stanzas, those short lines get even shorter— they shrink to two bare syllables. The poem's meter, like its message, is about insufficiency. It asks: "Is the arm of the Lord shortened that it *cannot* save?"

Christ cannot save in this poem. For the Christ it assumes doesn't stand in for us on the cross; there's no substitution, no proxy. Instead, everyone is crucified: "As many [crucifixions] be / As Persons – or Peninsulas –." The sites of Christ's suffering also expand democratically. Pilgrims need not venture to "Calvary," "Gethsemane," or "Judea," for Emily judges that these sites lie within us. They have become "a Province – in the Being's Centre –." They are, as she aptly puts it, "too near," and the closeness of the pain resonates through those two short (too short) syllables. Christ's death does nothing to alleviate our perpetual dying. Despite his death, Emily gripes in a letter, "Gethsemene and Cana are still a traveled route." Christ's supposedly saving death aside, the world is still suffering.

From an early date, the suffering of others was a central problem for Emily. "The seeing pain one can't relieve makes a demon of one," she muttered; "It will never look kind to me that God, who causes all, denies such little wishes." Sometimes, her letters make even small assaults—the death of her flowers in the garden—into a proof of God's absence or, worse, cruelty. Other times, it was the very real suffering of others that troubled her: "How many barefoot shiver I trust their Father knows who saw not fit to give them shoes." Whatever her tone here and elsewhere, she raises serious questions about how to reconcile the pervasive suffering of the world with the idea of a beneficent divine Providence. Theologians call this problem *theodicy*. Emily seems to be saying along with those theologians that if God is in charge of all things here below, he may not be such a marvelous God after all. Her searing question echoes back again: "Is God Love's Adversary?" It's a hard problem to reason away. Some people God does indeed *put through all of this*, as I'd feared my mother meant, only to kill them at the end.

Of all the proof of unjust suffering the world affords, Christ was for Emily the prime example. "God broke his contract to his Lamb," she posits, "to qualify the Wind –." Whatever good others claimed from "the Wind" of the Holy Spirit, Emily judged it was not enough to justify the anguishing death of Christ that preceded it. Failure, betrayal, isolation, agony: all at the hands of a loving God who had promised to be with him. "My God, my God, why hast thou forsaken me"?

Finally, in case this heaping unfairness were not enough to make you hear the haunting *cannot* in faith's promises, Emily points out that the Crucifixion does not even yield a perceptible result. Christ is no substitute for us in suffering. Instead he becomes merely a representative example of what we all suffer: "Our Lord – indeed – made Compound Witness –," she sums it up. Christ's death is a "Compound Witness" in that it merely witnesses to the anguish compounding across every human life. Christ can be a companion in your suffering, but he cannot keep you from suffering. On that bleak assertion of universal suffering, the poem ends: "And yet – / There's newer – nearer Crucifixion / Than That –." The Crucifixion is happening: now, and now, and now.

If the words *redemption* and *salvation* sounded hollow earlier, how much more bitter that word—*crucifixion*—sounds by the poem's end, when it lacks any glimmer of those other terms' intervening power. I turned to Emily in the hope that she might redeem for me one of those confusing terms. Instead, she's simply gutted them. Emily doesn't always say what I want to hear. Her refusal makes me realize how much I wished to affirm those terms. What would I give now for a little unexplained "ransom," some "atonement" to soften the assault of her poem's final lines?

Yet Emily does not yield. Pressed to give proof of her interior conviction of salvation, her own redemption, she would not consent. She simply would not or could not profess her faith. It seems that the preacher's "cannot" had become her own. Her poem too stands firm. It ends, untempered, on the Crucifixion. The final lines, with their flat *T* consonance (rhyming *yet* and *that*), leave us simply with the cross. Or rather, the final line leaves us with three crosses, for in Emily's writing, each *T* forms a straggly cross. Thus the three *T*s in "Than That" paint a familiar Crucifixion scene upon the page, in which three crosses lift into the sky.

I went to Emily seeking redemption, but her poem shows me instead how bitter this scene looks with just three crosses, raised upon the barren hillside of her poem: Christ and the two thieves; or Emily, you, and me. Her poem leaves us all on the cross.

> One Crucifixion is recorded – only –
> How many be
> Is not affirmed of Mathematics –
> Or History –
>
> One Calvary – exhibited to stranger –
> As many be
> As Persons – or Peninsulas –
> Gethsemane –
>
> Is but a Province – in the Being's Centre –
> Judea –
> For Journey – or Crusade's Achieving –
> Too near –
>
> Our Lord – indeed – made Compound Witness –
> And yet –
> There's newer – nearer Crucifixion
> Than That –

EASTER

⚜

OF ALL THE PASSION'S CAST OF CHARACTERS, Emily was fondest of the thieves. The one crucified besides Jesus, who begged, "Remember me," shows up in several of her poems. Her attachment to him is understandable, for there is something so poignant about the repentant thief who turns to hope at the hour of hopelessness and death. His request, "Lord, remember me when thou comest into thy kingdom," strikes the same chord of sudden belief as the words of the centurion, who suddenly bursts out, "Truly this was the Son of God." Yet the thief's profession rings with less fanfare, more humanity, perhaps because of his dire need. After all, the centurion speaks his word of Jesus' exaltation safely on the ground, while the thief sees the glory of the one beside him from the very cross.

No wonder Emily loved the thief. Even if the Paradise Jesus promises him should prove a sham, the thief's request holds within itself a certain kind of redemption. For, at his end, crucified and sure to die, the thief reaches out toward hope, believing against the evidence that the one who suffers with him will have a kingdom to share. Emily testifies somewhat starkly to the value of such a belief, should it turn out to be false: "Better an ignis fatuus / Than no illume at all –." The *ignis fatuus*, literally "foolish fire," is a glow of phosphorescence that lights up over swamps and bogs, fabled to lead astray travelers who, believing it a lantern or an inn, followed it and were lost. Emily's cynical image hints that faith might be such a foolish flame. Yet would you rather remain in the darkness? Who would not wish to be like that thief—robbing death of its destruction by a last grasp toward life, even, from present agony, toward the hope of Paradise? "I am so happy. I am so happy. I am so happy," Gerard Manley Hopkins spoke his final words before dying.

No angels swooped in to save the three men on Calvary; no trumpets blared to announce that Jesus' kingdom was come. Instead the thief heard Jesus say, "It is finished," and die before him. I wonder if, in taking Jesus' life, Death also stole from the thief his hope. Death robs from each of us, unfailingly, that thing most precious and precarious: life.

Of course, this story does not end on the hillside of Golgotha. Death, which steals upon all living things "as a thief in the night," would be robbed of its great prize. You know the tale: there's an opened tomb and a missing body. Mary Magdalene suspects a grave robbing, so she asks a passing gardener for clues. But the gardener's wounds prove his to be the body she seeks, even as his words reveal that he himself robbed the grave. Christ was not just crucified with robbers, he was the most accomplished thief of all. For the faithful say he stole away the very sting of death. In Christ, the thief is thieved.

I'd never have seen this side of Christ without Emily. Under Emily's tutelage (at least the tutelage of her more playful moods as we'll soon see), the whole Paschal story can read like a mystery-adventure tale, filled with crooks and bandits, surprise plot-turns, and a happy ending starring Christ, the robber. Although the poem into which this robber-Christ sneaks in the final lines may not rank among Emily's greatest, it has a wonderful last stanza that's worth the read.

> Dust is the only secret —
> Death — the only one
> You cannot find out all about
> In his native town —
>
> Nobody knew his Father —
> Never was a Boy —
> Had'nt any playmates
> Nor "Early history" —
>
> Industrious — Laconic —
> Punctual — sedate —
> Bolder than a Brigand —
> Swifter than a Fleet —
>
> Builds like a Bird — too —
> Christ robs the nest —
> Robin after Robin
> Smuggled to rest —

I love the surprise that comes each time I read this short biography of Death. After we learn all the knowns and unknowns that sum Death's portrait, suddenly, in the final lines, Christ appears and steals the poem. With a little shock of pleasure, I realize that the poem I thought was about Death is actually a poem about life, much as the events of Good Friday are transformed on Easter Sunday when Mary Magdalene meets Christ beside the tomb. Emily takes that single Easter robbery—one grave opened and one life stolen back from death—and spins its promise into a perpetual heist. "Christ robs the nest –" that Death continually stocks with his prey: "Robin after Robin / Smuggled to rest –."

To see Christ, who is always good and a very serious subject, do something a touch sneaky is terribly good fun. And how fun is it to envision Christ as a smuggler, sneaking us, his robins, past Death's nasty authorities? Here's a Christ who can keep company with the misfit heroes of the Scriptures, like Jacob who steals the birthright from his brother, tricks his father, and cons an angel into blessing him. How could we help but want to know this mischievous Christ, who once robbed Death and just keeps robbing him, snatching robins from Death's nest to smuggle them into the skies. And can't you see Death—whom Emily here says is so mean he "Had'nt any playmates"—coming home like a miser to his hoard, only to find the twigs snapt, his heap of robins gone. He'd growl as any good comic book villain would and clench his fists against his eternally mounting frustration. *Again!* he'd rage, *Christ! I'll get you for this.* But *rob*ins are meant to be *robb*ed; the very words are cousins, and Emily uses this aural link to stress the happy ending her poem promises. Christ the robber will come for his robins and free them from Death's nest. "Ineffable Avarice of Jesus," Emily brushes him with a warm regard, "who reminds a perhaps encroaching Father, 'All these are mine.'" Though the Father may be love's adversary, Jesus is entirely on our side. Greedy Jesus, the grave robber.

It's only an image, of course, one dreamed up by a poet who called herself a pagan, foreswore prayer, never gave a confession of faith, and left the church. It's not doctrine, certainly not Scripture. But this poem makes me want to be one of Christ's robins as no Scripture ever has. Besides, the whole of the Bible is filled with just such images, little glimpses of divine poetry that make the realities of the weary world more distant, the hope of heaven more near. The Son of Man coming on clouds of glory, the woman clothed with the sun, Elijah and his chariot of fire, even the repentant thief turning to hope from the agonies of the cross: these are images that make the promises of salvation more vivid to us. Add to the list Jesus the robber. It's not so far from what the Bible teaches in the book of Revelation, when the Son of Man announces, "I will come on thee as a thief," and "Behold, I come as a thief." O Death, where is thy sting? O grave, where is thy victory? Christ must have nabbed those, too.

One Holy Week, I encountered such an image, one of those sights that suddenly make the old scriptural stories feel new and vital. I was in the cloister garden of the monastery. It was Palm Sunday, and we were ready with our palms and hymns to begin the parade of the week's events. On the garden wall of warm, sun-baked brick, there hangs a wrought-iron sculpture of the crucified Christ. No cross looms behind him; there's just the cruciform of his body, stretched out across empty space. "And I," Jesus foreshadows his death in the Gospel of John, "if I be lifted up from the earth, will draw all men unto me." The body itself looks like one of those forged by the French nineteenth-century sculptor Auguste Rodin, all sinew and strength. On this particular day, Christ had company. Perched upon his shoulder—which we are told will bear the burden of us all—was a nest. Its twigs must have been carried there one beakful at a time. They wound up into the crown of thorns Roman soldiers wove twenty centuries ago. This Christ looks gentle, for all his strength, and that day his down-turned head seemed simply to be making room for the winged neighbors who had chosen to take refuge there.

For a moment, as I looked at the crown and the cross, and the shoulder and the nest, and the twigs and the sky, I thought it possible that I, too, could be borne upon that frame, smuggled with him into the skies. For Emily is right, "what indeed is Earth but a Nest, from whose rim we are all falling?" Knowing we all will fall, I want to nestle safely with those birds on that robber's shoulder, the robber who stole the grave back from death.

I didn't see the birds who built the nest, but I'm sure they were robins.

IMMORTALITY

I stand alive – Today –

LIFE

❦

I𝚗 1870𝚜 A𝙼𝙷𝙴𝚁𝚂𝚃, at forty, Emily was already a legend for her withdrawal from town life. While her friends gently teased her as the "Queen Recluse," the neighborhood also rustled with whispers less kind. They called her "the Myth" and strained for glimpses of her behind the hedge. *Disappointed love,* they whispered, *spinster, half-cracked.* Emily's niece, Martha Dickinson Bianchi, explains the fascination Emily held for the town: "If 'Miss Emily' could live without her fellow townsmen, they would not live without her . . . she seemed fated to be conspicuous in her very avoidance of notice."

The whispers pursue her still. That Emily was a "recluse" is widespread knowledge now, even for nonreaders of her poems. That fact features prominently in pop-cultural portraits and the mini-biographies that accompany her poems wherever they appear (magnets, bookmarks, anthologies). It's an unfortunate point to highlight from a life so full of other facets. It risks, for instance, obscuring the fact that she was a poetic genius. The word itself, *recluse,* is a large part of the problem; it conjures up images of unwashed hair, cat ladies, the creepy house on the corner where the weeds grow thick. I'd never use the word to describe Emily.

Like most myths, the myth of Emily's reclusiveness—rather, let us say *self-seclusion*—has a basis in truth. She did seclude herself, slowly, limiting her outings and encounters. As early as 1861, at thirty, she speaks of herself to her cousin as "I, who run from so many." Finally, Emily stopped going out and admitted only the rarest visitors, sometimes speaking with them from the other side of a propped-open door or listening from a perch high on the staircase. She turned to neighbors, Luke Sweetser and George Montague, to address her letters for her, as the very press of her pen to the page felt too private to be exposed to the public eye. Even dear friends like the editor Samuel Bowles, with whom she seems to have shared much that she shared with no one else, would arrive one day to find themselves suddenly turned away. Bowles remonstrated colorfully, as their close friendship allowed, *Emily, you wretch! Come down here, you damned rascal!* While his taunts lured her from her room, others were not so lucky, and she remained firm, sending a note of apology instead. One such note reads: "The Apostle's inimitable apology for loving whom he saw not, is perhaps monition to us, who are tempted to the same turpitude." She spins it well, but admittedly, this particular "turpitude" is hardly normal behavior. After her father's death, in 1874, she never went past the hemlock hedge that surrounded the house. She lived for twelve more years.

Seen in this light, Emily seems very strange indeed. But how many of us could withstand a similar winnowing of our identities—the single oddest fact or quality of our life pulled out of context and observed with scrutiny—and not seem strange? I know that I would not survive it gracefully. I'd appear a mass of neuroses and self-subverting behaviors, which, in some ways, I am, just not in all ways and not at all times. What about you? Imagine if, one hundred years later, your weirdest neurotic tic or personal hang-up had become the focal point of your portrait in the public eye.

And besides, what genius ever was normal? Is it not in the nature of genius to look aslant at the world, to engage it in a unique way? We glimpse such unique engagement visually in painting: one look at Van Gogh's skies, Cezanne's pears, Rothko's color, and we recognize that they saw uniquely. The vision is contagious, as through their lens the known world becomes for us unknown again, made fresh and unfamiliar through the power of genius to see things differently. "The soul must go by Death alone," Emily reasoned in her genius, "so, it must by life, if it is a soul." This was her difference, her way of seeing.

Emily's biographers, looking to explain her self-seclusion, gesture in explanation toward her father's overprotective tendencies, her mother's illnesses, the vocational demands of writing poetry, Emily's fear of exposure in print or in public, the wearying round of nineteenth-century social life, her independence of mind. Her niece, Matty, relates the memory of emerging from a punishment—*go to your room and think about what you did*—to find Aunt Emily smiling at the supposed trial: "Matty, child, no one could ever punish a Dickinson by shutting her up alone." Some biographers toss out dramatic words like *agoraphobic* and burrow into youthful letters to emerge with proof of her early abhorrence of crowds. Others mention her "ravenousness of fondness" for those she loved, a fondness too often disappointed by real encounters and that therefore took refuge in friendships experienced in letters, which Emily more effectively could idealize or control. "Is there not a sweet wolf within us that demands its food?" she asks.

While I'm not going to enumerate or evaluate the causes of Emily's seclusion, I would like to unfold, with Emily's help, one petal of this complex, multidimensional bloom, in the hope of making it seem less freakish. Because, of all the rationales for her seclusion, Emily wrote the most compelling one herself:

> Best Things dwell out of Sight
> The Pearl – the Just – Our Thought –
>
> Most shun the Public Air
> Legitimate, and Rare –
>
> The Capsule of the Wind
> The Capsule of the Mind
>
> Exhibit here, as doth a Burr –
> Germ's Germ be where?

She's asking about the sources of life. That last line could be glossed: where is the origin of life? (And she hides a warning within the sound of the two final words: *beware!*) The plant's "Germ"—a seed like a "Burr"—is borne unseen on the breeze, to spring up somewhere else, a sudden blossom. But that "Capsule" has to come from somewhere. "Where?" Emily asks, in the poem's final word. The mind also has capsules that work like a plant's physical burrs: carried along on "the Wind" (the familiar symbol for the Holy Spirit), the mind's seeds spring up, unexpectedly and in places unforeseen, into life. Emily's closing question, "Germ's Germ be where?" inquires into the hidden source of this internal growth. Where does the life behind such quickness originate? Where is the source of those seeds—mental, emotional, spiritual—that spark suddenly and beautifully into bloom?

There are conditions in which a person can ask these questions, just as there are conditions in which the growth they allude to can occur. Some plants need greenhouses; some fresh air; some partial sun; some shade. People grow the same way: in their own specific clime. For Emily, the necessary climate was "out of Sight." If she had married, had borne children, she likely would never have asked this question or written this poem. The conditions of that other life would have prevented it, just as the conditions of Emily's chosen life allowed the questions, the poem to grow. Look at her imagery in the second line: "The Pearl" cannot become a pearl without the oyster; the hermit needs his cave to become "Just"; and "Our Thought" forms only within the brain, nestled safely in the skull. Emily chooses these concrete examples to illustrate how and why "Best Things dwell out of Sight." In other words, she was a recluse as the pearl is one: because without the dark surrounds of sand and surf and shell—and time to grow—there would be no pearl. "How inspiriting to the clandestine Mind," the clandestine Emily exulted, "those words of Scripture, 'We thank thee that thou hast hid these things' –." Sometimes it is in hiding that we're found.

Still, *recluse* is the wrong word to describe Emily's choice. The word implies a certain disengagement from life. Recluses hide away; they withdraw because they cannot cope. They hole up as a strategy for avoidance. Hermits, on the other hand, like monks, step away from the world in order to engage its mystery more deeply. They struggle to achieve what Emily named "the solitary prowess / Of a Silent Life –." The monks I know will tell you that silence can be the loudest place around. The monastery is not an escape, but an encounter. And the one who called herself "The Wayward Nun – beneath the Hill –" stepped back from the crush and press of social life for the same reasons and in the same way that the hermit, the mystic, the anchoress in the church walls do: Emily secluded herself so as to engage life most deeply. Her persistent use of religious imagery to talk about her seclusion might also suggest a spiritual rationale for this choice: "The Soul that hath a Guest, / Doth seldom go abroad – / Diviner Crowd – at Home – / Obliterate the need –." Whether the guest was God or herself, she knew where it was to be met.

"Germ's Germ be where?" she asked. And she lived out the answer as it came to her. "Everywhere alone / As a Church remain –." Here. Life springs up right here.

AFTERLIFE

$\mathscr{S}$

EACH LIFE HAS A DEFINITE BEGINNING and an ultimate end. It bears a birthday and a last hour, as sure as the dates engraved on a tomb. "Mortality is fatal," Emily wields her wit tautologically in one of her earliest poems. Every mortal life must come to an end, and so even life itself is fatal at the last. Since the dead no longer speak, tombstones speak for them, tolling their brief span. 1830–1886. That was a life, begun and ended, as they all are.

Emily spent fifteen formative years, from nine to twenty-four, looking out her window onto a graveyard, eyeing the very plot where she eventually would lie. "I have just seen a funeral procession go by . . . ," she wrote in 1846, "so if my ideas are rather dark you need not marvel." On the days when funerals did not pass by, the stones still toned out the constant admonition, familiar from the Bible and funeral services, "for dust thou art, and unto dust shalt thou return." Some people thrive on such reminders, for the pressing thought of mortality spurs them to faith. Generations of preachers and missioners used this recollection to urge sinners to return to God before it's too late. Emily's own uncle published a horrifying Christian periodical for children, *The Sabbath School Visitor*, replete with stories of sudden tumbles down wells, quick-wasting diseases, and naughty lads and lasses who did not repent in time and so were rent from their happier siblings to spend eternity in hell. Children are led to the gallows, tossed into boiling water, and generally treated to a series of unfortunate accidents that either could have been avoided with the proper religious education or could have been better endured with love for Christ. The story "Charles's Last Sickness" concludes with Charles's peaceful acceptance of death and moralizes, "So *you* would feel, if you loved Christ as you ought, but remember you *must* die, whether you love him or not." Emily's father took a subscription for his children.

Scare tactics didn't move Emily to faith. Early letters from the period of Amherst's revivals, when she lived across from the graveyard, run thick with the threat of hell and the language of damnation: "How sad would it be for one of our number to go to the dark realms of wo, where is the never dying worm and the fire which no water can quench." Preachers employed this language to push the unrepentant toward God, and its presence in Emily's early letters shows just how powerfully it worked on a young imagination. But these threats ultimately pushed her in the opposite direction from the one intended—out the door. As Emily explained, "The Dust like the Mosquito, buzzes round my faith." Emily's faith was not in dust, even though the Bible promises that our dust will stand up and live. In the valley of dry bones, the Lord points to the dust and asks the prophet, "Son of man, can these bones live?" While the prophet demurs, "O Lord God, thou knowest," the Lord commands him, "Prophesy upon these bones, and say unto them, O ye dry bones, hear the word of the Lord. Thus saith the Lord God unto these bones; Behold, I will cause breath to enter into you, and ye shall live." Emily also offers to the dust a prophecy:

Behind Me – dips Eternity –
Before Me – Immortality –
Myself – the Term between –
Death but the Drift of Eastern Gray,
Dissolving into Dawn away,
Before the West begin –

'Tis Kingdoms – afterward – they say –
In perfect – pauseless Monarchy –
Whose Prince – is Son of none –
Himself – His Dateless Dynasty –
Himself – Himself diversify –
In Duplicate divine –

'Tis Miracle before Me – then –
'Tis Miracle behind – between –
A Crescent in the Sea –
With Midnight to the North of Her –
And Midnight to the South of Her –
And Maelstrom – in the Sky –

Life does not begin with our birth; it stretches "Behind" us into the "Eternity" that precedes us. Nor does life end with our death. Even without faith's promised "Kingdoms" and the "pauseless Monarchy" of God, life will stretch onward into the ages that will continue long after we are all just dates on a stone. In that central stanza, we watch Emily lean on one of her favorite strategies—the disavowing third-person plural *they*—to both reference and distance herself from faith's doctrinal promises. She'll make a quick aside to "a Hymn they used to sing when I went to Church" or whisper a little prayer that "Their Father in

Heaven remember them and her." Each *they* works as a perfect way to slip a bit of credulity in under the radar, a sort of poetic version of, "My friend is having a problem with her marriage." If Emily really disclaimed the idea of the kingdom of heaven, why would she mention it here at all? Instead, she leans upon the *they* (and on the cheeky tone) at the start of the second stanza, to allow herself to address theologically complex ideas about eternity that she could not quite claim in a sincere voice. God, of course, "they say" has a "perfect – pauseless Monarchy" and a "Dateless Dynasty." And the Incarnation? Oh, easy: "Himself – Himself diversify – / In Duplicate divine –." The line itself performs this "duplication" in the doubling up of the word *Himself.* It's all very wink-wink about the truths it also offers up as proof.

For proofs are what she's giving. Emily does not reject these notions, whatever her tone might seem to imply; she actually uses them for evidence of the third stanza's lifting claims: "'Tis Miracle before Me – then –." The keyword, which she sets off by bracketing it with dashes, is *then.* She draws her hope about what waits for her on the other side of death from the very promises she's teased in the preceding stanza. Her logic runs: if stanza two, "then" stanza three. Only by looking to God can we know that life continues on in "pauseless" and "dateless" progress. So Emily names herself in the final stanza a "Crescent in the Sea," because she knows that her little "Term" of life is just a slip of waning moon against the vast eternal sea of time. She's the grain of sand before infinity. As we all are. The position Emily claims is true of all of us: each of our lives occupies the scantest fraction of the time that stretches on both sides of us into all the lives that came before and will come after.

The thought of this ceaseless tide can be overwhelming. It might make us worry how one life can matter with so many lives. And where will all those souls go in the afterlife? Someone recently told me an incredible statistic that bears upon this question: there are more people now living than dead. For the whole of time and from the beginning of humanity, every soul—Cleopatra, Chaucer, JFK—every single body buried, burned, or in the sea, if you were to add them all up, every "Overcoat of Clay," as Emily terms the mortal body, you'd have a smaller number than the current living population of the world. There are more people on the earth at this moment than all the dead in it. The idea makes my own "Crescent in the Sea" feel very small indeed.

Yet rather than mourn that we're finite, Emily marvels here that for the few brief moments of this life, we participate in the infinite. If each individual stands as she pictures us, as a speck between two vast plateaus—an eternity behind, an infinity before her—then for the brief moment of her life, she is the "Term between" them; she is the convergence of those tides.

Have you never felt this? The wind gusts or the clouds churn, and finitude just slips away. It could be music, a fragrance on the breeze, a glimpse of stars above, but suddenly some key unlocks our sense of inner vastness. So William Wordsworth, facing the truth that we all "must vanish," nevertheless extols how "We feel that we are greater than we know." I felt this one midsummer, as I was sitting in the garden at Henry Wadsworth Longfellow's house, listening to a quartet playing chamber music. In an instant, some perfect combination of warm sun, waving boughs, and bows' harmony swelled my soul with a sense of magnitude. Emily captures the feeling of such

moments of awareness: "The Earth reversed her Hemispheres
– / I touched the Universe –." She elsewhere calls this feeling
"Convex – and Concave Witness –," mimicking in language
the disorientation just before one faints, when the world seems
to stretch and shift in all directions at once. At such moments,
the universe feels suddenly within reach, so she relates how
she, "A speck opon a Ball – / Went out opon Circumference – /
Beyond the Dip of Bell –." The place where that feeling lifts us
is one that neither bells nor birds can reach, where, at once,
death feels like a dreamt worry that, on waking, slips away.
"We all have moments with the dust," she admits, "but the dew
is given."

I trust you also have known, even once, that *dew*, the rare
intoxication of feeling suddenly, inexplicably, irrevocably more
than dust. We suddenly brush up against the infinity that
precedes, pervades, and encloses us. And instead of feeling
engulfed by the vastness, in such moments that vastness swells
within us. "Vastness –" Emily assures, "is but the Shadow of the
Brain which casts it –." That vastness is you.

The next time life asks you to *Remember that you are dust
and to dust you shall return,* remember instead this poem. Let it
persuade you of the hope that Emily came to hold: life does not
end as ashes to ashes and dust to dust, 1830–1886. Instead, it
moves as this poem does, from miracle to miracle, mystery to
mystery. "Those that are worthy of Life are of Miracle," Emily
determined, "for Life is Miracle." Just think, this miraculous
life awaited us on the other side of the darkness preceding our
birth. And it's darkness up ahead. "Emerging from an Abyss,
and reentering it – that is Life, is it not, Dear?" What miracle
awaits us beyond the grave?

RESURRECTION

Obtaining but his own extent
In whatsoever Realm –
'Twas Christ's own personal Expanse
That bore him from the Tomb –

DID CHRIST COME BACK TO LIFE with a great gasp and a
jolt, as the patient does beneath the paddles? Or did the life
trickle in, the way water perks up a wilting plant or rehydrates
a sponge? Imperceptibly, perhaps, the blue began to fade from
his lips, and color seeped into the ashy base of his brow, as in
the eastern sky at dawn. "Oh give it motion," Emily begs over a
dead body in one poem. When did Christ begin to move?

We know, at least, to add angels to the scene, since Luke tells
of dazzling youths who stayed in the tomb after Christ had left
it, to announce the resurrection. Perhaps the angels' radiance
lit the rock-hewn room—like a thousand tapers flickering in a
chapel shrine—when they first appeared inside, then bent to
stir the crucified man back to life. Or did he wake first, and did
his slowly adjusting eyes register in the craggy shadows rank
upon rank of angels who (who knows?) had kept vigil over
him across three long days of death? Expectant faces filling the
tomb in tiered, spectral rows, as Fra Angelico paints them in

the clouds of heaven, blue fusing to white warming to gold. What did they see as they watched by the body? Might that moment suggest what we shall see on that day Emily names, "Resumption Morn," mingling in her imaginings the promises of New Testament Easter and the imagery of the Old Testament flood: "When Cerements let go / And Creatures clad in Miracle / Go up by Two and Two –."

"Clad in Miracle" is all we can claim to know about what the bodies of the resurrection might look like. Neither biology nor medicine would recognize such an event. Even theology can't account for exactly what happened with Christ's body in the resurrection. It also can't resolve what will happen to ours. "I think just how my shape will rise –," Emily muses in an early poem, and it's the "shape" that matters most to many of us. Or will that new life bring merely a "Costumeless Consciousness," as Emily terms the fearful common understanding? St. Paul picks up the question on everyone's lips: "But some man will say, How are the dead raised up? and with what body do they come?" His next words are not encouraging to the inquirer, "Thou fool." He then goes on for twenty-three verses about "celestial bodies" and "terrestrial bodies," sowing and reaping, an extended analogy about the glory of the sun, moon, and stars, and the admonition, "flesh and blood cannot inherit the kingdom of God." His explanation is dense and not entirely clear: "This corruptible must put on incorruption." Got it? I don't.

No wonder Emily returned to this passage over and over, responding to different lines across the years, as if trying to parse them through poetry. It must have been widely known as one of her favorite biblical passages, since it was chosen to be read at her funeral. Yet in the only poem she wrote that literally quotes it with chapter and verse numbers, she tosses the whole passage out:

> "Sown in corruption"!
> Not so fast!
> Apostle is askew!
> Corinthians 1.15. narrates
> A circumstance or two!

The four contiguous exclamation points might suggest something of her ironic indignation. Yet she wasn't done with Paul or 1 Corinthians 15 at all. Another poem, written twenty years later, takes up and quotes Paul's question directly again, "'And with what Body do they come'?" before she tosses it aside as fast as Paul does, though in a different direction: "Then they *do* come, Rejoice!" For Emily, as for many of us, a resurrection of the body holds the vastest appeal, since the body is the only reality we know and the only reality by which we know those we love: "'Body'! Then real – a Face – and Eyes – / To know that it is them!" It was the body Emily wanted to know, to hold, to hold onto. So she rebelled against Paul's and preachers' insistence on the body's finitude and finality: "While the Clergyman tells Father and Vinnie that 'this Corruptible shall put on Incorruption' – it has already done so and they go defrauded." For Emily, the body was essential.

Indeed, Christ's body, which hung on the cross, then walked again, is at the heart of the promise and story of resurrection. That's why the Evangelists make so much ado about physical details: the stone rolled away from the empty tomb, the shroud left behind. They want to prove that Jesus literally came alive out of that tomb, in the very same body he had before. Otherwise doubters could sneer (and they did) that the resurrection appearances were just ghosts or visions. But a ghost does not take his body with him on his hauntings, and there was no body left in the tomb. To further prove that Christ is missing from the tomb—and not *just* missing from the tomb (there's another problem: the body could have been stolen)—the Evangelists show the risen Christ sitting down for a nice meal of fish with his disciples on the lakeshore. All these details aim to show that Christ is not in the tomb, not missing, not a ghost. "Why, Resurrection had to wait," Emily notes in the same spirit, "Till they had moved a Stone –." The physical realities of the resurrection scene—the stone, the wrappings, the body—point us to the spiritual realities they promise.

Yet the Evangelists also admit that Christ's risen body is patently not a body like every other body known since the world began. Although Christ's resurrected body continues to show the marks of his Passion—"Reach hither thy finger," he tells Thomas, offering his hand, his side—those wounds signal Christ's sustained identity, not his sustained nature. The wounds prove to us and Thomas that Christ is still Jesus; but they also show that he is by no means the same Jesus in quite the same way he was before. After all, he can no longer suffer from those wounds, nor can he receive new ones. And the greatest promise of all: unlike the raised Lazarus, he cannot die again. The risen Christ walks through walls and ascends into heaven, as no mortal could. In some stories, the risen Christ seems so transformed, his disciples don't even recognize him. Mary, come to mourn him, mistakes him at first for the gardener. How can this be? These contradictory narratives try to make clear the confusing fact that the risen Christ is at once the same and not the same, new and renewed.

In whatever untold way Christ's body changed as it moved from life to death to life, it's evident that this change changed everything. For when Jesus shut his eyes in death, then opened them in the tomb, the essential truths of the universe reversed: God can now die; man can now live beyond the grave. The early church, peering into the empty tomb, came to trust that this change would incorporate us all. So Paul pronounces his deep hope, "We shall not all sleep, but we shall all be changed." Emily picks up his line and turns it like a prism: "Were the Statement 'We shall not all sleep, but we shall all be changed,' made in earthly Manuscript, were his Residence in the Universe, we should pursue the Writer till he explained it to us. It is strange that the Astounding subjects are the only ones we pass unmoved."

Emily did not pass by these subjects unmoved. Where other seekers before her, like Paul, thrilled at the promise of change that the resurrection will bring—"In a moment, in the twinkling of an eye"—Emily clung to its promise of continuity. In four jam-packed lines on the resurrection, Emily traces not Christ's transformation, but the bold through-line that he draws between life and death:

> Obtaining but his own extent
> In whatsoever Realm –
> 'Twas Christ's own personal Expanse
> That bore him from the Tomb –

Emily exults that "In whatsoever Realm" he may occupy, Christ still obtains "his own extent." Admittedly, the poem is pretty thick, so let's loosen the lines and let them breathe.

Emily doesn't speak, as a theologian might, of Christ's nature, or being. No, instead, she introduces this strange word *extent*. And in the second half of the poem, the phrase "personal Expanse" isn't any clearer. Yet odd as this language sounds, its object is familiar: Emily points through these words to that unique realm of being that other writers might call the soul or the self. These more familiar terms evidently didn't appeal to Emily, since she constantly invents her own phrases to point to that internal being. Each time, she uses a term that gives the nebulous idea of the self a spatial heft. Here she talks about "extent" and "Expanse." In other poems, she calls the self "that profounder site," that "indestructible estate," and a "Sufficient Continent." *Site, estate, continent*—all place markers that suggest a material presence for the self you could stick a pin in or point to on a map. So Emily revels that "The smallest Human Heart's extent" can dwarf magnitudes like infinity and the cosmos. Again and again, in these instances and others, Emily chooses spatial terms to point to the self, perhaps so she can ground its abstraction through spatial metaphor. In the resurrection poem printed above, "Obtaining but his own extent," these spatial terms have added significance since they describe the risen Christ: like the Evangelists, Emily chooses her words carefully to lend the risen Christ a real, material presence in the world.

And not just in this world: the second line trumpets that Christ maintains his same extent in "whatsoever Realm" he may occupy. That space he carved out in the world and which was uniquely him, Christ carries it with him wherever he is. This persistent "extent" is nothing so material as a body, yet more concrete than a soul; it's not molecular and cannot be put under a microscope. And yet it must be even more precise than the absolutely unique atomic print that each of us carries and which composes us. For although atoms slip into the dust when we die and are buried, to become the spines and spindles of other creatures, Christ still carries his extensive self with him through death and after death. Whether Christ goes down to Hades, as the early Church Fathers thought, or lies dead in the tomb, or eats fish on the lakeshore, or ascends into heaven, he is still himself. He remains, still and ever, the same.

In fact, Emily argues that this constancy is the very cause of his resurrection. The second half of her poem reveals this causal link: "'Twas Christ's own personal Expanse / That bore him from the Tomb –." On first read, it seems as if Emily uses the terms *expanse* and *extent* synonymously. But they don't deal with space in the same way. *Extent* refers to an amount of space enclosed or defined; you could contain the extent of your property within a series of posts. But *expanse* points to an uncontained or uncontainable amount of space—a vista, a vastness. To say it another way: if *extent* deals with borders and measurements, *expanse* denotes breadth and the inability to be measured. In the case of Christ, the two terms interact rather uniquely: Christ's extent is Expanse. That measurable part of him cannot be measured; that contained part of him cannot be contained. The subtle distinction this poem traces between extent and expanse is Emily's answer to the question, "How did the resurrection happen?" It was Christ's Expanse, you see; death could not hold it. In the Incarnation, God poured his Expanse into the small extent of the human body. Yet his Expanse could not be contained by mortal limitations. His Expanse burst the boundaries of the body and the reign of death over it, and so Christ burst from the tomb on the third day. "The Granite crumb let go – / Our Savior," Emily sums up the resurrection, making death itself (as well as the huge boulder rolled before the tomb) a mere "crumb" compared to Christ's internal vastness.

This is lovely for Christ. Lovely for those angels who wept for three days only to see life begin stirring again, in the quick flicker of an eyelash. But what about us? While Christ may have an extent that is pure expanse, will our own littler extents prove expansive enough to make "the Granite crumb let go"? We are limited and human; no divinity tucked within. So the question rankles: will our own smaller extent be enough to burst death's bonds?

Emily's only answer to this question is "Yes." You cannot open her letters or poems without alighting on an assertion that the self continues beyond the grave. "You Cannot take itself / From any Human soul –," she argues. Or she comforts her aunt by saying, "There are no Dead, dear Katie, the Grave is but our moan for them." And again, "Dying dispels nothing which was firm before." And again, "To die is not to go – / On Doom's consummate Chart / No Territory new is staked – / Remain thou as thou Art." And again, "But that they have Abode – / Is absolute as God – / And instant – too –." And again, "We are eternal – dear." For all her doubts, Emily was certain about this one point, that the self will not dissolve in death as bodies do in earth. She affirmed the seemingly impossible hope: "power to be finite ceased / Before Identity was creased –." Identity is infinite, and Emily was sure that to be is to be immortal. If you have lived once, you will live always. These lines are just a few from the expansive stores Emily wrote on the subject. They all point to the same assurance. Emily trusted, ultimately, that "'It is finished' can never be said of us."

Christ was Emily's chief evidence for this belief. Looking to how he rose, still himself, after death, Emily did not doubt that this same continuity would be true for us all. See, this dense four-line poem "Obtaining but his own extent" was never meant to be solely about Christ and his escape from the tomb. Emily sent this poem in a letter to James D. Clark in 1882, and, in that context, the opening two lines don't point to Christ, but rather to Charles Wadsworth, the Philadelphia preacher she may have loved, who might have been her Master, and who had died. Wadsworth is the one whom she proclaims will continue to obtain "his own extent / In whatsoever Realm" he occupies. Christ, in the poem's second half, only proves this point about her friend. Another version of this poem, sent to Higginson, is even more inclusive: "Obtaining but *our* own extent / In whatsoever Realm –." This tiny shift in pronouns has huge implications. We see that Emily offers Christ as an example, but not the unique example, of resurrection. In that crucial "our," Emily reveals her belief that we also will continue beyond the grave. You, me, her. Christ is just the "Tender Pioneer," as she names him in another poem, who blazes before us, for us, the path through death, to life again. God "sent his Son to test the Plank," she imagines the bridge over the great ravine. "And he pronounced it firm –."

It's as if Christ's vast Expanse has opened in death a wide way—a battering ram, a bulldozer could not have cut a broader swath. Now you and I have only to pass along behind him, into "whatsoever Realm" awaits. With "His sure foot preceding –," Emily chides us into hope: "Base must be the Coward / Dare not venture – now –."

> Obtaining but our own extent
> In whatsoever Realm –
> 'Twas Christ's own personal Expanse
> That bore him from the Tomb –

SILENCE

"Now, my George Eliot," Emily lamented her favorite author's death. She learned of it in newsprint, yet felt it much nearer. That proprietary "*my*" tells a great deal about Emily's love for her. Emily hung George Eliot's picture in her bedroom, though freely admitting that it was not for love of her face: "God chooses repellent settings, dont he, for his best Gems?" And it was not just Eliot's death that made her so dear. When asked, years earlier, on the first publication of *Middlemarch*, what she thought of it, Emily had responded with feverous warmth: "What do I think of glory – except that in a few instances this 'mortal has already put on immortality.' George Eliot is one. The mysteries of human nature surpass the 'mysteries of redemption,' for the infinite we only suppose, while we see the finite." The finitude of Eliot, even before it closed, seemed to Emily much more like the infinity other believers recognized in the titans of faith. So when Elizabeth Gaskell's much-awaited biography of Mary Ann Evans came out, telling all, Emily staunchly defended to friends "her" George Eliot's apparent lack of piety: "None of us know her enough to judge her, so her Maker must be her 'Crowner's Quest' – Saul criticized his Savior till he became enamored of him – then he was less loquacious –." To prove Eliot's piety, Emily makes an argument from her silence. As someone who wishes to explore Emily's piety, I'm stunned by this passage. Because if Emily argued thus for Eliot, should I so argue for Emily?

At times it is tempting to make an argument from her silence. While Emily writes quite profoundly on some matters of faith, there are many matters she entirely passes over. So many things of God get not one word from her pen. She appears, for instance, never to have heard that a Second Coming was coming. And salvation doesn't arise much after her thirties, either as a concept or a hope. Rather, she tends to shake off God's reward scheme, even violently. She shouts to God, "'Crowns of Life' are servile Prizes," and in another draft of the poem, tosses the prize back to the one who'd offered it, "Try it on Yourself –." More provoking than such ire, which at least suggests engagement, is how often religious themes seem like tricks of vocabulary, words turned to her purposes. The Trinity, Mary, the Incarnation, the Holy Spirit, Sin, Satan, even the Crucifixion and resurrection: Emily can exploit all of these as common reference points, which she bends for her own effect, whether mischief or illustration. Even Jesus often seems more of a symbol than a Savior. It appears that this tendency dates to childhood, as a prose fragment records a brief biographical incident that reveals Emily's early levity toward the one event most believers don't joke about, "We said she said Lord Jesus – receive my Spirit – We were put in separate rooms to expiate our temerity and thought how hateful Jesus must be to get us into trouble when we had done nothing but Crucify him and that before we were born –."

God the Father, too, can smack more of muse or mythic figure than one true God worshiped with fear and trembling. In fact, she several times compares God to another mythical white-bearded man: "The Fiction of 'Santa Claus' always reminds me of the reply to my early question of 'Who made the Bible' – 'Holy Men moved by the Holy Ghost.'" In other words, a nice lie to tell your children. So even an early emotive response to the promises of faith could be shrugged off with lightheartedness: "The cordiality of the Sacrament extremely interested me when a Child, and when the Clergyman invited 'all who loved the Lord Jesus Christ, to remain,' I could scarcely refrain from rising and thanking him for the to me unexpected courtesy, though I now think had it been to all who loved Santa Claus, my transports would have been even more untimely." Read alongside such pervasive scoffs and chuckles, the gaps in the record can sometimes seem to prove Emily's overriding skepticism, her (pithy) rejection of the whole Christian system.

Then I read from Emily's own pen this surprising contention, "Saul criticized his Savior till he became enamored of him – then he was less loquacious –," and all her silences might just tip the other way. Might Emily's relative silence about the Savior prove, by her own argument, just how "enamored" she was of him?

> Speech is one symptom of affection
> And Silence one –
> The perfectest communication
> Is heard of none
>
> Exists and it's indorsement
> Is had within –
> Behold said the Apostle
> Yet had not seen!

These lines echo Emily's defense of George Eliot, arguing that words are only one form of communication—silence is another; that, between the two, speech might not be the best way of showing deep "affection." She'd argued the same point about Eliot: her reticence may have proved she loved, since she simply may have loved too much to talk about it. While this is a slippery logic to apply to others' hidden inner lives, we know from firsthand experience how hard it can be to speak about the most important emotions and experiences. In the centuries before ours, of course, conventions of propriety would have dictated some reticence, even among close friends, about personal subjects. How many of us have heard parents or friends prove this point with stories of a family member—often of an older generation—who loved deeply but never named it? It's not too far of a stretch, even in our Twitter- and Facebook-crazed world, to imagine some continuation of this tendency into our own day. You might tweet about what you did on Saturday; would you tweet about what God revealed to you in prayer? Emily reiterates this point for herself in her letters: "The broadest words are so narrow we can easily cross them – but there is water deeper than those which has no Bridge." She knew from experience that no words could bridge that deepest "water" within her. Sometimes it seems as if we speak everything *but* the deepest water that no words can bridge.

In the poem above, Emily proves this point by taking up, as a test case, one of the most powerful instances of speech in recorded history: "the Apostle" Paul. Paul's letters to the budding Christian church have shaped Western civilization. Yet Emily dismisses his and other apostles' speech—the very New Testament itself—as a mere "symptom" of a form of silent communication. Above speech, the poet praises "the perfectest communication," which "is heard of none." There are revelations, Emily means to say, that come in communication beyond speech, and she points to the apostles for proof of it. The poem makes its point in oracular fashion, the lines lurching and jumping from idea to idea without connecting the thoughts. Take a line like, "Yet had not seen!" It's missing both subject (he) and object (Jesus): "Behold said the Apostle / Yet [he] had not seen [Jesus]!" The reader is left to fill in the blanks. It's as if Emily truncates the lines to prove her point about the limitations of speech and the value of silence, since she composes the poem of scraps of language that almost break down into silence. After making her point that the best form of communication "Exists," although it is known only to the one who has experienced it ("it's indorsement / Is had within –"), she goes on to offer a snapshot of the apostles' accomplishments as proof. The apostles who did not see Jesus in his life—Paul chief among them—still cried, "Behold," and spread the truth they knew in some other way. How did they know this truth? They heard it in the "perfectest communication" with God, which is "heard of none" but them.

Emily evidently values this communicative silence so highly that she has to invent a superlative form of the ultimate superlative to describe it: "perfectest." *Perfect* was simply not a strong enough word. And while the apostles went on to turn their internal experiences into powerful words, her poem makes the point that not everyone does. Speech is just "one symptom of affection." How many have loved the Lord and never shouted it from the rooftops? How many have never breathed a word of it? Not everyone will write a Gospel. So who dares to know what another person's silence might hold? This is the argument that Emily makes about Eliot after her death: "The gift of belief which her greatness denied her, I trust she receives in the childhood of the kingdom of heaven." It's an amazing assertion, coming from her: Emily passes onto Eliot a "gift of belief" that many readers believe she denied herself. Yet it sounds like the utterance of a believer.

So should we say the same for Emily? Shall we give her that "gift"? This poem reminds me that Emily's poetry is but "one symptom of affection." I recall, too, how well Emily knew the power of silence, even within speech. "The appetite for silence is seldom an acquired taste," hints one born with a taste for it. Emily was silent on many things. How often she would place a dash in the line or the stanza, just as it neared revelation, to leave the rest unsaid. Look back at those lines above: she leaves so much unsaid in order to make her reader puzzle out the rest. She declared, "Aloud / Is nothing that is chief," and so must have kept many chief things silent.

Just what the dimensions of her own depths were, just what Emily heard in the silence, none of us can know. As she queried George Eliot after she was gone, I often ask of Emily: "Amazing human heart, a syllable can make to quake like jostled tree, what infinite for thee?" In reply, I hear only the silence.

IMMORTALITY

I live with Him – I see His face –
I go no more away
For Visitor – or Sundown –
Death's single privacy

The Only One – forestalling Mine –
And that – by Right that He
Presents a Claim invisible –
No Wedlock – granted Me –

I live with Him – I hear His Voice –
I stand alive – Today –
To witness to the Certainty
Of Immortality –

Taught Me – by Time – the lower Way –
Conviction – every day –
That Life like This – is stopless –
Be Judgment – what it may –

WHILE EMILY WAS SILENT ABOUT MANY MATTERS, there
was also what she called "the Flood subject." Immortality
was a flood for her because the thought came in waves and

drowned everything else; a flood because she could not escape the thought and so submerged herself in it; a flood because, one day, she too would be taken under the waters; a flood because so many of her eighteen hundred poems show her trying to row her way to safety. "I suppose we are all thinking of Immortality," she confided, "at times so stimulatedly, that we cannot sleep." Her broad and stimulated thoughts on this key subject become focused, in later years, on the single thought of reunion. "I fear we shall care very little for the technical resurrection, when to behold the one face that to us comprised it is too much for us, and I dare not think of the voraciousness of that only gaze and its only return." If the resurrection shall not include reunion with loved ones, if it is only "a rendezvous where there is no Face," Emily wasn't particularly interested.

While we all long for a "Vista of reunion" after death, the reunion with certain beloveds holds an attraction even more dear. I confess I find more appealing than the traditional view of heaven's throne the glimpse that Dante gives of hell, in which Paolo and Francesca swirl eternally together. Like John Keats, I picture that "second circle of sad Hell" as not actually all that sad. Keats imagines the scene I share a wish for: "pale were the sweet lips I saw, / Pale were the lips I kiss'd, and fair the form / I floated with, about that melancholy storm." The storm may be melancholy, but at least you're with the one you love. Emily explains the problem with this desire in her playful paraphrase of a line Jesus speaks in Matthew's Gospel: "in Heaven they neither woo nor are given in wooing –." (Jesus had said, "For in the resurrection they neither marry, nor are given in marriage.") She concludes, "what an imperfect place!" My wishes for forever, like Emily's, retain a persistently terrestrial bent. If only she is right and "Forever – is composed of Nows –." Now is the only forever I want.

Emily toyed with this same concern in two of the longest poems she wrote, "I cannot live with You –" and "Because that you are going." In both, she unfolds her fear that on the last day, it's not Jesus' face she'll be looking to see. She worries that "The 'Life that is to be'" will prove "A Residence too plain / Unless in my Redeemer's face / I recognize your own –." Fearing that such a preference will lead Christ to exclude her or her beloved from heaven, she knows that she could have a tough decision coming. Should she glimpse her beloved's face going down, she fears that she might just choose hell together over heaven apart. "And were You lost," she whispers, "I would be –."

This preference betrays, to say the least, troublesome priorities. We're instructed, "thou shalt love the Lord thy God with all thy heart, and with all thy soul, and with all thy mind, and with all thy strength: this is the first commandment," but isn't it something of a lost cause if you've already given your heart to another? Emily was guilty of love's idolatry—and she knew it. She often spoke to Sue in language verging on the blasphemous: "Susan's Idolator keeps a Shrine for Susan." And when, at last, she fell in love and had that love returned, her deep reservoirs of reverence flooded toward Judge Lord. "Oh, my too beloved, save me from the idolatry which would crush us both –." But the truth was that she didn't want to be saved from it. The letters she wrote to him exult in their newfound, late-come, overpowering love. Even four years after she'd uttered to him that plea, she was still boiling away: "The trespass of my rustic Love upon your Realms of Ermine, only a Sovereign could forgive – I never knelt to other – The Spirit never twice alike, but every time another – that other more divine. Oh, had I found it sooner! Yet Tenderness has not a Date – it comes – and overwhelms." Let's note: the Sovereign she's kneeling to here is not God. Nearly every letter to Judge Lord borrows the language of the Lord and offers it to Lord (the earthly, not the heavenly one; his name, not His title). She wonders aloud, "While others go to Church, I go to mine, for are not you my Church, and have we not a Hymn that no one knows but us?" Perhaps, through this sacred language alone, could Emily make sense of the adoration she felt.

While I don't follow the view that figures God as some holder of the eternal ticket book, delightedly meting out punishments for each small offense we commit, the first commandment does demand, "no other gods before me." And any lover can testify firsthand to love's possessive side. Preferring love to Love threatens to swerve us straight into idolatry. And though Emily may justify herself with a bold defense—"Why should we censure Othello, when the Criterion Lover says, 'Thou shalt have no other Gods before Me'?"—the fear rings through: that the "Criterion Lover" will censure her.

It's supposed to be the easiest thing in the world, love of God, love of neighbor. The faithful uphold that the two loves are not merely compatible, but even complementary. The more you love your neighbor, the more you love God; the more you love God, the more you love your neighbor (and the more God loves you: "Well done, thou good and faithful servant"). The whole thing looks, from the outside, like a foolproof plan.

Objectively, Emily gets the connection. She ticks off the rote formula, "and love, you know, is God." In a more theological mood, she can muse with the best of them on the heavenly origins of all earthly love: "The Love a Life can show Below / Is but a filament, I know, / Of that diviner thing," namely, God's divine love. And she calls God names like "Awful Father of Love," and "the 'Throne' of Tenderness — the only God I know —." Yet playful as these names are, they hint at irony or double-handedness. The *awful* seems tinged more with the primary meaning, "terrible," than the archaic one, "full of awe." Her God of Love is certainly not a figure to whom you might unfold the secrets of the heart. You can't get cozy with a throne. Yet I once knew a nun who told me, in all earnestness, that she slept each night wrapped tight in Jesus' arms. This nun knew that "God is love" is no abstraction, but an act: God loves. That is a much warmer phrase.

But what if love is God for us? Is the phrase reversible? Most days now, I simply hope that heaven will be half as good as this life. Even if I recognize, with Emily, that God is the "Source of Love" (and this is as orthodox as she gets on the subject), the "Source" remains rather at a distance, as the remote sun is the source of our earthly light. Love, on the other hand, earthly love, is quite near. Love can be right at hand.

> I live with Him — I see His face —
> I go no more away
> For Visitor — or Sundown —
> Death's single privacy
>
> The Only One — forestalling Mine —
> And that — by Right that He
> Presents a Claim invisible —
> No Wedlock — granted Me —

I live with Him – I hear His Voice –
I stand alive – Today –
To witness to the Certainty
Of Immortality –

Taught Me – by Time – the lower Way –
Conviction – every day –
That Life like This – is stopless –
Be Judgment – what it may –

"I live with Him – I see His face" every blessed day. My beloved is at hand, sometimes on the right hand, sometimes on the left, before, behind, beside me. How can God compete with that delight, with the everyday and the enticements of shared days? This is why Emily prefers love to Love. "'Tis easier than a Saviour," she reasons, "– it does not stay on high and call us to its distance; its low 'Come unto me' begins in every place." While theology tells that we have seen the face of God in the "Saviour," Jesus isn't around much these days—not to talk to, not to see. But those we love are: "I live with Him – I see His face – / I go no more away." Is it any wonder, then, that a beloved face becomes the architecture of our happiness, the span of our hopes? "I go no more away" from my beloved because there is nowhere else I want to be, not even heaven if he's not there. "I live with Him," and that is all the life I want, in this life and in the life to come. For I don't simply "live with Him," in the sense of cohabitate with him, I also live by him and in him and for him, and most days, it feels like there is no "Visitor – or Sundown –" who can interfere with that glorious fact.

Except death. No matter how many times I read this poem, I feel sucker-punched by that fourth line every time. The opening lines' whirl of gratitude dissolves when "Death's single privacy" hits, a terrible blow, reminding me that death can at any moment claim the ones I love. It's an awful turn. And it just keeps going: death and its prior "Claim" occupy the entire next stanza too. Emily makes that phrase, "Death's single privacy / The Only One — forestalling Mine —," straddle two stanzas, and the enjambment illustrates powerfully the grasping power of death, which stretches right across any obstacles or safety nets we might put in place. It extends into our little worlds, forestalling love's claims and preempting love's rightful privacy. Although "I go no more away" from my beloved, death can at any moment stretch out a hand and take him away from me. "No Wedlock" could be "granted" powerful enough to keep us safe from death's invasive grasp. There *is* no such "lock," since death always has the key. Whether or not we choose to look at the fact, everyone we love will one day be "claimed."

Death would seem to have earned the final word on this topic, since death has the final word on all human topics. "And through a Riddle, at the last — / Sagacity, must go —," and only death knows the answer. But this poem doesn't end on death's somber note. In spite of death's "Claim invisible" on us all, Emily goes on to argue for immortality. Death may straddle the first two stanzas, but immortality spans the second pair with a reach just as broad.

Emily's argument for immortality begins, surprisingly enough, with a refrain of the opening line's domestic note, "I live with Him — I hear His Voice." Emily never knew shared domesticity, of course, never truly "lived with Him" in the sense I enjoy with my beloved. But we can share life with a friend who lives hundreds of miles away; can hear the voice of our mother in our head long after we have left her home. Emily could pronounce "I live with Him – I hear His Voice" because by love he'd become so much a part of her that where she was, he was. She could "hear His Voice" in her head. This would be true even on the other side of "Death's single privacy." In love, we can draw near to those we cherish even after death has claimed them: not in the flesh but in the heart. That voice never falls silent.

After celebrating this fact, the next line charges into another mood altogether, those stalwart tones I tend to think of as Emily's scaffold voice. With ringing assurance, she declares her trust in the face of the abyss: "I stand alive – Today – / To witness to the Certainty / Of Immortality –." She reveals that her "Certainty" does not arrive by prayer, by fasting. It does not descend in a sudden revelation or through mystic communion with God. No, it comes, she explains at the start of the last stanza, "the lower Way," that is to say, "by Time," in the little acts of the everyday. By hearing his voice and sharing life with him in this lower way of the day-to-day, Emily wins the incredible, wonderful "Conviction – every day – / That Life like This – is stopless – / Be Judgment – what it may –."

Emily may end on the risky resolution, "Be Judgment – what it may –," but the effect is one of hope, not fear. "The Judgment" was just another of her playful names for God, one by which she mocked the tendency of her contemporaries to assign God such a snarly personality. God the Judge, always wielding the gavel, always pronouncing: *guilty*. Who would want to love a God always brandishing the threat of the fiery pit? Isn't that blackmail? Surely this is not what John meant when he said, "God is love." By the end of her days, Emily was more convinced than ever that, so far from begrudging our borderline idolatrous loves, God will reunite lovers and beloveds at the last. "If 'God is Love,'" she reasoned, then "He will refund us finally / Our confiscated Gods –."

"I live with Him – I hear His Voice –," Emily sings, and this line is the key. For her beloved's voice teaches her to hold as true the very hope the Gospels champion: "All that are in the graves shall *hear his voice*, And shall come forth." The voice she heard may have had a different speaker than the one the Gospels meant, but isn't the message the same? Her poem's promise, "That Life . . . is stopless," is the great promise of the Gospels. The hope of immortality, of love stretched beyond the grave, is after all God's great gift to humanity in Christ come down and raised from death to life again. So Emily calls Christ the "Bisecting Messenger" of Paradise, because he is the axis at which heaven and earth meet, like the still point of two bisecting lines. Earthly love, like that Jesus demonstrated throughout his life, is supposed to teach us, not impede God's love. The contemplative nun who sleeps in Jesus' arms learns in that love to trust in eternal life. The monastic Brothers who commit to live together in Christ learn, through community and its love, to hope for the coming kingdom. From families and partners and friends, Emily and I and many others learn this same lesson in a "lower Way," through the daily acts of love.

"I live with Him – I hear His Voice – / I stand alive – Today –." Every day, our life together works its slow conversion on my soul. Doesn't love teach me what is good, ask me to be better, cherish me as precious, and fill me with such gratitude that all my days are praise? Does this love not drive me to the truest prayers I speak, because (though lax in prayer for myself) love drives me to beg God earnestly for *his* good? Every year at the monastery's Good Friday services, the moment that moves me to tears is not the Veneration of the Cross, the Passion Gospel, the sermon, or the Eucharist, but a line that comes in a hymn we sing toward the end of the service:

> And then for those, our dearest and our best,
> by thy prevailing presence we appeal:
> O fold them closer to thy mercy's breast,
> O do thine utmost for their souls' true weal;
> from tainting mischief keep them pure and clear,
> and crown thy gifts with strength to persevere.

As archaic as the language is, I can never reach the end of that verse without welling up. Honestly, I can never make it past "our dearest and our best." And on Easter morning, when we ring the bells and sing the Paschal hymn, I feel the closest I ever do to the trust of immortality by seeing the love radiating from the face beside me. So I cling to the hope of immortality, solely because I long to be with my beloved beyond the grave. While I cannot yet, as Emily does, "witness" with assurance to my immortality, I think I would go to the scaffold for his. He must continue. "Love will not expire," Emily swears. I live with him, I see his face, I hear his voice, and I do witness to the hope of immortality. For my love for him teaches me to trust that the one who is breath and being for me cannot cease to be.

In the last years of her life, Emily began to close her letters to those she loved with the line, "I give his Angels charge –."

She uses the phrase in letter after letter, perhaps because it was *for* them and even *by* them that she believed—simply because she needed there to be a heaven to enfold those she loved. In her final months, she took charge of the angels as Jacob once did, closing her letters, "I will not let thee go, except I bless thee." I nod her words back to her, "Pugilist and Poet, Jacob was correct –."

Thus when my grandfather died, my grandma looked at me from across sixty years of marriage and said with quiet assurance, "I believe there is another life." It was the first time she'd ever spoken of it to me. Her husband, my grandpa, must have taught her, by going first, to know that it was true. Emily trusted from her own experience that this was so: "To live lasts always, but to love is firmer than to live. No Heart that broke but further went than immortality." When those we love are gone from earth, the love does not die with them. Our love goes with them to immortality and perhaps takes a bit of us with it. So Emily predicted it would occur: "It may surprise you I speak of God –," she wrote Judge Lord. "I know him but a little, but Cupid taught Jehovah to many an untutored Mind – Witchcraft is wiser than we –." All lessons of love here below may well be part of that divine "Witchcraft" by which God woos us to believe his best promises.

Several years ago, I took my questions about heavenly love and earthly love to Br. Curtis, and he stilled me with a question: "I wonder if you might consider that Eric is God's revelation of love to you?" Somehow, I had never believed that God could love so well. Now I wonder, what other explanation could possibly account for the gift?

I live with Him – I see His face –
I go no more away
For Visitor – or Sundown –
Death's single privacy

The Only One – forestalling Mine –
And that – by Right that He
Presents a Claim invisible –
No Wedlock – granted Me –

I live with Him – I hear His Voice –
I stand alive – Today –
To witness to the Certainty
Of Immortality –

Taught Me – by Time – the lower Way –
Conviction – every day –
That Life like This – is stopless –
Be Judgment – what it may –

BEAUTY

The Bird her punctual music brings

ECSTASY

Take all away from me, but leave me Ecstasy,
And I am richer then, than all my fellow men –
Is it becoming me, to dwell so wealthily, when at my very door
Are those possessing more, in boundless poverty?

GOD TOOK EMILY AT HER WORD: before he took her, he took "all away." Father first—the man who loomed in life towered more in death, and his absence from the family circle gave daily pain. "My mind never comes home." Her mother died slowly of this loss, and Emily nursed her through years of neuralgia and paralysis before she "quietly stole away," leaving the rest of them "Homeless at home." Those sick years were marked by further losses, each its own devastation: her confidant, Samuel Bowles; Charles Wadsworth, whom she named "my dearest earthly friend"; Dr. Holland, her own friend and dear friend Elizabeth Holland's husband; others too, school fellows, teachers, ministers, neighbors, wives and husbands and children of acquaintances near and far. "There are too many to count, now, and I measure by Fathoms, Numbers past away –." Then her nephew, Gilbert, the family's joy at eight, was lost in days to typhus. With him gone, it seemed there was nothing left to take. But then, her beloved Judge Lord (who but two years before had asked to marry her) died of a stroke: "I hardly dare to know that I have lost another friend, but anguish finds it out."

With that last anguish, Emily literally was stricken with grief. She later told the story to her cousins Fanny and Loo:

> Eight Saturday noons ago, I was making a loaf of cake with Maggie, when I saw a great darkness coming and knew no more until late at night. I woke to find Austin and Vinnie and a strange physician bending over me, and supposed I was dying, or had died, all was so kind and hallowed. I had fainted and lain unconscious for the first time in my life. Then I grew very sick and gave the others much alarm, but am now staying. The doctor calls it "revenge of the nerves"; but who but Death had wronged them?

Her wronged nerves were still fragile, and the letter closes shortly thereafter, almost in haste: "But it is growing damp and I must go in. Memory's fog is rising." Two years later, the final fog would close around Emily. Those last were sorrowing years.

It's too easy, as a reader, to avoid such sorrow, to ignore or minimize it. Losses become lists. Even a biography gets shortened into the brief chronology printed near its covers. We skip on this list from event to event, we tally the births, marriages, and deaths, and this sum seems to express something of the life lived between the dates. But Emily, like many, never recovered from certain events. The chronological entry, "1883 October 5: Gilbert (nephew) dies, age eight," while true, proves misleading. Gib died in 1883, true, but also in 1884, 1885, and 1886. "The little boy we laid away never fluctuates," Emily sighed, "and his dim society is companion still." His death ripped through Emily's experience of life. Absent, Gib never ceased being present to her, and Aunt Emily bore until her end that sorrowful paradox. She turned it over and over, lamenting how he could have died, wondering where he might now dwell: "'Open the Door, open the Door, they are waiting for me,' was Gilbert's sweet command in delirium. *Who* were waiting for him, all we possess we would give to know –."

If Gilbert's death struck her and stayed, other losses brought equal rupture. She mourned, "the Death of the Loved is all moments – *now* –," and she pointed to the day that Wadsworth died: "Love has but one Date – 'The first of April' 'Today, Yesterday, and Forever' –." In fact, it's hard to think of a loss that mattered less or more in those final years, for they all mattered, and their accumulation mattered most. The letters from Emily's last years become, by necessity, an unremitting elegy: she sends out letters sharing news of deaths, offering comfort in the face of death, commemorating anniversaries of deaths, remembering those who were gone. "Memory is a strange Bell –," she marveled in the midst of such demand for it. "Jubilee, and Knell."

To separate "Jubilee, and Knell"—in our reading, in our remembering of her—risks to cheapen both experiences and make them false. Without the knell, jubilee sounds naïve; without the jubilee, knell becomes morbid. Emily often suffers this separation at the hands of readers. She appears either eternally sixteen in cheer or preternaturally morbid as she dwells on and waits for death. Once again we see how it is difficult to credit others with the same complexity we know in ourselves. How many fights between friends or spouses have come about precisely because we ask the other person to feel more univocally about some matter than we do? Remember the outrage many expressed when Mother Teresa's private correspondence with her confessor was published, and her crises of faith were revealed? Her role for us, like that of other saints, was to be solid, sure. We needed her—at least *her*—to be confident in God, so that we could steal a bit of the reflected glow. Learning that she had shadows, too, felt to many like a betrayal. We can require in others the very wholehearted certainty that we ourselves cannot feel.

Yet sometimes we get a glimpse into the complexity of someone else's inner life. For instance, the letter Emily sent next door to Sue, on the day Gib died, is one of the most ecstatic in her whole repertoire. "The Vision of Immortal Life has been fulfilled," she begins and then continues on, through the whole letter, in a long crescendo:

> Dear Sue –
> The Vision of Immortal Life has been fulfilled –
> How simply at the last the Fathom comes! The Passenger and not the Sea, we find surprises us –
> Gilbert rejoiced in Secrets –
> His Life was panting with them – With what menace of Light he cried "Dont tell Aunt Emily"! Now my ascended Playmate must instruct *me*. Show us, prattling Preceptor, but the way to thee!
> He knew no niggard moment – His Life was full of Boon – The Playthings of the Dervish were not so wild as his –
> No crescent was this Creature – He traveled from the Full – Such soar, but never set –
> I see him in the Star, and meet his sweet velocity in everything that flies – His Life was like the Bugle, which winds itself away, his Elegy an echo – his Requiem ecstasy –
> Dawn and Meridian in one.

Wherefore would he wait, wronged only of Night, which
he left for us –
Without a speculation, our little Ajax spans the whole –

Pass to thy Rendezvous of Light,
Pangless except for us –
Who slowly ford the Mystery
Which thou hast leaped across!

Emily.

The letter swings from metaphor to metaphor, as if she's rifling
through them, looking for one to answer, perhaps even amend,
the loss. A crescent! A star! A bugle! "Dawn and Meridian in
one." What metaphor will fill the void of what is gone? Emily
unrolls them, one after another, and the abundance spills over,
the overflow itself suggesting better than the words themselves
the intensity of Emily's grief. The resulting letter is exquisite—
almost too much so for real life, almost certainly too much so
for a grieving mother to receive. It's hard to imagine reading a
letter like this on the day you've just lost your youngest son.
While beauty is welcome in joy, it can affront despair. Emily
certainly would not write this letter to a stranger, who would
likely have struggled to know what to make of it. But Emily
builds upon the long, shared life of language that she had
with Sue. Where others might turn to the familiar language
of commonplace or Scripture—"May he rest in peace"—Emily
calls upon the register that she and Sue knew from the lifetime
of letters and poems they exchanged. Ecstasy. For all her grief,
Emily sings "his Requiem ecstasy."

"Take all away from me, but leave me Ecstasy," she wrote
in 1885, the year before she died. She was sick as she wrote,

and not just sick with grief. Her handwriting—once bold, firm hieroglyphs—now shakes in faint penciled waves on the page. Only to see those wavering words is to know that she was dying as she wrote them.

> Take all away from me, but leave me Ecstasy,
> And I am richer then, than all my fellow men –
> Is it becoming me, to dwell so wealthily, when at my very door
> Are those possessing more, in boundless poverty?

Imagine writing such words as these from your deathbed. To think that Emily scraped the base of her soul, after so much sorrow, and found there the residue not of bitterness or grief, not nostalgia or regret, but ecstasy. That discovery gives her the right to the claim she makes here: "I am richer then, than all my fellow men –." Even at my age, I have some idea how rare this perspective must be. Many people, I think, never use the word *ecstasy*, even in the happiest moments of their lives. Others, burdened by the weight of sad years, might consider that Emily was fooling herself if she could make this announcement after such loss. I can imagine that another reader, one who has known too deep a grief, might say that if Emily could still find ecstasy, she had not truly suffered. I scan again the list of her lost: Father, Mother, Bowles, Wadsworth, Dr. Holland, Gib, Judge Lord. I remember the shaking of her pencil on the page—feeble letters forming strong words—and to me, the word *ecstasy* sounds with wonder. I hear that word like a bell, tolling from a great height and a long distance. It calls out to me my ignorance: *you don't yet know, you don't yet know.*

I do know that Emily was not born with this grace. (I can't but call this gift of perspective *grace*.) Even Emily noted that "Glee intuitive and lasting is the gift of God." When in the youth of her writing, Emily was prone to ecstatic pronunciations, extreme and fleeting, with no spine, like adolescent love or the quick ecstasy others point to with the word. In one such flight, a young Emily pronounces on the nature of ecstasy itself: "For each extatic instant / We must an anguish pay / In keen and quivering ratio / To the extasy –." She presents this ratio as a learned truth, but it feels ungrounded, more hyperbole or hypothesis than knowledge. In 1859, when she wrote those lines, Emily had lived only a fraction of the anguish and ecstasy life had in store for her. In this case, I'd agree with the skeptics: her ecstasy feels naïve; it's jubilee without knell.

But by 1885, when she wrote the poem "Take all away from me," she'd known both anguish and ecstasy. She'd reckoned for real the "keen and quivering ratio" life draws between the two. And once she'd fathomed the anguish fully—I blink to see—Emily actually reversed the ratio she once drew between the two. Rather than judge her ecstasy too small for the anguish life exacts, she finds that ecstasy outlasts any anguish. "You speak of 'disillusion,'" she addressed Maria Whitney, mourning along with her the loss of Samuel Bowles. "That is one of the few subjects on which I am an infidel. . . . To have been made alive is so chief a thing, all else inevitably adds. Were it not riddled by partings, it were too divine." Emily continued to consider, even through that sweep of partings, that life was such a gift, any additional joy was extra, more abundance. Her ecstasy came from the sense that life itself is so divine, "all else inevitably adds."

If Emily had stopped there, with that observation, her perspective would still merit our admiration, rare as such a perspective is. How many come through grief with joy like hers intact? But Emily does not stop there. After having recognized her rare wealth, she goes on to raise the fundamental question of *caritas*, that Latin word wonderfully holding within it both love and charity. Looking to her stores in her poem "Take all away from me," Emily asks: "Is it becoming me, to dwell so wealthily, when at my very door / Are those possessing more, in boundless poverty?" She knew that poverty could come in many forms. And while Jesus declared, "Blessed are the poor in spirit. . . . Blessed are they that mourn," Emily gave priority to another group to which she herself belonged: "Blessed are they that play, for theirs is the kingdom of heaven." Play. Glee intuitive and lasting. Ecstasy. Emily was blessed with this gift and she knew it. With such interior riches, knowing that so many just beyond the door were poor in spirit, heart, mind, or soul, Emily wonders if she does not owe it to the world to share.

We might discern her answer to this question in the way she gave her wealth away. Sometimes she sent a poem or a handful of poems. Often, to brighten sadness, she included blossoms she'd grown in her greenhouse, along with a few lines. "Winter under cultivation / Is as arable as Spring" was not just true of plants. She sent cakes and jellies on occasion to sweeten bitter days. Most often, though, in her later years, she wrote letters—sometimes long ecstatic requiems like the one she sent Sue on the day of Gib's death, sometimes the briefest promise of companionship in suffering: "When thou goest through the Waters, I will go with thee." Or she would turn familiar words of faith a new way, hoping perhaps to offer, through the surprise, the comfort that the more time-worn phrases could not give. Take this note sent to a friend who had lost a child: "'Come unto me.' Beloved Commandment. The Darling obeyed." It's hard to know how these gnomic condolences were received. That her correspondents kept the notes might tell something of their response. But what we do know is that Emily composed these notes with care, going through multiple drafts, and that she sent them with the sincere hope of consoling the bereaved. For years after a death, she would keep the anniversary, sending encouraging words to those who mourned. She sent these gems even to strangers whom she'd heard to be bereaved, a remarkable practice in one rightly known to be reclusive at the last.

While it's estimated that a fraction (perhaps a tenth) of all the letters Emily actually wrote have come down to us today, the breadth of her correspondence still astonishes. Ask why Emily wrote so broadly, so beautifully, and so often, and you might hear that her correspondence was a form of coterie publishing, by which she sent her verses out to select readers. Or you might hear tell of a dwindling in Emily's poetic energies in later years, that she began crafting her letters with poetic care when she could no longer write poems with ease. There's a measure of truth in both of these explanations. But neither pinpoints the full cause of her correspondence, nor does either account for its deeply sympathetic nature in her later years. The letters are a flood of compassion. I find a deeper, more resonant answer in the last lines of this poem. As her grief assailed her, Emily still had ecstasy to spare. She looked around herself and asked: "Is it becoming me, to dwell so wealthily, when at my very door / Are those possessing more, in boundless poverty?"

This was not the first time she'd asked that question. In a poem written a quarter century earlier, Emily exposes her sense of the obligation her gift for ecstasy imposed upon her. Taking a cup of "unaccustomed wine" to soothe a sufferer with "parching" lips, she returns a second time to find the sufferer dead. Emily resolves:

> And so I always bear the cup
> If, haply, mine may be the drop
> Some pilgrim thirst to slake –
>
> If, haply, any say to me
> "Unto the little, unto me,"
> When I at last awake –

Jesus encouraged his disciples to offer a "cup of cold water," literal and metaphorical, to all who thirst, encouraging them, "Inasmuch as ye have done it unto one of the least of these my brethren, ye have done it unto me." Emily saw people around her thirsting for water that she felt she could provide, and so she bore the cup. She sent her words, the one thing she had to offer "Unto the little, unto me."

But only on her own terms. She never passed off the cup for others to bear to strangers. I'm speaking, of course, about her refusal to publish. When prominent editors solicited poems and manuscripts from her, Emily consistently refused to hand any of them over. She even refused when one of her close friends—the famed novelist of the time Helen Hunt Jackson—flattered, cajoled, and threatened Emily in an attempt to woo her toward publication: "You are a great poet," she wrote Emily, "and it is a wrong to the day you live in, that you will not sing aloud. When you are what men call dead, you will be sorry you were so stingy." That was in 1875. Nine years later, Emily still resisting, Jackson was still at the charge:

> It is a cruel wrong to your "day & generation" that you will not give them light. . . . Surely, after you are what is called "dead," you will be willing that the poor ghosts you have left behind, should be cheered and pleased by your verses, will you not? – You ought to be. – I do not think we have a right to with hold from the world a word or a thought any more than a *deed*, which might help a single soul.

In this appeal to *caritas*, Jackson had chosen a powerful plea. For Emily distilled the Scriptures into this single thought: "The Savior's only signature to the Letter he wrote to all mankind, was, A Stranger and ye took me in." *Caritas*, even the help of just a single soul, was key. She boils down Jesus' injunction yet further, "Last – Least – / The Cross' – Request –."

In a way, Jackson was right, and Emily *was* stingy in choosing to keep her poems out of the presses and away from those wider readers of her day whom they could have reached and helped. This appeal had been launched as early as 1862, when Emily reported to Higginson that two editors had been pressuring her for poems, calling her "penurious" when she refused to use her poems to help the world. For all the risk of publishing—the forced titles, corrected punctuation, regularized rhyme, and tamed imagery that were inflicted on her posthumously published poems—Emily also recognized the risk she took in keeping her poems to herself. "He has obligation / Who has Paradise –," she paraphrases to herself Jesus' warning. "For unto whomsoever much has been given, of him shall be much required." Emily had Paradise. Would she share? For many years, she did send her poems, haltingly, hesitatingly, to editor friends in powerful positions: Samuel Bowles at the *Springfield Daily Republican*, Dr. Josiah Holland at *Scribner's*, Thomas Wentworth Higginson at the *Atlantic*, as if to test how they would respond. She would gauge her response on theirs. Would they see Paradise in her poems?

If Emily was aware of the obligations incumbent on her gifts, she also knew that Jesus (in another mood) advised against offering pearls to swine. What would a pig do with Emily's poems but snort at them; muck them up? By the time publication was finally offered to her, too late, Emily had found a different way to repay her obligations. She'd share her gift with fewer recipients, yet with a greater likelihood of success. The connection was always personal. This is one reason we have so many variant versions of her poems: Emily often tweaked and tailored the verses she included in her letters to make them speak specifically to the recipient's circumstances. You can't do this with an anonymous public. And while publishing enters the world of commerce, "Publication – is the Auction / Of the Mind of Man –," Emily's correspondence and the verses it contained remained always in the realm of gift, a wholly human exchange, carefully crafted with the specific recipient in mind. She doled her poems out one by one—a cup of cold water for you, and one for you, and for you—to those who needed them most, and who could receive the help they offered. "I wish I might say one liquid word to make your sorrow less," she wrote, doling out one more cup.

Emily sent this poem, "Take all away from me," to three different recipients in the last year of her life. I wonder if those readers knew her work enough to note the oddness of the poem for its writer. Instead of working in four-, six-, seven-, or eight-syllable lines, as she so often does, Emily here writes in lengthy lines of twelve syllables each. To a reader accustomed to Emily's habitually brief verses, these lines seem to stretch on forever. And in the line where she asks that crucial question, "Is it becoming me, to dwell so wealthily," she adds yet another six syllables. That enormous eighteen-syllable line is among the longest in all her work. Her wealth so overflows, it pours into the very meter of her poem. Through this superabundance, Emily answers her poem's final question: with such abounding wealth, what can she do but give it away? She knows her call: "Mine be the Ministry / When thy Thirst comes –."

Ecstasy, after all, does not mean merely rapture or joy. *Ecstasy*, at its root, means to stand outside oneself. Eight lines here, six lines there, and by a vast extent of letters, Emily sent her ecstasy—by which I mean her self—out into an impoverished world.

> Take all away from me, but leave me Ecstasy,
> And I am richer then, than all my fellow men –
> Is it becoming me, to dwell so wealthily, when at my very door
> Are those possessing more, in boundless poverty?

PORTRAIT

WHEN THOMAS WENTWORTH HIGGINSON, early in their correspondence, asked Emily to send him her portrait, she demurred: "Could you believe me – without?" She sent no picture. Instead, she penned a portrait for him, calling herself "small, like the Wren." Although she went on to detail that her hair was "bold, like the Chestnut Bur," and her eyes the color of "the Sherry in the Glass, that the Guest leaves –," I suspect Higginson heard little that followed the word *wren*. For that word fixed Emily in his mind as a diminutive creature, faint and plain. When Higginson finally met Emily, then nearly forty, he confirmed that impression: "A step like a pattering child's in entry & in glided a little plain woman." Little and plain—like the wren.

We later readers find it hard not to repeat Higginson's mistake. Our only photograph of her shows Emily as a wisp of a girl at sixteen, just recovering from illness. Her slim fingers fiddle with a flower. She looks fragile (if fierce of eye). Picturing this image and recalling some of her sappier poems from adolescence, we can fall into the trap of reading Emily, throughout her work, as akin to the lark, the hummingbird, who flit across her writings. Remembering the rumors about the broken heart, the white dress, the reclusiveness, we can follow Higginson, too, in thinking of her as a sort of "eccentric poetess," as he dubbed her in a letter to his sisters. He reports: "She came to me with two day lilies which she put in a sort of childlike way into my hand & said 'These are my introduction' in a soft frightened breathless childlike voice – & added under her breath Forgive me if I am frightened; I never see strangers & hardly know what I say." Neither soft, frightened, breathless, nor childlike would be adjectives I'd use to describe Emily's voice upon the page—unless she's donning them as a pose. All four of them together, without some tempering agent of irony or jest? Never. I meet her much more tellingly in the next lines of Higginson's report: "but she talked soon & thenceforward continuously – & deferentially – sometimes stopping to ask me to talk instead of her – but readily recommencing." Emily holds court. I like this glimpse far better.

Unfortunately, the prevailing mythology has clutched to the first half of his portrait. This preference may be based partly in truth, but surely also in the fact that it makes for a better story. After a second visit with Emily, Higginson reports back that his wife's previous comment about Emily, "Oh why do the insane so cling to you?"—(do you hear the clucking tongue?)—"still holds." Insane is a much better story. So Emily gets pictured in that (in)famous white dress, lowering gingerbread to neighborhood children from her upper-story tower room, whispering her floral introductions. She appears insubstantial and a little bit crazed. When we read from Emily's own pen that she was "small, like the Wren," it's easy to think back to the daguerreotype, the myths, the dress, and nod in pity at her birdlike (Higginson would say "childlike") fragility.

But this portrait misses the point. Birds are vast creatures for their size. From her five-foot-six-inch vantage, Emily pronounces, "The tiniest ones are the mightiest – The Wren will prevail –." Birds are bold and cocky creatures too.

> The Bobolink is gone – the Rowdy of the Meadow –
> And no one swaggers now but me –
> The Presbyterian Birds can now resume the Meeting
> He gaily interrupted that overflowing Day
> When opening the Sabbath in their afflictive Way
> He bowed to Heaven instead of Earth
> And shouted Let us pray –

If Emily shall be a bird, in our memories, let's make her one of the "Rowdy" ones—the bobolink, the jay—it's how she saw herself. "Unless we become as Rogues," she winked, "we cannot enter the Kingdom of Heaven –."

Her sense of humor, if an acquired taste, is very real. Her roguish interruption of the solemn "Presbyterian Birds" around her may even have been one reason she stopped attending church. Emily reports in an early letter to Austin about a particularly egregious sermon that she listened to "in a state of mind very near frenzy, and feared the effect too much to go out this afternoon." The "fear" of further frenzy was likely just an excuse to stay home from a second exposure to this less-than-inspiring preacher (though he apprently did inspire her laughter). Austin knew his sister well enough to catch her tone and enjoy the joke with her. We get a wonderful glimpse inside the church where Emily's hilarity took place from her niece, Matty. She describes the church in vivid detail, and it helps—in our own day of churches with carpeted interiors, coffee bars, stadium lighting, and rock bands—to picture the context of Emily's youthful religious upbringing:

> There were high pews painted white, with doors fastened securely by brass buttons. . . . These doors were too often

carelessly slammed, but that only set off the noise made by the sexton just as the sermon ended, throwing open the doors of the two cast-iron box stoves with violence and hurling strange-looking geometrical wood, called felly wood, into their vast satanic depths, so that the farmers and their families, who remained for the afternoon service at one o'clock might warm their half-frozen members and refill their foot stoves. . . . The light, much weather-stained walls, patched and cracked, were brought into bold relief by the heavy mahogany pulpit and the really immense red damask curtain dropped for a background. . . . The pulpit was so high the minister was obliged to infer the effect of his sermon chiefly from the tops of the heads and bonnets before him.

We know that at least one bonnet bobbed, not with agreement, but amusement. So when Matty goes on to describe the kettles hung overhead to catch the thick, black creosote that dripped from the stovepipes and the clanging of the iron catches on the enormous sanctuary doors, we can picture the rather forbidding environment in which the Dickinsons attended Sabbath meetings. This context gives texture to the outburst of Emily's glee. For while Matty may describe "the noon interval" as a time when everyone crowded around the stoves and "neighborly visiting was indulged in, with low sad tones," Emily offers a strikingly different report to Austin: "The morning exercises were perfectly ridiculous, and we spent the intermission in mimicking the Preacher, and reciting extracts from his most memorable sermon. I never heard father so funny." Picture the Dickinson clan, even starched Edward, as the loud group in the corner, stifling the laughter that only becomes so deliciously irrepressible at solemn moments.

Emily's taste for jest, gentle and biting, never dwindled. When all Amherst swooned in awakening (again), Emily smirked out her window at the spectacle her overdressed and imperious neighbor made: "I know of no choicer ecstasy than to see Mrs. [Sweetser] roll out in crape every morning; I suppose to intimidate antichrist." It was an old joke with her cousins Fanny and Loo, one Emily had prodded them with a few years earlier: "Mrs. S gets bigger, and rolls down the lane to church like a reverend marble."

Even serious topics, such as sin, could become a fuse for humor. Emily reveals her method in a rare moment of transparency, "The truth I do not dare to know / I muffle with a jest." So when the preacher bellowed sin and damnation, a topic we know could trouble her, Emily "jested" instead at his inconsistency in terminology from one Sunday to the next: "Our Pastor says we are a 'Worm.' How is that reconciled? 'Vain – sinful Worm' is possibly of another species." She expands on her snip in a subsequent letter: "What a privilege it is to be so insignificant! Thought of intimating that the 'Atonement' was'nt needed for such atomies." One day she heard: sin makes us a worm in the eyes of God; the next day: in the atonement, God saves us from sin. Putting the two messages together, she concluded: what a strange God to be willing to die to save a worm.

If doctrine could be teased into fun, its source could too. "I fell to reading the Old & New Testament," she reported to her long-term friend Joseph Lyman. "I had known it as an arid book but looking I saw how infinitely wise & how merry it is." It takes a special genius to see the Bible's merriment. Emily had that gift, and so she often punned and funned with the Bible, using its earnest reception by most readers as a foil for her wit: "If prayers had any answers to them, you were all here to-night, but I seek and I don't find, and knock and it is not opened. Wonder if God is just – presume he is, however, and t'was only a blunder of Matthew's." Emily's song was not some heartbroken warble. As we've seen in these pages, she was often tart, often irreverent, often wry. And she was all of these ways, above all, with God. "I hope God will forgive me," she expressed the common wish, then shifted it, "as he'll have to many times, if he lives long enough."

As wrong as it would be to miss her humor—and it's easy to do—it would be just as wrong to confuse Emily's tartness and swaggering for a mere rejection of the truths she teased. Her niece attempted to set the record straight, apologizing that "although Emily took liberties with the Puritan vernacular and dogma . . . these impish flashes were no more to the underlying God-consciousness of the real Emily than the gargoyle on the roof is to the heart of the Cathedral within." While I consider some of Emily's rebellious diction to have had more teeth than Matty seems to have wished her readers to think in the 1910s and 1920s, her image is striking. And the point remains that God could certainly take a little joking amid the attentions of the overtly, perhaps even overly, pious. God might just understand how one could poke fun and still *be* pious.

As we know from earthly relationships, teasing often proves intimacy and affection. In my friendship with the Brothers, the signal moment was when I stopped looking toward them with reverence long enough to make a joke. (Okay, so it was a joke about the medieval philosopher Abelard's famous castration, and I made it in the chapel during Holy Week, not the most tasteful choice, but it meant—and so I made it and so they laughed—that we were friends.) "I believe," Emily proposed, "the love of God may be taught not to seem like bears." And I agree with the letter's next phrase too: "Happy the reprobates under that loving influence." While others tiptoed about the Almighty like a sleeping bear, the reprobate Emily swaggered and sang out of love.

In fact, Emily's bobolink poem is far rowdier than it seems in the version printed above. The manuscript, never resolved into a fair and final copy, has a maelstrom of alternative word choices and variant lines. It swaggers all over the place. Here's what the manuscript looks like:

If we visualize all the possible alternative ways we could read the poem, it looks something like this:

The Bobolink is gone – the Rowdy of the Meadow –

And no one swaggers now but me –

The Presbyterian Birds can now resume the Meeting

He gaily interrupted that overflowing Day   boldly

When opening the Sabbath in their afflictive Way

He bowed to Heaven instead of Earth

And shouted Let us pray –   When supplicating Mercy
                                    In a portentous way –

  Sweet from a surreptitious Twig   to every Heaven above

  Gay from an unannointed Twig   to all the saints he knew

                                           every God he knew

  He recognized his Maker –

  He overturned the Decalogue –   and bubbled let us pray –

  He swung upon the Decalogue   He gurgled – Let us pray –

Each line opens into an array of alternate options, a sort of choose-your-own-adventure. Has the bobolink "recognized his Maker –" or "overturned the Decalogue"? Will he shout, bubble, or gurgle that final liturgical invitation, "Let us pray –"? I love reading Emily's poetry with the variants on display because it allows all the possibilities she had storming in her mind to thunder in ours. It puts us in the boil of the creative process alongside her, and we experience her work as she did: open-ended, still alive with possibilities. Suddenly, we can read her imagery more subtly, with a sense of how she weighted it. A phrase like "overturned the Decalogue" can sound fierce on its own—the tone of an irate Jesus driving the money lenders from the temple—but when you pair that line with its alternative, "swung upon the Decalogue," suddenly the poem is a playground and the bobolink is on a romp with God. He's boldly-gaily bowing to heaven-saints-God, gay-sweet from a surreptitious-unannointed twig, while bubbling-gurgling-shouting, "Let us pray –." Although the poem may not be traditionally readable in this form, it does suggest something of the boundless energy Emily brought to her verse and her life. It also shares some of that vibrancy with us.

Her neighbors in the adjoining pews, the "Presbyterian Birds" she names here, may have been offended at the zest the bobolink shows, sounding its raucous string of notes over the fields, but God couldn't have minded. Emily's rowdy, backward prayers might just have pleased God more than the "afflictive" attentions of the average Sabbath meeting. Dour faces in church are depressing enough from an earthly vantage. What must "the Sky" think? And forget too the choirs of cherubim, martyrs, and puritans in the world to come; Emily imagines heaven with "Bobolinks around the throne / And Dandelions gold," because she knows that God, creator of all things, must also love the boisterous birds and rapacious weeds.

Emily encourages the wayward, the irreverent: "The crucifix requires no glove." Grasp it tight and firm in your sweaty palm, you will not offend; twirl it like a baton, it will not break. God likes a lark as well as we do. And, thanks to Emily, I believe God loves a bobolink.

GRASPED BY GOD

I heard, as if I had no Ear
Until a Vital Word
Came all the way from Life to me
And then I knew I heard –

I saw, as if my Eye were on
Another, till a Thing
And now I know 'twas Light, because
It fitted them, came in.

I dwelt, as if Myself were out,
My Body but within
Until a Might detected me
And set my Kernel in –

And Spirit turned unto the Dust
"Old Friend, thou knowest Me",
And Time went out to tell the News
And met Eternity

"GRASPED BY GOD" is Emily's phrase. The three words tantalize from a scrap, a thrilling islet in the sea of papers she left behind.

They tantalize because they point to an experience of great power, but don't describe it. I'm convinced that Emily must have had the experience of being "grasped" herself, precisely because she chooses that word, *grasped*. The word *conversion*, by way of contrast, functions as an exterior label that interprets, after the fact, an internal event. It does not capture the event itself. So an interpreter, in the objective vein, might describe conversion as "encountering God" or "finding God." But such words do not seize the essence of that experience. They make it sound as if, in such moments, God is a friend bumped into, unexpectedly, on the street, or a quarter found under the couch. They don't convey the shock or thrill of it. Ah, but *grasped*, yes, *grasped* rings true. For *grasped* has a *gasp* in it, as if the wind were just knocked out of you. Or rather, as if a breath were suddenly pulled into you. Try it: gasp. So, in such moments of being grasped, you feel a sudden inspiration. Emily must have known this gasp to name it so; she must have been grasped.

The first time I was grasped by God, it felt like a floodlight. Literally, I felt, on my flesh and to my bones, like I was standing under a floodlight, beamed full bore from the heights onto my head. "*Feu*," Blaise Pascal scrawled on the page that records the night that turned his own life toward God. "*Certitude, certitude, sentiment, joie, paix.*" In my certitude, sentiment, joy, and peace, I only felt the light.

The second time, ten years later, it was honey. There's no other way to describe the feeing: as Br. Curtis spoke the words of my baptism, I felt as if thick honey, warm as candle wax, was streaming over my head, pooling in the hollows of my eyes, to pour over the outcroppings of cheekbones, nose, lips, and chin. And it was sweet. I could smell its fragrance all around me. I felt it everywhere, dripping down and down.

Twice I was grasped by God. One hand was honey, the other light, but each time the hand was God's. I know that, just as I know that I could never have believed without these graspings. I've often thought that these proofs of God are a proof of the weakness of my own capacity for belief. I have needed such signs, where others have been able to move forward, to love God, without the proof. "Blessed are they that have not seen, and yet have believed." My necessity alone must be the reason these experiences were given to me. And I know—against my reason and against my skepticism—that they were given to me, just as I know intuitively that, without them, I would not believe. Yet, given the honey, given the light, I find (thank God) I have no other choice.

Time seems to funnel around such moments, siphoning into clear sets of Before and After. Emily shows this temporal shift quite well in her wonderful poem on being grasped by God.

> I heard, as if I had no Ear
> Until a Vital Word
> Came all the way from Life to me
> And then I knew I heard –

I saw, as if my Eye were on
Another, till a Thing
And now I know 'twas Light, because
It fitted them, came in.

I dwelt, as if Myself were out,
My Body but within
Until a Might detected me
And set my Kernel in –

And Spirit turned unto the Dust
"Old Friend, thou knowest Me",
And Time went out to tell the News
And met Eternity

Each of the poem's first three stanzas shares the same structure, narrating a before and after state. "I heard / I saw / I dwelt" one way "until"—until nothing was the same. Once the Word, the Light, the Might came to her, everything changed forever. Emily is especially clever about the way she shows this change in the first stanza: it begins and ends with the same words, "I heard," so that the stanza looks as if it has merely traveled full circle with no change. But appearances deceive. These changes are not visible, since they happen within. From the first "I heard" to the second, the whole nature of what it means to hear has altered. One might say that, far from everything being the same as it was before, nothing will ever be the same again.

The third time I was grasped by God—I don't deserve it, but it keeps happening, each time I lose the thread—I felt not windlessness, but wind. I had entered Notre-Dame by accident, with the hope of seeing the sunset through the great rose window of the western facade. Suddenly, we lookers-on were thrust aside to let the procession for the Mass pass by. I remember thinking of Paul Claudel, the twentieth-century French playwright who was famously grasped by God near the second pillar leading to the entrance to the choir: *"En un instant mon cœur fut touché et je crus."* He explains:

> In an instant, my heart was touched and I believed. I believed, with such force of attachment, with such an upheaval of my entire being, with a conviction so powerful, with such certainty as left no room for doubt of any kind, that since then, no book, no reasoning, no circumstances of a troubled life, could shake my faith, nor even, to tell the truth, touch it.

I never entered the cathedral without thinking of Claudel, wondering which was the pillar, as if by standing beside it I could know the same overthrow. Pushed aside that day, I watched as the procession came in pairs, first choirboys, priests in cassocks and nuns in veils, then candle bearers, thurifer and crucifer, the Word luminous in silver casing, and a whole cast of celebrants in embroidered chasubles and copes, glimmering in the half-light, and then last of all and all on his own, the bishop of Paris. I knew him by his miter and the wooden shepherd's crook he carried. As they passed, the always-new-yet-familiar feeling began to stir in me, like starlings' wings before they rise. Then—out of nowhere and for no reason, yet undeniably as light or honey—the bishop of Paris looked me in the eye; his own eyes simmered with the hint of a laugh. I thought, inexplicably, "I know him." Then he inclined his head—*to me*—a tiny bow—*I was standing among thousands*—and whispered to me, *"Bonjour."* I knew at once that it was not him but God who was greeting me.

How can I describe what happened next? Wind. On my face and fingertips, so sudden and palpable, I think I may actually have stumbled back a step or two in surprise. Or maybe I curtsied. I think I did. I did curtsy, as if in the presence of, well, a King. It makes no sense, and yet, as Emily demurs, "Conversion of the Mind / Like Sanctifying in the Soul – / Is witnessed – not explained –." This bishop mouthed to me a mere "Hello," and with that word, a wind rose, and suddenly it was spring inside the cathedral. No—more than that—I'm no longer in the cathedral at all, I'm somewhere in the atmosphere, buoyed amid the clouds. For a moment, you see, I don't know where I am. Perhaps, to borrow St. Paul's tantalizing phrase for his experience of being grasped by God, perhaps I was "caught up to the third heaven." But no, that's not right either, for there I was, looking the bishop in the eye while he looked in mine. I only know that single word, *bonjour*, swept through my skin with a bright quickening wind, freshening me with great gulps of new beginnings. And so I felt each time. Whether the freshening came with light, honey, or wind, I sensed a new beginning begin.

In my experience, *after* has a disappointing way of becoming much like *before*. Although the moments of being grasped by God seem to rearrange time around them, they still happen in time. And time moves on. Tick, tock. We temporal beings cannot stay side-by-side with eternity, even if we're convinced, in that one eternal instant, we will. I've watched many friends slide back from an encounter with eternity to the daily round of time and, in the banal aftermath, come to doubt that they were ever grasped by God at all.

One dear friend and a brilliant skeptic, Niki, has fought hard against faith for so long—although admittedly she consented enough to enroll in divinity school, to accompany me to the monastery, to debate theology over wine, and to weep during the Holy Week services. Nevertheless, her guard was up and she was *not* a believer, you hear? Then one spring she visited a monastery on an island in Greece (you see what I mean, she's clearly not interested in God), and I received a breathless e-mail written at an airport computer terminal, "I am a Christian, but then you knew that already." My joy could not have been less than hers. By the time her plane had landed in Boston and she met me to share the tale—it had only been two days—she'd explained away the experience: it was only the pressures of school and personal concerns; the powerful stimulus of the environment; the examples of the Sisters. Whatever it was, it wasn't God, certainly not, not for her. While I maintain that something real happened to her on that island, for her it was already over. We'll see.

I know I thought, after my first encounter with the light, that I would stay enlightened, just like that, unto eternity. But I did not; the dark inched in. And I registered the change with such self-reproach. So many people lose their faith in God by disaster, by loss that severs their trust and hope. My loss was avoidable, a loss by atrophy. Yes, I felt sure that I had ruined, through my own carelessness, the irreplaceable gift I had been given—that "Kernel" Emily names in the third stanza of her poem, which "Might" sets inside her. So this very poem became for me a further proof of my failure, my fallenness, and each of Emily's exalted *untils* punished me. They reminded me that I too had had the word, the light, the might, *until* I had lost them.

Her poem became, to borrow another of Paul's expressions, "a thorn in the flesh." But time moves on, and God is good. And every time I wandered too far, God found a way to grasp me and pull me back.

I know that many people do feel rare moments of contact with God in their lives. They too have been grasped. Emily had at least three such experiences, and the three this poem records may be only the beginning. See, I now believe that her poem does not relate a single experience told three ways, but three separate experiences. Emily heard a Word. Time passed, the word fell silent. She saw a Light. Time passed, the light grew dim. She felt a Might. Time passed, the might began to fade. So it happens, again and again. However sublime or subtle the experience of God, this fading simply happens. It need not be ushered in by a tragedy any greater than that of time's passage and it may be no more avoidable than the movement of time, for we time-bound creatures simply cannot sustain a single state—exalted or banal—across great sweeps of time. I don't think Might expects us to, nor does Might blame us for the loss.

I believe this because even after I'd lost my "Kernel" twice, the Spirit spied me in the eyes of a bishop going to Mass in a Parisian church and said, with a simple "*Bonjour*" and a twinkle in the eye, "Old friend, thou knowest Me." And then, just as Emily said it would happen, "Time went out to tell the News / And met Eternity."

I heard, as if I had no Ear
Until a Vital Word
Came all the way from Life to me
And then I knew I heard –

I saw, as if my Eye were on
Another, till a Thing
And now I know 'twas Light, because
It fitted them, came in.

I dwelt, as if Myself were out,
My Body but within
Until a Might detected me
And set my Kernel in –

And Spirit turned unto the Dust
"Old Friend, thou knowest Me",
And Time went out to tell the News
And met Eternity

REVELATION

LIKE MANY READERS OF EMILY'S POEMS, I've gone on pilgrimage to Amherst in the attempt to flesh out her enigma, draw her from page to person. I've toured the Homestead, with its whitewashed rooms and tokens suggestive of a nineteenth-century upper-middle-class life—some china, chairs, a fireplace grate. I've nodded to the bed, a deep sleigh, where she died. I've strolled the garden paths and walked the streets of downtown Amherst, where most of the buildings I seek are gone and a little university town hums away, unperturbed by the loss. I've slept a night in the meadows her window overlooked. An inn has since arisen where the hay bales spilled. That night I heard the wildest thunderstorm of my life and, with each clap, I mouthed her words again, "To pile like Thunder to it's close / Then crumble grand away / While everything created hid / This – would be Poetry –." I've walked the street in Cambridge where she lived with Fanny and Loo while undergoing treatment for her eyes, enduring the terrifying fear that she would go blind. I've visited the libraries that house her manuscripts, paged through the careful fascicles, late scrawled scraps, envelopes, receipts, handbills, and I've held three versions of one poem mingling stormily on a single page. And I've visited her grave—a fence, some birdsong.

She wasn't in any of those specific places. But she was everywhere: in the buzzing squadron sounding chaos around her too-tidy garden, "Bees are Black – with Gilt Surcingles – / Buccaneers of Buzz –." In one old tree, "Whose fingers comb the Sky – / Then quiver down, with tufts of tune – / Permitted Gods – and me –," which lifted above the vacant house, as well as in some young, lusty weeds pushing between the orderly flagstones of the walk. Emily's contemporary, Walt Whitman, famously ends his *Song of Myself*, "I bequeath myself to the dirt to grow from the grass I love," inviting his readers, "If you want me again look for me under your bootsoles." I looked, but not for him.

"I am glad you are in the open Air –," Emily commended dear Elizabeth Holland, "that is nearest Heaven –." In the natural world, I feel close to her, for this world was her chapel, her love for it her prayer. When I'm in the open air, I hear her words and even believe that she's in heaven.

> Through the Dark Sod – as Education –
> The Lily passes sure –
> Feels her White foot – no trepidation –
> Her faith – no fear –
>
> Afterward – in the Meadow –
> Swinging her Beryl Bell –
> The Mold-life – all forgotten – now –
> In Extasy – and Dell –

Emily finds in the lily a whole theology of eternal life. An able preacher, the lily teaches us how to die ("Feels her White foot – no trepidation –"), as well as how to hope for resurrection ("The

Mold-life – all forgotten – now – / In Extasy – and Dell –"). To those so inclined to see, a simple flower preaches immortality. For education, we need look no farther than the field. Emily was always looking. "'Consider the Lilies,'" she smiled, is "the only Commandment I ever obeyed." Writing on nature was her holy task.

Religious readers have long perceived the created world as the second book of God. Even the Psalms ring with such teachings: "The heavens declare the glory of God; and the firmament sheweth his handywork." Can you hear what they declare? "Their line is gone out through all the earth." Just listen, and the Psalms will point you to the thirsty hart, the hills and rivers, blooming palm trees, the strength of the horse, each with a different lesson (longing for God; praise of God; the triumph of the wicked or the maturity of the faithful; and the futility of human striving, respectively). So Emily steps into a grand tradition, knowing that the lily, looked at rightly, teaches the same immortal truths the Scriptures maintain, only in more colorful messages. "Consider the lilies of the field," Jesus commands in that line she loved: "how they grow; they toil not, neither do they spin: And yet I say unto you, That even Solomon in all his glory was not arrayed like one of these. Wherefore, if God so clothe the grass of the field, which to day is, and to morrow is cast into the oven, shall he not much more clothe you?" Whether or not she credited the promise the lilies passed on, Emily needed no inducement to study them, preferring nature's style of revelation—especially the "liquid Commandment" about the lilies—to that preached in the Bible or to the pews: "Were all it's advice so enchanting as that," she teased, "we should probably heed it."

A year's worth of sermons and hymns, Psalms and Scriptures waited just beyond the door. In the "sacrament of summer days," she found a communion of "consecrated bread" and "immortal wine." Fall brought the mowers to the meadows and, with them, thoughts of the final harvest: "Our man has mown today, and as he plied his scythe, I thought of *other* mowings, and garners far from here." Winter's "certain Slant of light" narrowed the gap between the finite and the infinite, bringing "Heavenly Hurt" and an awareness of the grave. And each spring, "Nicodemus' Mystery / Receives it's annual reply" in the flowers' reminders of the second birth and the hope of resurrection. The whole world bloomed with the promises that the Bible made sound strange and formal, and yet which, encountered out of doors, became believable and true. "Nature and God – I neither knew," Emily resists, then admits, "Yet Both so well knew Me / They startled, like Executors / Of My identity –." The God she fled from in the pews she met beneath the open sky, where "The Star's Etruscan Argument" was waiting to "Substantiate a God." All she had to do was look up. The birds passed on divine "benediction / And badinage." All she had to do was listen. And flowers bloomed so blissfully on every side, how could she not pronounce that "with no disrespect to Genesis, Paradise remains."

"I was thinking, today . . . ," she mused, "that the 'Supernatural,' was only the Natural, disclosed – / Not 'Revelation' – 'tis – that waits, / But our unfurnished eyes –." God is all around us, revealed in the natural world. If only we could see, we'd pray with Emily, "In the name of the Bee – / And of the Butterfly – / And of the Breeze – Amen!" This tiny three-line poem is not just jest. The bee, like God the Father, is a creator (father of many flowers); the butterfly, like God the Son, rises from its cocoon grave; and the breeze, like God the Spirit, moves everywhere and touches all. Here is the Trinity: alive in every summer day.

"Not 'Revelation' – 'tis – that waits." Poem by poem, Emily furnishes our eyes.

BEAUTY

The Bird her punctual music brings
And lays it in it's place –
It's place is in the Human Heart
And in the Heavenly Grace –
What respite from her thrilling toil
Did Beauty ever take –
But work might be Electric Rest
To those that Magic make –

FOR "PUNCTUAL MUSIC," no bird can compete with the robin. Emily wryly ascribes to robins "the punctuality / Of the New England Farmer –" since, like the farmer, robins work dawn to dusk. Among the first birds to sing at sunrise and last to sound at sunset, the robin also appears earliest in spring and stays latest into the winter. Sometimes, in fact, robins do not migrate at all, but roost with thousands of other robins to wait out the cold. While other birds have flashier feathers, better migration spots, the robin admittedly lives "In humble circumstances –." So Emily laughingly locates the robin in "Transport's Working Classes –."

Yet, there's nothing humble about the robin's song. I think you'd recognize it, even if (like me) you can't generally tell one birdsong from another. Robins have a uniquely heartening trill that ornithologists try to describe with words like *continuous, melodic,* and *caroling.* They transcribe its song, *cheerily, cheer up, cheer up, cheerily.* Judging from sheer presence, the robin must have been Emily's favorite bird, as it figures in over forty poems and fifty letters. In this record, the robin trumps the next-best birds—jay, sparrow, and bobolink—by 500 percent. At nineteen, she chirps, "I seem to myself a robin," and she appears never to have lost the identification. Did the robin's "Durham Breast," tinged the hue of Durham's dried tobacco, make her love them best, Durham-hued as she was? Or was it the robins' songs that made her love them so dearly? She does pronounce, "The Robin's my Criterion for Tune –," and often points in her songs to theirs. "I raise only robins on my farm," she boasts and imagines the robins as somehow sharing in the writerly task: "They are writing *now*, their Desk in every passing Tree." *Cheerily, cheer up, cheer up,* she heard them from her writing desk that lifted up into the branches just beside her, only a windowpane between them. You might have heard this sound echoing from a lone tree top, as the sun sets, for although the robin hunts for food on the ground, in a characteristic zigzag run, it saves its song for high perches. *Cheerily, cheer up, cheer up.* Who could help but feel cheered to hear, after all the other birds have flown, the robin's bright refrain lifting from a barren branch into the waning sky?

"Wherefore sing," a young Emily asked such a solitary bird singing at the end of her garden, "wherefore sing, I said, since nobody *hears?*" For answer, Emily tells that she watched "One sob in the throat, one flutter of bosom – '*My* business is to *sing*' – and away she rose!" Emily goes on to muse, "How do I know but cherubim, once, themselves, as patient, listened, and applauded her unnoticed hymn?" She wrote this mawkish little scene in 1862, in the thickest years of her writing. In 1862, before she gave up the idea of publication, Emily was keenly aware of herself as such a solitary singer, with no one to *hear*.

"Wherefore sing"? We might well turn Emily's question on herself. For poets, as for birds, the drive toward song remains mysterious. Ornithologists answer the birdsong question with the science of mate attraction. Yet even in their scientific answers, they admit that science cannot fully account for birds' songs. Instead, they gesture toward another explanation, one that poets tend to offer for their drive to song, as well as for that of the birds whom they identify as fellow workers in a common cause. That answer can be given in a single word: *beauty*. Poets and birds, they sing for the beauty of it.

"Beauty crowds me till I die," Emily sang. From her upper-story room, from her writing desk, from her abundant garden, beauty never stopped mobbing her. She goes on to pray to this omnipresence: "Beauty mercy have on me / But if I expire today / Let it be in sight of thee –." The beauty she invokes is larger than the birds who contribute their "punctual music" and the poets who add their rhymes. It's vaster than the flowers, even than the sum of all the flowers' prismatic beauty. In fact, this beauty stretches beyond the dimensions of the beautiful, natural world Emily so often and so joyously praised.

For Emily speaks of beauty in the same language theologians use to speak of God. She says: "The Definition of Beauty is / That Definition is none –." Theologians say God is indefinable. She says: "Estranged from Beauty – none can be – / For Beauty is Infinity –." Theologians say God is omnipresent and infinite.

She says: "Beauty – be not caused – It Is –," and the line sounds strikingly reminiscent of the line, "Before Abraham was, I am." Indeed, theologians say that God is causeless, *prima su*, pure Being. Elsewhere, Emily equates beauty with truth, another name God claims: "I am the way, the truth, and the life." And she even speaks of sorrow, like Christ's death on the cross, as working "To bend the eye / Best Beauty's way." The "Best Beauty" to which the cross points is God. So, in poem after poem, Emily paints beauty with God's attributes—infinity, omnipresence, immortality—not because she has supplanted God with an alternate deity, Beauty, but rather because she understands that God is at the root of all beauty. In a rare moment of clarity, she explains: "There is a syllableless Sea / Of which it [Beauty] is the sign." Beauty is the signpost pointing the way to that "syllableless Sea," God. Although we can't speak a syllable about God, beauty invites us to sound our praise. As it had done for countless theologians, philosophers, and artists before her, beauty led Emily to God.

The divinely guiding beauty she praises can come in many forms. It can be natural, artistic, interpersonal. For me, Fra Angelico's depiction of Paradise in *The Last Judgment* makes real the heaven it promises, because it holds so much joy. And the crisis of praise at the close of Handel's *Messiah* testifies to God, simply because there must be a deity to inspire and receive it. When a neighbor sent her son over to sing for Emily, she replied, "I had felt some uncertainty as to my qualification for the final Redemption, but the delightful Melody has entirely fitted me – Congratulate your son on his divine Gift –." Beauty, in such moments, argues better than any preacher could the case for God. So Emily marvels, "How vast is the chastisement of Beauty, given us by our Maker!" A chastisement, perhaps, because when we stray, it's beauty that calls us back.

Birds were for Emily particularly good messengers of the Maker's beauty. She describes their work in this poem:

> The Bird her punctual music brings
> And lays it in it's place –
> It's place is in the Human Heart
> And in the Heavenly Grace –
> What respite from her thrilling toil
> Did Beauty ever take –
> But work might be Electric Rest
> To those that Magic make –

The bird's song lands in both the "Human Heart" and the "Heavenly Grace," and so it forms a bridge between the two locations. The bird's ability to link these two realms made Emily liken birds to "troubadours"—medieval poets of courtly love—since they bring to us songs from the heavenly courts, where God, the "Paragon of Chivalry," reigns. On occasion, Emily goes even further and declares outright that birds are angels in disguise, explaining, "Angels have that modest way / To screen them from Renown –." While all birds could be angelic messengers, Emily gives robins the highest rank, perhaps because their tune entranced her best. Robins she names "Gabriels."

I met such a messenger on my last visit to Emily's house in Amherst. Or rather, I should say, this messenger met me. I was walking at sunset in the patch of woods that Emily's window overlooks, between the Homestead and the Evergreens, where Austin and Sue lived. Sun streamed in bright bars through the towering trees that were mere saplings when Emily lived there. Motes twinkled in the light. And there was a robin, perhaps ten feet ahead, on the path. It stood still, steadily regarding me. Have you ever really been looked at by a bird? Well, this robin was watching me. And then, when it had taken my measure, it did not take wing, it did not run— robins always run—it did nothing that normal birds normally do when they're aware of nearby people. This robin tilted its head toward the west and, still watching, opened its beak and sang.

The song was untranscribable. It was indescribable, though I imagine Emily could have done it justice: "Like Trains of Cars on Tracks of Plush" or some such riff. The robin kept singing and singing, for minutes, all the while looking back, as if to make sure I was still listening. I was a bit stunned, because I remembered what Emily said about robins: I knew she called them *Gabriels.* I knew she believed that birds "Breathe in Ear more modern / God's old fashioned vows –." But it was also silly—absurd, really—to think that this robin had anything to do with her, or God, or for that matter, me. Come on, it's a bird. Obviously it's just a robin singing, from the ground, on an open path in the woods, a few feet from two people, whom it won't stop watching while it sings. Robins do that all the time. Really, stop. That's just a robin; it's just a song.

When the just-a-robin had finished its just-a-song, it spied us again for a long moment with those insistent eyes, then turned and calmly stepped its way down the path.

What was the bird's message? That's the question I couldn't stop from asking myself, even as the bird was singing. It's not so different from the one Emily asked her solitary bird, in 1862,

"Wherefore sing?" As I've marveled at her poems, reread her letters, and met Emily again and again through her words, I've realized that the answer to the two questions is the same. There was no secret bird language inside the notes that I should—like a Pentecostal worshiper—translate in the Spirit. The robin's message *was* the song. And the song was beauty.

"I told my Soul to sing –," Emily declares in the line I've taken for this book's title, and I thank God she did. She met the world, its grief and joy, with song: "The first Day's Night had come – / And grateful that a thing / So terrible – had been endured – / I told my Soul to sing –." Her song rises first from trouble and then from gratitude. So too, the tune I've hummed here with her has ensued from struggle, but above all from my gratitude: that she was born, lived a reflective life, and wrote these poems remains among the most grateful facts of my life. The question of *why* she sang fades before the sheer, gratuitous gift *that* she sang, as well as the overwhelming beauty of *what* she sang. I can't say that her poetry has saved me or solved all my spiritual troubles, but she never promised it would. "I told my Soul to sing –" is not the end of the story, nor the end of that poem. In the very next lines, her soul responds with yet further complications: "She said her strings were snapt – / Her Bow – to atoms blown – / And so to mend her – gave me work / Until another Morn –." For all the time I've worked alongside Emily at mending those "snapt" and worn places in my soul, I have not gotten particularly adept in prayer. I'm certainly not immune to doubt. But her songs are woven through me now. And, as the same poem goes on to say, "That person that I was – / And this One – do not feel the same –." Lifting my eyes from our shared work, I see that it is "another Morn –." A new day. The birds are beginning. What to do now? I'll tell my soul to sing.

How else can I repay the gift of beauty that Emily's poems have been to me? They've bolstered me, as the punctual music of the bird cheers us when we wait for dawn; they've stilled me, as the robin's did that day by its singular genius; they've lifted me, through their intelligence and grace, toward God. There are many paths to God. I feel so grateful to have found my way to this one, with Emily for my guide.

I hope you'll choose to venture further with her now. Eighteen hundred poems await you and over a thousand letters, and you know she loved to say, "I will not let thee go, except I bless thee." Rocky and brambly as the way is, I can promise you that there are birds everywhere, piping the most beautiful songs.

> The Bird her punctual music brings
> And lays it in it's place –
> It's place is in the Human Heart
> And in the Heavenly Grace –
> What respite from her thrilling toil
> Did Beauty ever take –
> But work might be Electric Rest
> To those that Magic make –

ACKNOWLEDGMENTS

ALTHOUGH EMILY MAINTAINED that "Gratitude is not the mention of a tenderness, but its mute appreciation," I mention here a few of the many individuals who've made this book possible. My understanding of Emily Dickinson gratefully rests upon the work of several generations of scholars, biographers, and editors, especially Thomas H. Johnson and R. W. Franklin, Richard Sewall, and Alfred Habegger, without whose work this book could never have been. Any faults in this portrait and its readings are my own. I'm grateful to Susan Halpern at Harvard's Houghton Library and Peter Nelson and Margaret Dakin at Amherst College Archives and Special Collections for their assistance during research visits and in obtaining the photographs of manuscripts included in this volume. My thanks go to Melissa Flashman for championing this book and to Jon M. Sweeney for his editorial insight in shaping it, as well as to the whole team at Paraclete. I thank Barbara Newman, for fostering the book and its author. To the Brothers of the Society of Saint John the Evangelist I owe more than I can express. Their monastery housed much of this book's wrestling and continues to offer endless blessing. Finally, I thank my parents, Debby and Richard Hennessy, for their loving support in this and every other project, and Niki Kasumi Clements, for being an incomparable reader and friend. And lastly (firstly) my beloved husband, Eric: "the Creek turns Sea – at thought of thee –."

NOTES

All quotations of Dickinson's poems are reprinted by permission of the publishers and the Trustees of Amherst College from *The Poems of Emily Dickinson: Varorium Edition*, edited by Ralph W. Franklin, Cambridge, MA: The Belknap Press of Harvard University Press, Copyright © 1998 by the President and Fellows of Harvard College. Copyright © 1951, 1955, 1979, 1983 by the President and Fellows of Harvard College. All poems will be cited by Franklin's number and first line below.

All quotations of Dickinson's letters are reprinted by permission of the publishers from *The Letters of Emily Dickinson*, edited by Thomas H. Johnson, Cambridge, MA: The Belknap Press of Harvard University Press, Copyright © 1958, 1986, The President and Fellows of Harvard College; 1914, 1924, 1932, 1942, by Martha Dickinson Bianchi; 1952 by Alfred Leete Hampson; 1960 by Mary L. Hampson. All letters will be cited by Johnson's number, as well as recipient and date, when known.

Front Matter

"Prove it me" . . . F682, So well that I can live without

"Let Emily sing for you" . . . L278, ED to Louisa and Frances Norcross, 1863

INTRODUCTION

"infidel" . . . L860, ED to Maria Whitney, 1883

"gypsy" . . . F349, He touched me, so I live to know; F131, Tho' my destiny be fustian

"rogue" . . . L915, ED to Cornelia Sweetser, 1884. The Bible and Midas were also characterized as roguish and Rogue (L562 and L543 respectively).

"one of the lingering *bad* ones" . . . L36, ED to Abiah Root, 1850

"surly – and muggy – and cross" . . . L30, ED to Jane Humphrey, 1850

"quite vain" . . . L69, ED to Abiah Root, 1852

"*wicked*" . . . L31, ED to Abiah Root, 1850

"a Pagan" . . . L566, ED to Cornelia Sweetser, 1878; L976, ED to Helen Hunt Jackson, 1885

"one of those brands" . . . . L30, ED to Jane Humphrey, 1850

"past 'Correction in Righteousness'" . . . L650, ED to Elizabeth Holland, 1880

"Eve, alias Mrs. Adam" . . . L9, ED to Abiah Root, 1846

"Simon Peter" . . . L645, ED to Judge Lord, 1880

"Barabbas" . . . L282, ED to Thomas Wentworth Higginson, 1863

redhead . . . There has been a certain reluctance to describe this striking feature of the poet. Her schoolmate Emily Fowler Ford suggests that her hair was "lovely auburn, soft and warm"; a relative described her hair as "soft, 'tawny' . . . somewhat like the soft ears of an Irish setter dog"; and Miss Marian, the seamstress who sewed the family's dresses, reports, "Her hair was warm-looking. It was not red." These three distinct testimonies are quoted in *The Years and Hours of Emily Dickinson*, ed. Jay Leyda (New Haven: Yale University Press, 1960), 2:478–80. Martha Dickinson Bianchi, the poet's niece, describes her locks as "of that same warm bronze-chestnut hue that Titian immortalized" in her introduction to *The Single Hound* (Boston: Little, Brown & Co., 1914), xvi. A photograph of a lock of Emily's hair has been published in the lush volume of Jerome Liebling's photographs, *The Dickinsons of Amherst* (Hanover, NH: University Press of New England, 2001), 213. Her hair is distinctly red; no other term will do. Notably, her father also had red hair, and her brother, Austin, was famous in town for his unruly head of red hair. Perhaps the feature was less offensive—bold as it was—on the men in the family.

"I'm Nobody! Who are you?" . . . F260, I'm nobody! Who are you?

"If I can stop one Heart from breaking" . . . F982, If I can stop one heart from breaking

"'Hope' is the thing with feathers –" . . . F314, "Hope" is the thing with feathers

"This is my letter to the World" . . . F519. This was a popular poem of hers from the start, as it was one of the fourteen poems that Thomas Wentworth Higginson selected to publish in *The Christian Union* in September 1890, to help prepare the way for the first volume of her poems, where it also serves as the epigraph.

"was not temptation" . . . L889, ED to Maria Whitney, 1884

"*unmerited* remembrance – 'Grace'" . . . L200, ED to Mary Emerson Haven, 1859

Emily Dickinson plush dolls . . . Take, for instance, the item description for the "Emily Dickinson Little Thinker" doll, available for $16.95 on the site "Shakespeare's

Den": "Emily Dickinson was an outgoing child, but matured into an introspective and reclusive adult. Nevertheless, she wrote beautiful, perceptive poetry that revealed amazing insight into life and her often frequented subject of poetry: death. Dickinson is considered a quintessential American poet."

a significant and ultimately failed love . . . The most recent (and wonderfully readable) biography, *My Wars Are Laid Away in Books*, by Alfred Habegger, sums up what can be said about this love affair like this: "There was a man, probably a minister; he was married and in other ways out of reach and unsuitable; his feelings for her had little in common with hers for him; she knew little about him and began to project her powerful desires and fantasies on him; their correspondence became increasingly troubling for her; they met, perhaps in 1860, perhaps only once, parting in a way that looked quite ordinary to a bystander; and in the poems she wrote afterward she returned again and again to this impossible relationship, developing its latent elements in fantastic ways" (New York: Random House, 2001), 421.

ten poems did appear in print . . . The ten poems published in her lifetime were: F2, Sic transit gloria mundi; F11, Nobody knows this little rose; F207, I taste a liquor never brewed; F124, Safe is their alabaster chambers; F95, Flowers – well – if anybody; F122, These are the days when birds come back; F236, Some keep the sabbath going to church; F321, Blazing in gold and quenching in purple; F112, Success is counted sweetest; F1096, A narrow fellow in the grass.

"The Heaven – unexpected come" . . . F361, Like flowers that heard the news of dews

"the Foreigner" . . . F976, Besides this May

"that Bold Person, God" . . . F1074, What did they do since I saw them?

"Itself" . . . F791, My worthiness is all my doubt

"the imperceptible" . . . L391, ED to Elizabeth Holland, 1873

"Tyranny" and "a Mastiff" . . . F1332, Abraham to kill him

"Old Suitor Heaven" . . . F1595, We shun it ere it comes

"Vagabond" and "Sorcerer from Genesis" . . . F1598, The clock strikes one

"the Mysterious Bard" . . . F178, To learn the transport by the pain

"the Sky" . . . L521, ED to Elizabeth Holland, 1877

"Might" . . . F996, I heard as if I had no ear

"Deity" . . . The name occurs twenty-three times in the poems. Among others: F654, Beauty be not caused – It is; F627, I think I was enchanted.

"Omnipotence" . . . F429, You'll know it as you know 'tis noon

God is the thirty-ninth most frequently occurring word . . . Let me express my debt of gratitude to S. P. Rosenbaum and Cynthia MacKenzie for their invaluable work in compiling concordances to the poems and letters of Emily Dickinson. According to these concordances, the word *God* occurs 130 times in the poems and 151 times in the letters. After that, the list of occurrences for divine names, in instances where the word reasonably can be interpreted to point to God, runs as follows: *Lord* (poems: 25, letters: 20), *Savior* (poems: 9, letters: 13), *Maker* (poems: 6, letters: 10), *Jehovah* (poems: 7, letters: 3), *Sovereign* (poems: 7, letters: 1, counting occurrences as nouns rather than adjectives), *Creator* (poems: 6), *Redeemer* (poems: 1, letters: 4), *Almighty* (poems: 2, letters: 1).

"Papa above! / Regard a mouse" . . . F151, Papa above!

"Home is the definition" . . . L355, ED to Perez Cowan, 1870. For instances of her use of the word *home* to refer to heaven, see L593 and L153.

"Foxes have Tenements" . . . L979, ED to Elizabeth Holland, 1885

"great Argument" . . . John Milton, *Paradise Lost*, in *The Riverside Milton*, ed. Roy Flannagan (Boston: Houghton Mifflin, 1998), lines 24–26.

"a M.S. collection" . . . L813b, Thomas Niles to ED, 1883. This request was in response to Emily's inclusion of F291, It sifts from leaden sieves, in an earlier exchange. That poem was composed in 1862.

"When I state myself" . . . L268, ED to Thomas Wentworth Higginson, 1862

"the Stranger" . . . L243, ED to Edward S. Dwight, 1861; see also L535, ED to Adelaide Hills, 1878

"the Savior" . . . F295, Savior! I've no one else to tell. As mentioned above, the word appears nine times in the poems, from 1862 to 1880. It also makes a number of appearances in the letters, including L222, ED to Catherine Scott Turner, 1860.

"Judgment" . . . See, for instance, Fascicle 32's consecutive poems F698, I live with him – I see his face, and F699, The power to be true to you.

"Love" . . . Dickinson directly references the traditional Christian formulation "God is love" in her poem F1314, Because that you are going. She spins it in a Trinitarian direction in poems F287, While it is alive, and F1674, Is it too late to touch you, dear?

"That Hand is amputated now" . . . F1581, Those dying then

"God seems much more friendly" . . . L492, ED to Elizabeth Holland, 1877

"Narcotics cannot still the Tooth" . . . F373, This world is not conclusion

"It comforts an instinct" . . . L503, ED to Thomas Wentworth Higginson, 1877

"Let Emily sing for you" . . . L278, ED to Louisa and Frances Norcross, 1863

"I will not let thee go" . . . Genesis 32:26. For all scriptural passages, I will quote the King James Version, as that is the translation Emily knew and riffed on throughout her writings. This line was a particular favorite: Emily quotes the line in F145, A little east of Jordan. At the end of her life, Emily also reversed the formula in the final notes she sent to several friends, "I will not let thee go, except I bless thee": L1035 to Sarah Tuckerman, 1886; L1042 to Thomas Wentworth Higginson, 1886.

"Our Old Neighbor – God –" . . . F689, It was too late for man

"belle of Amherst" . . . L6, ED to Abiah Root, 1845. The phrase enters into common usage—and along with it a certain portrait of Dickinson—with William Luce's 1976 play of the same title.

"This World is not conclusion" . . . F373, This world is not conclusion

"Some keep the Sabbath going to Church" . . . F236, Some keep the Sabbath going to church

"The Bible is an antique Volume" . . . F1577, The Bible is an antique volume

"My period had come for Prayer" . . . F525, My period had come for prayer

"I hesitate which word to take" . . . L873, ED to Elizabeth Holland, 1883

"A Book is only" . . . L794, ED to Elizabeth Holland, 1882

Chapter 1: Belief

"I could not find my 'Yes' –" . . . F346, He showed me hights I never saw

CONVERSION

"I shall keep singing!" . . . F270, I shall keep singing!

"They thought it queer" . . . The line comes from Clara Newman Turner's "My Personal Acquaintance with Emily Dickinson," quoted in Richard Sewall, *The Life of Emily Dickinson* (Cambridge, MA: Harvard University Press, 1974), 269. As Sewall relates, the incident is a cobbling together of family legend and the accounts of schoolfellows such as Clara Newman Turner. Martha Dickinson Bianchi, Emily's niece, tells the story much the way I relate it here, concluding, "And be it said to her eternal glory . . . Emily stood alone," *The Life and Letters of Emily Dickinson* (Cambridge, MA: Riverside Press, 1924), 26. Alfred Habegger's *My Wars Are Laid Away in Books* downplays the incident, while offering a detailed portrait of Miss Lyon and the proceedings at Mount Holyoke during Emily's tenure there.

"Christ is calling everyone here" . . . L35, ED to Jane Humphrey, 1850

nine revivals that flooded Amherst . . . Sewall quotes Professor Edward Hitchcock's *Reminiscences of Amherst College*, wherein Hitchcock notes the following revival years at Amherst College during Emily's early life: 1834, 1835, 1839, 1842, 1846, 1850, 1853, 1855, 1857, 1858, 1862 (Sewall, 24). It is worth mentioning that Emily's letters from 1846 and 1850, in particular, show a marked spike in religious themes.

"I am standing alone" . . . L35, ED to Jane Humphrey, 1850

"melt" . . . L10, ED to Abiah Root, 1846

"I felt that I was so easily excited" . . . L10, ED to Abiah Root, 1846

"I continually hear Christ saying" . . . L10, ED to Abiah Root, 1846

"Many conversed with me seriously" . . . L10, ED to Abiah Root, 1846

"I hope the golden opportunity" . . . L10, ED to Abiah Root, 1846 [emphasis mine]

"I know that I ought now" . . . L11, ED to Abiah Root, 1846 [emphasis mine]

"I do not feel that I could *give up*" . . . L13, ED to Abiah Root, 1846 [emphasis mine]

"I have not yet *given up*" . . . L20, ED to Abiah Root, 1848 [emphasis mine]

"I may never, never again" . . . L23, ED to Abiah Root, 1848

"You must pray when the rest" . . . L35, ED to Jane Humphrey, 1850; she makes a similar request at the close of L36 to Abiah Root in 1850.

"The few short moments" . . . L11, ED to Abiah Root, 1846

"I hereby give myself to God" . . . The note, dated May 1, 1873, is reprinted in Jay Leyda's *Years and Hours of Emily Dickinson*, 2:200.

"This timid life of Evidence" . . . F725, Their hight in heaven comforts not. The spelling of "dont" without an apostrophe, here and elsewhere, is Emily's.

"See how the Lord in his love" . . . *The Rule of Saint Benedict in English*, Prologue (Collegeville, MN: Liturgical Press, 1980), 16.

"a school for the Lord's service" . . . . *The Rule of Saint Benedict in English*, Prologue, 18

"Let us run with patience" . . . Hebrews 12:1

"We shall run on the path" . . . *The Rule of Saint Benedict in English*, Prologue, 19

"I work to drive the awe away" . . . L891, ED to Louisa and Frances Norcross, 1884

"My Business is Circumference" . . . L268, ED to Thomas Wentworth Higginson, 1862

"My business is to *sing*" . . . L269, ED to Elizabeth Holland, 1862

"I feel that I shall never be happy" . . . L10, ED to Abiah Root, 1846. Loving Christ and being a Christian were clearly not the same thing for Emily. In this same letter to Abiah where she mentions that she wants to love Christ, she also three times declares that she was not, is not, will not be, a Christian. It seems evident from this reluctance that it was the institution, not the institutor, of the faith that repelled her.

"Lord, open our lips" . . . Morning Prayer II, *The Book of Common Prayer* (New York: Oxford University Press, 1990), 80.

"I am alone before my little" . . . L11, ED to Abiah Root, 1846

SCRIPTURE

Emily's Bible is in the Houghton Library's collection. The edition is *The Holy Bible, Containing the Old and New Testaments: Translated Out of the Original Tongues* (Philadelphia: J.B. Lippincott & Co, 1843). Emily's copy is viewable in its entirety online at http://nrs.harvard.edu/urn-3:FHCL.Hough:4906292.

"Father is reading the Bible" . . . L42, ED to Austin Dickinson, 1851

"Father calls him 'Timothy'" . . . L333, ED to Susan Dickinson, 1869

"All grows strangely emphatic" . . . L950, ED to Elizabeth Holland, 1884

"a tremendous Book" . . . L693, ED to Louisa and Frances Norcross, 1881

"With God all things are possible" . . . Matthew 19:26

"I held a Jewel in my fingers –" . . . F261, I held a jewel in my fingers

"Don't tell . . . but wicked as I am" . . . L185, ED to Elizabeth Holland, 1856

"your throbbing Scripture" . . . L562, ED to Judge Lord, 1878

"Her father was not severe" . . . L342b, Thomas Wentworth Higginson to his wife, Mary, 1870

"whom shall I accuse?" . . . L952, ED to Catherine Sweetser, 1884

"Now unto the King eternal" . . . 1 Timothy 1:17

"Mine – by the Right of the White Election!" . . . F411, Mine by the right of the white election!

"I had rambled too far" . . . L11, ED to Abiah Root, 1846

"When I was a child" . . . 1 Corinthians 13:11–12

DOUBT

"Though the great Waters sleep" . . . F1641. As R.W. Franklin notes, all seven versions of the poem vary slightly, but not significantly—a capital here, a comma there. I follow him in printing the latest version for which a manuscript still exists, in this case the one that Emily tucked into her 1885 note to Judge Lord's executor, Benjamin Kimball.

"What a Comrade" . . . L1031, ED to Katherine Prince, 1886

"*all* are friends" . . . L967, ED to Benjamin Kimball, 1885

"I sing, as the Boy does" . . . L261, ED to Thomas Wentworth Higginson, 1862

"off charnel steps" . . . L298, ED to Louisa and Frances Norcross, 1864

"We dignify our Faith" . . . L209, ED to Catherine Scott Turner, 1859

"The shore is safer, Abiah" . . . L39, ED to Abiah Root, 1850

"I was told that the Bank" . . . L319, ED to Thomas Wentworth Higginson, 1866

"a Pagan" . . . L566, ED to Cornelia Sweetser, 1878; L976, ED to Helen Hunt Jackson, 1885

"one of the lingering" . . . L36, ED to Abiah Root, 1850

"You have experienced sanctity" . . . L413, ED to Thomas Wentworth Higginson, 1874

"Of Life to own –" . . . These lines, part of L413, to Thomas Wentworth Higginson, are first printed as their own poem in Thomas H. Johnson's 1955 edition of *The Poems of Emily Dickinson* (Cambridge, MA: The Belknap Press of Harvard University Press, 1955). Franklin follows suit, printing them as F1327 in his more recent edition.

"Are you certain" . . . L827, ED to Charles H. Clark, 1883

"Moving on in the Dark" . . . L871, ED to Susan Dickinson, 1883

"One guess at the Waters" . . . L822, ED to Elizabeth Holland, 1883. Water imagery
    was evidently central for Emily in parsing the great questions. Look to F1250, If
    my bark sink, where she uses it to show trust about these questions, and F960,
    The heart has narrow banks, where it expresses the dissolving power of doubt.

"Fathoms are sudden Neighbors" . . . L804, ED to James D. Clark, 1883

"Death – so – the Hyphen" . . . F1486, Those not live yet

"that Great Water in the West" . . . F750, We thirst at first – 'tis nature's act

"It is the speck" . . . L367, ED to Louisa and Frances Norcross, 1871

"That the Divine has been human" . . . L523, ED to Richard Mather, 1877

"I believe we shall" . . . L785, ED to Louisa and Frances Norcross, 1882

"The Risks of Immortality" . . . L353, ED to Thomas Wentworth Higginson, 1870

"Remoteness is the founder of sweetness" . . . L388, ED to Louisa and Frances
    Norcross, 1873

"Water, is taught by thirst" . . . F93, Water is taught by thirst

"How Human Nature dotes" . . . F1440, How human nature dotes. The absence of
    an apostrophe in the contraction is Emily's.

"A Diagram – of Rapture!" . . . F212, A transport one cannot contain

"Sermons on unbelief" . . . L176, ED to Susan Gilbert (Dickinson), 1854

"The unknown is the largest need" . . . L471, ED to Louisa and Frances Norcross,
    1876

"we thought Darwin had thrown" . . . L750, ED to Judge Lord, 1882

"Too much of Proof" . . . F1240, So much of heaven has gone from earth

"To believe the final line" . . . L912, ED to Susan Dickinson, 1884

"the Balm of that Religion" . . . F1449, Ourselves we do inter with sweet derision

"uncertain certainty" . . . F1421, Of Paradise' existence

"We both believe, and disbelieve" . . . L750, ED to Otis P. Lord, 1882

"write them upon the table" . . . Proverbs 7:3

"And write thy name thyself" . . . Emily's embroidered sampler is quoted in Leyda, *Years and Hours of Emily Dickinson*, 1:99.

"the recallless Sea" . . . F1654, Still own thee – still thou art

"while she skimmed the milk" . . . The full passage runs, "I know that Emily Dickinson wrote the most emphatic things in the pantry, so cool and quiet, while she skimmed the milk; because I sat on the footstool behind the door, in delight, as she read them to me." This recollection appears in Louisa Norcross's letter to *Woman's Journal*, March 1904, quoted in Polly Longsworth's *The World of Emily Dickinson* (New York: Norton, 1990), 3.

"drift called 'the infinite'" . . . L785, ED to Louisa and Frances Norcross, 1882

"I cannot tell how Eternity seems" . . . L785, ED to Louisa and Frances Norcross, 1882

"I wonder how long we shall wonder" . . . L190, ED to Joseph Sweetser, 1858

BELIEF

"We cannot believe for each other" . . . L591, ED to Maria Whitney, 1879

"*Oui, mais il faut parier*" . . . This line translates, "Yes, but it's necessary to wager. It's not voluntary, you're already underway." Blaise Pascal, *Pensées*, "Preuves de la religion par le people juif, les prophéties et quelques discours," Série II, #397 in *Œuvres Complètes*, ed. Michel le Guern (Paris: Gallimard, 2000), 677.

"The Crash of nothing, yet of all –" . . . F1532, More than the grave is closed to me

"Soul, Wilt thou toss again?" . . . F89, Soul, wilt thou toss again? The battle for the soul appears in her poetry at a later date, as well. See F629, The battle fought between the soul, as well as F988, Said death to passion, and F973, Death is a dialogue between.

"Was ever the concentrated contest" . . . Thomas Wentworth Higginson, "An Open Portfolio," *The Christian Union* 42 (September 25, 1890): 392–93.

Decision theorists have parsed . . . The graphs, variables, and equations I cite here are taken from Alan Hájek's article on "Pascal's Wager" in *The Stanford Encyclopedia of Philosophy* (Summer 2011 Edition), ed. Edward N. Zalta, http://plato.stanford .edu/archives/sum2011/entries/pascal-wager/. As complicated as this initial parsing is to the untrained eye, the article goes on for three thousand words to summarize the major strands of objection to Pascal's logic and this equation. Those objections have further equations to illustrate them. I will try no one's patience by attempting to understand or quote those here.

"Do you wish to understand" . . . Augustine, *Tractates on the Gospel of John* 29.6

"For I do not seek to understand" . . . Anselm, *Proslogium* 1

"we believe / But once – entirely –" . . . F1280, Who were "the Father and the Son"

"the loss of an Estate –" . . . F632, To lose one's faith surpass

"Peter, do you love me" . . . John 21:15–17

"I continually hear Christ saying" . . . L10, ED to Abiah Root, 1846

"Give me thine Heart" . . . . L608, ED to Abigail Cooper, 1879. As Johnson notes, Emily is quoting from Proverbs 23:26.

"He showed me Hights I never saw –" . . . F346, He showed me hights I never saw. I've followed R. W. Franklin in adopting Emily's variant word "larger" for "steadier" in line 11. I've also retained her spelling of "hight" here and elsewhere.

"a distant – stately Lover –" . . . F615, God is a distant stately lover

"'No' is the wildest word" . . . L562, ED to Judge Lord, 1878

"Remember, Dear, an unfaltering *Yes*" . . . L908, ED to Susan Dickinson, 1884

"When a Child and fleeing" . . . L412, ED to Elizabeth Holland, 1874

"Some keep the Sabbath going to Church –" . . . . F236. This poem was published during Emily's lifetime, in 1864, by her neighbor and her cousin, who put out the literary publication *The Round Table*.

"The bells are ringing" . . . L77, ED to Susan Gilbert (Dickinson), 1852

"let Redemption find you" . . . L522, ED to Thomas Wentworth Higginson, 1877. In this passage, as elsewhere, I've retained the apostrophe that Emily inserts into the possessive form of its.

"Love is like Life – merely longer" . . . . F287, While it is alive. The image of this manuscript is reprinted courtesy of Amherst College Library Archives and Special Collections, where the original resides.

"Lord, I believe" . . . Mark 9:24

PROOF

"That I did always love" . . . F652, That I did always love

The Master letters manuscripts are in the possession of Amherst College Archives and Special Collections, who kindly gave permission to reprint these images here.

"My closest earthly friend" . . . L765, ED to Thomas Wentworth Higginson, 1882

"my Shepherd from 'Little Girl'hood" . . . L766, ED to James D. Clark, 1882

"my Clergyman" . . . L790, ED to Judge Lord, 1882

"my dearest earthly friend" . . . L807, ED to James D. Clark, 1883

"My Philadelphia" . . . L750, ED to Judge Lord, 1882

"intimacy of many years" . . . L766, ED to James D. Clark, 1882

"Dickenson" . . . L248a, Charles Wadsworth to ED, 1862. Wadsworth writes what Thomas H. Johnson, editor of the letters, terms "a solicitous, pastoral letter" in response to some trial about which she had written him. What that trial was scholars cannot agree. And while there is no evidence that Emily took him up on his offer to "write me, though it be but a word," she must have, since he would visit her for the second time nearly twenty years later.

"He rang one summer evening" . . . L766, ED to James D. Clark, 1882

"I knew him a 'Man of sorrow'" . . . L776, ED to James D. Clark, 1882

"No Bird – yet rode in Ether" . . . L233, ED to unknown, 1861. Franklin prints this line as part of a separate couplet, F190, No rose, yet felt myself a'bloom.

"One drop more from the gash" . . . L233, ED to unknown, 1861. The three Master letters are L187, L233, and L248. They are also published separately in *The Master Letters of Emily Dickinson*, ed. R. W. Franklin (Amherst, MA: Amherst College Press, 1986).

"supple Suitor" . . . F1470, Death is the supple suitor

"Our Lord – thought no" . . . F538, Must be a wo

"Faith – the Experiment of Our Lord –" . . . F191, "Morning" means "milking" to the farmer

"'Faith' is a fine invention" . . . F202, "Faith" is a fine invention

"plucks at a twig of Evidence –" . . . F373, This world is not conclusion

"Experiment escorts us last –" . . . F1181, Experiment escorts us last

"Except I shall see" . . . John 20:25

"Thomas' faith in Anatomy" . . . L233, ED to unknown, 1861

"I could not see to see" . . . F591, I heard a fly buzz when I died

"Faith is <u>Doubt</u>" . . . L912, ED to Susan Dickinson, 1884

Chapter 2: Prayer

"Prayer is the little implement" . . . F623, Prayer is the little implement

HYMN

"Trust you enjoy your closet" . . . L110, ED to Austin Dickinson, 1853

"'Oh could we climb where Moses stood'" . . . F114, Where bells no more affright the morn. As Franklin notes, the first two lines Emily quotes from Watts read, "Could we but climb where Moses stood, / And view the landscape o'er."

"I dont wonder" . . . L30, ED to Jane Humphrey, 1850. The lack of an apostrophe in the contraction is Emily's.

"I rose – because He sank –" . . . F454, I rose because he sank

"a little hymn" . . . L307, ED to Louisa Norcross, 1865

"I have promised three Hymns" . . . L674, ED to Thomas Wentworth Higginson, 1880

"Let Emily sing for you" . . . L278, ED to Louisa and Frances Norcross, 1863

paired for the first time in *The Southern Harmony* . . . Steve Turner discusses this pairing in *Amazing Grace: The Story of America's Most Beloved Song* (New York: HarperCollins, 2002), 124. The image of "New Britain" comes from the Library of Congress's digital edition of William Walker's *The Southern Harmony and Musical Companion: Containing a Choice Collection of Tunes, Hymns, Psalms, Odes, and Anthems* (Philadelphia: Thomas, Cowperthwait & Co., 1847), viewable at http://lccn.loc.gov/unk84126581.

"God is indeed a jealous God –" . . . F1752, God is indeed a jealous God

"Susie, when they sang" . . . L88, ED to Susan Gilbert (Dickinson), 1852

"Almost the last tune that he heard" . . . L414, ED to Louisa and Frances Norcross, 1874

"You think my gait 'spasmodic'" . . . L265, ED to Thomas Wentworth Higginson, 1862

"Humming – for promise –" . . . F378, Better than music!

PRAYER

"Prayer is the little implement" . . . F623, Prayer is the little implement

"Let Emily sing for you" . . . L278, ED to Louisa and Frances Norcross, 1863

"not reared to prayer" . . . L280, ED to Thomas Wentworth Higginson, 1863

"we did not learn" . . . L242, ED to Samuel Bowles, 1861

"Knew I how to pray" . . . L976, ED to Helen Hunt Jackson, 1885

"It is Sunday – now – John" . . . L184, ED to John L. Graves, 1856

"They are religious – except me" . . . L261, ED to Thomas Wentworth Higginson, 1862

"'I say unto you,' Father would read" . . . L432, ED to Elizabeth Holland, 1875

"I prayed, at first, a little Girl" . . . F546, I prayed, at first, a little girl

"My period had come for Prayer –" . . . F525, My period had come for prayer

"Austin and I were talking" . . . L650, ED to Elizabeth Holland, 1880

"Prayer the Churches banquet" . . . George Herbert, "Prayer," in *The Poetical Works of George Herbert* (New York: D. Appleton & Co, 1855), 61–62. The copy in the Houghton collection is inscribed "S.H. Dickinson."

"I cannot ope mine eyes" . . . George Herbert, "Mattens," *The Poetical Works of George Herbert*, 76–77.

"It was then my greatest pleasure" . . . L11, ED to Abiah Root, 1846

"A Grant of the Divine –" . . . F560, Did our best moment last

"God it is said replies in Person" . . . F1148, Tell as a marksman were forgotten

"Prayer – / The Only Raiment I should need –" . . . F662, I had no cause to be awake

"And shape my Hands –" . . . F292, I got so I could hear his name

"Of Course – I prayed –" . . . F581, Of course I prayed

"I threw my Prayer away –" . . . F711, I meant to have but modest needs

"I dwell in Possibility –" . . . F466, I dwell in possibility

"Dare you see a Soul at the 'White Heat'" . . . F401, Dare you see a soul at the "White Heat"

"I dreaded that first Robin, so" . . . F347, I dreaded that first robin so

"I felt a Funeral, in my Brain" . . . F340, I felt a funeral in my brain

"Through the Straight Pass of Suffering" . . . F187, Through the straight pass of
suffering

"Unto like Story – Trouble has enticed me –" . . . F300, Unto like story trouble has
enticed me

"I shall keep singing!" . . . F270, I shall keep singing

"I heard, as if I had no Ear" . . . F996, I heard as if I had no ear

"'Heavenly Father' – take to thee" . . . F1500, "Heavenly Father" – take to thee

"If pain for peace prepares" . . . F155, If pain for peace prepares

"Of God we ask one favor" . . . F1675, Of God we ask one favor

"Oh God / Why give if Thou must take away" . . . F1114, A shade opon the mind
there passes

"My chancel – all the plain" . . . F29, All these my banners be

INTERCESSION

"I kneel and thank God for it" . . . L170, ED to John L. Graves, 1854

"I ask God on my knees" . . . L212, ED to Mary Bowles, 1859

"though not reared to prayer" . . . L280, ED to Thomas Wentworth Higginson, 1863

"a wish that would almost be a Prayer" . . . L566, ED to Cornelia Sweetser, 1878

"Our freckled bosom bears" . . . L242, ED to Samuel Bowles, 1862. The apostrophes
in the possessive pronouns, here as elsewhere, are Emily's.

"long interceding lips" . . . F1768, There comes an hour when begging stops

"'Thou shalt not' is a kinder sword" . . . F1768, There comes an hour when begging
stops

"Prayer has not an answer" . . . L790, ED to Judge Lord, 1882

"You are like God" . . . L830, ED to Maria Whitney, 1883

"I fumble at my Childhood's Prayer –" . . . F185, A wife at daybreak I shall be

"My Tactics missed a rudiment –" . . . F525, My period had come for prayer

"Please, Sir" . . . F231, We dont cry – Tim and I

"Oh Jesus – in the Air –" . . . F377, At least to pray is left – is left

"I found the words to every thought" . . . F436, I found the words to every thought

"Wonderfullest things are ever" . . . Herman Melville, *Moby-Dick*, ch. 23, "The Lee Shore" (Evanston: Northwestern University Press and The Newbury Library, 1988), 106.

"Abyss has no Biographer –" . . . L899, ED to Martha Gilbert Smith, 1884

"I pray we could come to this darkness" . . . Pseudo-Dionysius, "The Mystical Theology," Ch. 2, *Pseudo-Dionysius: The Complete Works*, Classics of Western Spirituality (Mahwah, NJ: Paulist Press, 1987), 138.

"shedding all and freed from all" . . . Pseudo-Dionysius, "The Mystical Theology," Ch. 1, 135.

"You'll know it – as you know 'tis Noon" . . . F429, You'll know it as you know 'tis noon

"Father – I bring thee – not myself –" . . . F295, Father – I bring thee not myself. The version of the poem I recited to myself that day is the one Emily transcribed into Fascicle 12, one of her sewn books from 1862. I prefer (and so must have memorized) one of her variant readings for line 3, "imperial" for "departed." This is how I recalled it to myself and so how I print it here. Emily herself seems to have had a very fluid and aural memory for her own verse, slipping lines and words around to play with sense and sound. She wrote an alternate version of this poem, "Savior! I've no one else to tell," which Franklin speculates that she sent to Sue.

"The Missionary to the Mole" . . . F1240, So much of heaven has gone from earth

"After a while, dear" . . . L731, ED to Elizabeth Holland, 1881

JESUS

"Jesus! thy Crucifix" . . . F197, Jesus! thy crucifix. There are two extant copies of this poem, one (copy *A*) Emily sent in a letter to Samuel Bowles in 1861. The other (copy *B*) she wrote into Fascicle 12 around 1862. As is sometimes the case, the two versions show minor differences in underlining, capitalization, and punctuation. Copy *B* explodes with exclamation points. While Franklin gives priority to the latest version of a work—and so prints *B*, the Fascicle version, in his reader's edition of the *Poems*—I gravitate toward the stiller punctuation of the earlier version and so choose to print *A*, from the letter to Bowles.

"I am Jesus –" . . . F825, "Unto me"? I do not know you

"And 'Jesus'! Where is *Jesus* gone?" . . . F222, Dying! Dying in the night

"What are you looking for" . . . John 1:38 (NRSV)

"Grant me, Oh Lord, a sunny mind –" . . . F123, Besides the autumn poets sing

"God of the Manacle" . . . F754, Let us play yesterday

"When Jesus tells us about his Father" . . . L932, ED to Adelaide Hills, 1884

"If I believed God looked around" . . . F546, I prayed, at first, a little girl

"The loveliest sermon I ever heard" . . . L385, ED to Frances Norcross, 1873

"Could Pathos compete" . . . L393, ED to Susan Dickinson, 1873

"'They have not chosen me' – he said –" . . . F87, "They have not chosen me" – he said

"God keeps His Oath to Sparrows" . . . F195, Victory comes late. The tone of this rather piercing poem suggests that Emily is not too confident that the "oath" has any value. In fact, the poem is a rather striking testament to the reverse: if the fall of every sparrow is counted, why do so many fall?

"The whole Life of Christ was a Cross" . . . Thomas à Kempis, *Of the Imitation of Christ*, ch. 12, "On the Royal Way of the Holy Cross" (London: Rivingtons, 1876), 101–2.

"Awake, why sleepest thou O Lord?" . . . Psalm 44:23

"Say, Jesus Christ of Nazareth –" . . . F377, At least to pray is left – is left

"Let us make man" . . . Genesis 1:26

"Lord, remember me" . . . Luke 23:42

"Remember me" . . . F1208, "Remember me" implored the thief!

"Recollect the Face of me" . . . F1306, Recollect the face of me

"Many will say to me" . . . Matthew 7:22–23

"This seems a hard saying to many" . . . Thomas à Kempis, *Of the Imitation of Christ*, 97

Emily's Calvinist roots . . . While the Dickinson family, in Emily's generation and her parents' generation, was Congregationalist, the deeper roots—of the family and the town—push into Calvinist territory.

"I fear my congratulation" . . . L406, ED to Sarah Tuckerman, 1874

"Christ – omitted – Me –" . . . F762, Promise this – When you be dying

"Mr. S. preached in our church" . . . L200, ED to Mary Haven, 1859

"what would become of those" . . . L175, ED to Dr. and Elizabeth Holland, 1854

"though in that last day, the Jesus Christ" . . . L173, ED to Susan Gilbert (Dickinson), 1854. The apostrophe in the possessive "it's" is Emily's.

Emily may never have been baptized . . . Her latest biographer, Alfred Habegger, makes a convincing point that Austin and Emily may not have been baptized as infants given that neither of the Dickinson parents were yet members of the church in full standing, the requirement for baptism. Lavinia was baptized on August 4, 1833 (Habegger, *My Wars Are Laid Away in Books*, 86). Martha Dickinson Bianchi, it might be worth noting, does seem to assume that her aunt was baptized, referring to her middle name as "the 'Elizabeth' of baptism" (*Emily Dickinson Face to Face* [Boston: Houghton Mifflin, 1932], 32).

"The name They dropped opon my face" . . . F353, I'm ceded – I've stopped being their's. The spelling of "opon" is Emily's.

"The light of Christ" . . . The Great Vigil of Easter, *The Book of Common Prayer*, 285

Do you desire . . . Holy Baptism, *The Book of Common Prayer*, 301

you are sealed . . . Holy Baptism, *The Book of Common Prayer*, 308

"No Verse in the Bible has frightened" . . . L788, ED to James D. Clark, 1882

GOD

"If I ascend" . . . Psalm 139:8–10

"bears the Soul as bold" . . . F978, Faith is the pierless bridge

"Grace – perhaps – is the only hight" . . . L678, ED to Elizabeth Holland, 1880

"Let the phantom love" . . . L609, ED to Mary Bowles, 1879

"They say that God is everywhere" . . . L551, ED to Elizabeth Holland, 1878

"God grows above –" . . . F525, My period had come for prayer. The spelling of "opon" in the later verse is Emily's.

"My Business – with the Cloud" . . . F292, I got so I could hear his name

"The Infinite a sudden Guest" . . . F1344, The infinite a sudden guest

Maranatha . . . The Aramaic word is preserved in 1 Corinthians 16:22. It can also be translated "our Lord has come."

The manuscript of F1344, The Infinite a sudden guest, belongs to Amherst College Archives and Special Collections, with whose permission it is reprinted here.

Chapter 3: Mortality

"The tranquiller to die –" . . . F1082, That such have died enable us

INCARNATION

"Cherish Power – dear –" . . . L583, ED to Susan Dickinson, 1878. Emily makes almost identical comments about preferring power in two letters, 292 and 330.

"Adamant" and "God of Flint". . . F478, Just once! Oh least request!

"The Jehovahs – are no Babblers –" . . . F692, Only God detect the sorrow

"The Savior must have been" . . . F1538, The savior must have been

"Ah, what a royal sake" . . . F230, For this accepted breath

"Perhaps you think Me stooping" . . . F273, Perhaps you think me stooping

"'Tis true – that Deity to stoop" . . . F791, My worthiness is all my doubt. The spelling of "opon" is Emily's.

"Could condescension be" . . . F1715, A word made flesh is seldom

"Let this mind be in you" . . . Philippians 2:5–11

"To be human is more" . . . L519, ED to Thomas Wentworth Higginson, 1877

LEARNING TO DIE

"Let down the Bars, Oh Death –" . . . F1117, Let down the bars, oh death

"Nobody here could look on Frazer" . . . L255, ED to Louisa and Frances Norcross, 1862. Emily was free with her spelling of Frazar ("Frazer"), as she was with many names.

"Austin is chilled" . . . L256, ED to Samuel Bowles, 1862

"'Tis populous with Bone and stain –" . . . F704, My portion is defeat today

"The possibility – to pass" . . . F243, That after horror – that 'twas us. This stanza evidently stood on its own for Emily as she sent it without the preceding lines to Thomas Wentworth Higginson in 1862.

"How cordial is the mystery!" . . . F1594, Pompless no life can pass away

"Ah! democratic Death!" . . . L195, ED to Dr. and Elizabeth Holland, 1858

"the emerald recess" . . . L952, ED to Catherine Sweetser, 1884

"That *Bareheaded life* –" . . . L220, ED to Samuel Bowles, 1860

"I am the good shepherd" . . . John 10:14

"I cannot imagine" . . . L10, ED to Abiah Root, 1846

"First – Chill – then Stupor –" . . . F372, After great pain a formal feeling comes. Another poem where she imagines freezing to death is F967, Two travellers perishing in snow.

"Three times – the Billows threw me up –" . . . F514, Three times we parted – breath and I. She returns to this three-part structure of drowning in F1542, Drowning is not so pitiful.

"The Forehead copied stone –" . . . F614, 'Twas warm at first like us

"Looking at Death, is Dying – " . . . F341, 'Tis so appalling – it exhilarates –

"Flood subject" . . . L319, ED to Thomas Wentworth Higginson, 1866

"Life is death we're lengthy at" . . . L281, ED to Louisa and Frances Norcross, 1863. The lines are also printed as a couplet, F502.

"that Etherial Gain" . . . F288, My first well day since many ill

"Rafter of Satin and Roof of Stone –" . . . F124, Safe in their alabaster chambers

"as harmless as a Bee" . . . L294, ED to Susan Dickinson, 1864

"Now we have given our Mr Bowles –" . . . L535, ED to Henry and Adelaide Hills, 1878

"the Stranger" . . . L243, ED to Edward S. Dwight, 1861

"Neither fearing Extinction" . . . L968, ED to Benjamin Kimball, 1885

"'So loved her that he died'" . . . L892, ED to Catherine Sweetser, 1882

"The statement of the Lord" . . . F390, Do people moulder equally

The manuscript and this photograph of F1117, Let down the bars, oh death, belong to Amherst College Archives and Special Collections.

"and I will dwell" . . . Psalm 23:6

MORTALITY

"Called back" . . . L1046, ED to Louisa and Frances Norcross, 1886

"Step lightly on this narrow Spot –" . . . F1227, Step lightly on this narrow spot

"That Such have died enable Us" . . . F1082, That such have died enable us

"a Chapeau of fire" . . . F150, Like her the saints retire

"Read – Sweet – how others – strove –" . . . F323, Read – Sweet – how others strove

"Clear strains of Hymn" . . . F323, Read – Sweet – how others strove

"saints – with new – unsteady tongue –" . . . F230, For this accepted breath

"The bravest die" . . . F1530, Facts by our side are never sudden

"Oh how the sailor strains" . . . L248, ED to unknown, 1862. This is the final of the three Master letters.

"I want to take hold of your Hand" . . . L577, ED to Martha Gilbert Smith, 1878

"Is Immortality a bane" . . . F1757, Is immortality a bane

"Beckoning – Etruscan invitation –" . . . F300, Unto like story trouble has enticed me

CRUCIFIXION

"One Crucifixion is recorded – only –" . . . F670, One crucifixion is recorded only

"the fair schoolroom of the sky –" . . . F215, I shall know why when time is over

"Is God Love's Adversary?" . . . F792, ED to Elizabeth Holland, 1882

"When a few years old –" . . . L503, ED to Thomas Wentworth Higginson, 1877

"Even in Our Lord's" . . . L353, ED to Thomas Wentworth Higginson, 1870

"When we think of the lone effort" . . . L727, ED to Louisa and Frances Norcross, 1881

"I suppose your friend – the Stranger –" . . . L243, ED to Edward S. Dwight, 1861

"Queen of Calvary" . . . F347, I dreaded that first robin so

"Empress of Calvary" . . . F194, Title divine is mine!

"So Savior – Crucify –" . . . F283, I should have been too glad, I see

"Sabacthini" . . . F283, I should have been too glad, I see. Christ's final words on the cross are recorded as "Eli, Eli, lama sabachthani," in Matthew 27:46. Emily's spelling here is free, as it often was.

"My God, my God" . . . Matthew 27:46

"See! I usurped *thy* crucifix" . . . F1760, Proud of my broken heart since thou did'st break it

"Gethsemene and Cana are still" . . . L598, ED to Adelaide Hills, 1879. The spelling of "Gethsemene" is Emily's.

"The seeing pain one can't relieve" . . . L234, ED to Louisa and Frances Norcross, 1861

"How many barefoot shiver" . . . L207, ED to Dr. and Elizabeth Holland, 1859

"God broke his contract" . . . F1465, How ruthless are the gentle

EASTER

"Remember me" . . . For instance, F197, Jesus! thy crucifix, discussed earlier in this section. See also F1208, "Remember me" implored the thief!; F1306, Recollect the face of me.

"Lord, remember me" . . . Luke 23:42

"Truly this was the Son of God" . . . Matthew 27:54

"Better an ignis fatuus" . . . F1581, Those dying then

"I am so happy" . . . Paul Mariani, *Gerard Manley Hopkins* (New York: Viking, 2008), 425. G. F. Lahey recounts the same scene in *Gerard Manley Hopkins* (London: H. Milford, Oxford University Press, 1930), 147.

"It is finished" . . . John 19:30

"as a thief in the night" . . . 1 Thessalonians 5:2

"Dust is the only secret –" . . . F166, Dust is the only secret. The inverted spelling of "Had'nt" in the seventh line is Emily's. Franklin prints in his reading edition copy *B*, the fascicle copy. I chose to print copy *A,* which Emily sent to Sue, and which varies slightly in phrasing and punctuation. The fascicle version abounds more amply in exclamation points.

"Ineffable Avarice of Jesus" . . . L899, ED to Martha Gilbert Smith, 1884

"I will come on thee as a thief" . . . Revelation 3:3

"Behold, I come as a thief" . . . Revelation 16:15

"And I, if I be lifted up" . . . John 12:32

"what indeed is Earth but a Nest" . . . L619, ED to Elizabeth Holland, 1879

Chapter 4: Immortality

"I stand alive – Today –" . . . F698, I live with him – I see his face

LIFE

"Queen Recluse" . . . Samuel Bowles coined the term in an 1863 letter to Austin, whom he asks to give "to the Queen Recluse my especial sympathy – that she has 'overcome the world.' – Is it really true that they ring 'Old Hundred' & Aleluia' perpetually, in heaven – ask her." For Bowles, Emily's reclusiveness was evidently linked to a sort of (teasable) religious temperament. Bowles's letter is reprinted in Jay Leyda's *The Years and Hours of Emily Dickinson*, 2:76.

"the Myth" . . . Mabel Loomis Todd, who would become Austin's mistress and the first editor of Emily's poems, had a hearty hand in perpetuating these rumors. She wrote her parents in 1881, after two months in Amherst, "I must tell you about the *character* of Amherst. It is a lady whom the people call the *Myth*." Mabel goes on to call her "the climax of all the family oddity," describing all the familiar traits: the reclusiveness, the dressing in white, the lowering of treats to neighborhood children, etc. Quoted in Sewall, *The Life of Emily Dickinson*, 216.

"If 'Miss Emily' could live without" . . . Martha Dickinson Bianchi, *Emily Dickinson Face to Face*, 36. While Martha's writings on Emily have been put on the back shelf for scholarly purposes not concerned with Dickinson's reception history, as too indebted to family legend and a certain romanticizing of the poet aunt, they provide a wonderful counterpoint to the whispers about how weird Emily was. In her writings we meet Emily in the flesh, quirky still, but real. So for instance, we hear how Emily once spotted Mattie headed out in bright red heels and remarked, "Going to a wake, I take it, dear?" (33). We meet her in such comments.

"I, who run from so many" . . . L245, ED to Louisa Norcross, 1861

Emily, you wretch! . . . Emily's cousin Gertrude M. Graves narrates this scene in a 1930 *Boston Sunday Globe* article, which Thomas H. Johnson quotes in his note to Emily's 1877 letter (515) to Bowles, the one she sent after him to apologize for her initial refusal to descend.

"The Apostle's inimitable apology" . . . L944, ED to Eben and Mary Loomis, 1884

"The soul must go by Death alone" . . . L321, ED to Elizabeth Holland, 1866

"Matty, child, no one could ever punish" . . . Martha Dickinson Bianchi, *Emily Dickinson Face to Face*, 66. Emily spells her name "Mattie" consistently, while the woman herself spells it "Matty."

"ravenousness of fondness" . . . L824, ED to Maria Whitney, 1883

"Is there not a sweet wolf" . . . L824, ED to Maria Whitney, 1883

"Best Things dwell out of Sight" . . . F1012, Best things dwell out of sight

"How inspiriting to the clandestine Mind" . . . L853, ED to Susan Dickinson, 1883

"the solitary prowess" . . . F790, Growth of man like growth of nature

"The Wayward Nun – beneath the Hill –" . . . F745, Sweet mountains – ye tell me no lie

"The Soul that hath a Guest" . . . F592, The soul that hath a guest

"Everywhere alone" . . . F594, What I hoped I feared

AFTERLIFE

"Mortality is fatal" . . . F2, Sic transit gloria mundi. Emily's two earliest poems were both written as valentines, the first in 1850, the second in 1852. This second poem was published in the *Springfield Daily Republican*, along with the editorial comment wishing that "a correspondence, more direct than this" would be established between the newspaper and the writer. Emily would go on to form a close friendship with the editor, Samuel Bowles.

"I have just seen a funeral" . . . L9, ED to Abiah Root, 1846

"for dust thou art" . . . Genesis 3:19

"So *you* would feel" . . . "Charles's Last Sickness," from the January 1837 *Sabbath School Visitor*, is quoted in Habegger's *My Wars Are Laid Away in Books*, 101.

"How sad would it be" . . . L10, ED to Abiah Root, 1846

"The Dust like the Mosquito" . . . L235, ED to Mary Bowles, 1861

"Son of man, can these bones live?" . . . Ezekiel 37:3–5

"Behind me – dips Eternity –" . . . F743, Behind me dips eternity

"a Hymn they used to sing" . . . L521, ED to Elizabeth Holland, 1877

"Their Father in Heaven remember" . . . L263, ED to Louisa Norcross, 1862

"Overcoat of Clay" . . . F973, Death is a dialogue between

"must vanish" . . . William Wordsworth, "Conclusion," *The River Duddon, a Series of Sonnets* (London: Longman, Hurst, Rees, Orme, and Brown, 1820), 35.

"The Earth reversed her Hemispheres –" . . . F633, I saw no way – The heavens were stitched

"Convex – and Concave Witness –" . . . F830, The admirations and contempts of time

"A speck opon a Ball –" . . . F633, I saw no way – The heavens were stitched. The spelling of "opon" is Emily's.

"We all have moments with the dust" . . . L337, ED to Louisa Norcross, 1869

"Vastness – is but the Shadow" . . . L735, ED to Thomas Wentworth Higginson, 1881

"Those that are worthy of Life" . . . L294, ED to Susan Dickinson, 1864

"Emerging from an Abyss" . . . L1024, ED to Susan Dickinson, 1885

RESURRECTION

"Obtaining but his own extent" . . . F1573, Obtaining but his own extent. As I discuss later, there are two versions of this poem. Here I print copy A, which was sent to James D. Clark and is also printed as L776.

"Oh give it motion" . . . F1550, Oh give it motion – deck it sweet

"Resumption Morn" . . . F165, I have never seen "volcanoes"

"When Cerements let go" . . . F192, 'Tis anguish grander than delight

"I think just how my shape will rise –" . . . F252, I think just how my shape will rise

"Costumeless Consciousness" . . . F1486, Those not live yet

"But some man will say" . . . 1 Corinthians 15:35

"flesh and blood cannot inherit" . . . 1 Corinthians 15:50

"This corruptible must put on" . . . 1 Corinthians 15:53

"'Sown in corruption'!" . . . F153, "Sown in dishonor"!

"'And with what Body do they come'?" . . . F1537, "And with what body do they come"? She further engages the question of the resurrection body in F1448, With pinions of disdain, and F1627, The spirit lasts but in what mode.

"While the Clergyman tells Father" . . . L391, ED to Elizabeth Holland, 1873

"Why, Resurrection had to wait" . . . F1545, A pang is more conspicuous in spring

"Reach hither thy finger" . . . John 20:27

"We shall not all sleep" . . . 1 Corinthians 15:51

"Were the Statement 'We shall not all sleep'" . . . L568, ED to unknown, 1878

"In a moment" . . . 1 Corinthians 15:52

"that profounder site" . . . F1696, There is a solitude of space

"indestructible estate" . . . F1359, You cannot take itself

"Sufficient Continent" . . . F1113, All circumstances are the frame

"The smallest Human Heart's extent" . . . F1178, The life we have is very great. *Expanse* and *extent* are variant choices for one word in F1432, I have no life to live, itself an earlier version of the poem, "I have no life but this."

"The Granite crumb let go –" . . . F243, That after horror – that 'twas us

"You Cannot take itself" . . . F1359, You cannot take itself

"There are no Dead" . . . L338, ED to Catherine Sweetser, 1870

"Dying dispels nothing" . . . L523, ED to Richard H. Mather, 1877

"To die is not to go –" . . . F1354, Two lengths has every day

"But that they have Abode –" . . . F1460, Than heaven more remote

"We are eternal – dear" . . . L577, ED to Martha Gilbert Smith, 1878 "power to be finite ceased" . . . F1515, Estranged from beauty none can be

"'It is finished' can never be said" . . . L555, ED to Elizabeth Holland, 1878

"Obtaining but *our* own extent" . . . F1573, Obtaining but his own extent [emphasis mine]. The "our" version was sent to Thomas Wentworth Higginson, L767, in 1882.

"Tender Pioneer" . . . F727, Life is what we make it

"sent his Son to test the Plank" . . . F1459, How brittle are the piers

"His sure foot preceding –" . . . F727, Life is what we make it

SILENCE

"Now, *my* George Eliot" . . . L710, ED to Louisa and Frances Norcross, 1881

"God chooses repellent settings" . . . L692, ED to Elizabeth Holland, 1881. The spelling of "dont" without an apostrophe is Emily's.

"What do I think of glory" . . . L389, ED to Louisa and Frances Norcross, 1873

"None of us know her". . . L979, ED to Elizabeth Holland, 1885

"'Crowns of Life' are servile Prizes" . . . F1386, "Faithful to the end" amended. There are five versions of the poem. The "servile Prizes" line comes from a manuscript that dates to 1876 and was also sent to Thomas Wentworth Higginson. The "Try it on" version exists in both draft and fair copy form, but was not sent to anyone as far as we know.

"We said she said Lord Jesus –" . . . Prose Fragment 51 in *Letters of Emily Dickinson*

"The Fiction of 'Santa Claus'" . . . L794, ED to Elizabeth Holland, 1882

"The cordiality of the Sacrament" . . . L926, ED to Clara Newman Turner, 1884

"Speech is one symptom of affection" . . . F1694, Speech is one symptom of affection. The apostrophe in the possessive pronoun is Emily's.

"The broadest words are so narrow" . . . L413, ED to Thomas Wentworth Higginson, 1874

"The gift of belief" . . . L710, ED to Louisa and Frances Norcross, 1881

"The appetite for silence" . . . Prose fragment 106 in *Letters of Emily Dickinson*

"Aloud / Is nothing that is chief" . . . F1057, Embarrassment of one another

"Amazing human heart" . . . L710, ED to Louisa and Frances Norcross, 1881. Emily used the same line in letter 715 to Dr. Holland.

IMMORTALITY

"I live with Him – I see His face –" . . . F698, I live with him – I see his face

"the Flood subject" . . . L319, ED to Thomas Wentworth Higginson, 1866

"I suppose we are all thinking" . . . L332, ED to Perez Cowan, 1869

"I fear we shall care very little" . . . L969, ED to Maria Whitney, 1885

"a rendezvous where there is no Face" . . . L856, ED to Susan Dickinson, 1883

"Vista of reunion" . . . L896, ED to Charles H. Clark, 1884

"second circle of sad Hell" . . . John Keats, Sonnet 20, "On a Dream after Reading of Paolo and Francesca in Dante's Inferno," in *The Poems of John Keats* (London: Everyman, 1992), 249.

"in Heaven they neither woo" . . . L750, ED to Judge Lord, 1882

"For in the resurrection they neither marry" . . . Matthew 22:30

"what an imperfect place!" . . . L750, ED to Judge Lord, 1882

"Forever – is composed of Nows –" . . . F690, Forever is composed of nows

"I cannot live with You –" . . . F706

"Because that you are going" . . . F1314

"The 'Life that is to be'" . . . F1314, Because that you are going

"And were You lost" . . . F706, I cannot live with you

"thou shalt love the Lord" . . . Mark 12:30

"Susan's Idolator keeps a Shrine" . . . L325, ED to Susan Dickinson, 1868

"Oh, my too beloved" . . . L560, ED to Judge Lord, 1878

"The trespass of my rustic Love" . . . L750, ED to Judge Lord, 1882

"While others go to Church" . . . L790, ED to Judge Lord, 1882

"no other gods before me" . . . Exodus 20:3

"Why should we censure Othello" . . . L1016, ED to Mabel Loomis Todd, 1885

"Well done, thou good and faithful servant" . . . Matthew 25:21

"and love, you know, is God" . . . L669, ED to Louisa and Frances Norcross, 1880

"The Love a Life can show Below" . . . F285, The love a life can show below

"Awful Father of Love" . . . F1200, Whatever it is she has tried it

"the 'Throne' of Tenderness" . . . L689, ED to Elizabeth Holland, 1881

"God is love" . . . 1 John 4:8

"Source of Love" . . . L828, ED to Catherine Sweetser, 1883

"'Tis easier than a Saviour" . . . L536, ED to Mary Bowles, 1878

"And through a Riddle, at the last –" . . . F373, This world is not conclusion

"The Judgment" . . . F699, The power to the true to you; see also F711, I meant to
    have but modest needs, and F619, Did you ever stand in a cavern's mouth

"If 'God is Love'" . . . F1314, Because that you are going

"All that are in the graves" . . . John 5:28–29 [emphasis mine]

"Bisecting Messenger" . . . F1421, Of Paradise' existence

"And then for those" . . . William Bright, "And now O Father mindful of the love,"
    Hymnal 1982 (New York: Church Hymnal Corp, 1982), hymn 337.

"Love will not expire" . . . L357, ED to Louisa and Frances Norcross, 1870

"I give his Angels charge –" . . . L975, ED to Mary Warner Crowell, 1885; L991, ED
    to Catherine Sweetser, 1885; L1012, ED to Samuel Bowles the younger, 1885.

"I will not let thee go" . . . L1035, ED to Sarah Tuckerman, 1886; L1042, ED to
    Thomas Wentworth Higginson, 1886.

"Pugilist and Poet". . . L1042, ED to Thomas Wentworth Higginson, 1886

"To live lasts always" . . . L364, ED to Susan Dickinson, 1871

"It may surprise you" . . . L562, ED to Judge Lord, 1878

Chapter 5: Beauty

"The Bird her punctual music brings" . . . F1556, The bird her punctual music brings

ECSTASY

"Take all away from me, but leave me Ecstasy" . . . F1671, Take all away from me but leave me ecstasy. There are six versions of this poem, beginning with one written on an advertising flyer announcing a sale. In her later years, Emily often composed on whatever scraps of paper were at hand, so poems squeeze onto the flap of an envelope or nestle in the margin of a recipe. The other versions of this poem were sent in letters to Eben and Mary Loomis, Helen Hunt Jackson (three draft compositions of this letter remain), and Samuel Bowles the younger. This last version is the one used here.

"My mind never comes home" . . . L414, ED to Louisa and Frances Norcross, 1874

"quietly stole away" . . . L782, ED to Cornelia Sweetser, 1882

"Homeless at home" . . . F1603, To the bright east she flies. The poem was sent to Maria Whitney (L815) in 1883.

"my dearest earthly friend" . . . L807, ED to James D. Clark, 1883

"There are too many to count" . . . L882, ED to Elizabeth Holland, 1884

"I hardly dare to know" . . . L891, ED to Louisa and Frances Norcross, 1884

"Eight Saturday noons ago" . . . L907, ED to Louisa and Frances Norcross, 1884

"But it is growing damp" . . . L907, ED to Louisa and Frances Norcross, 1884

"1883 October 5: Gilbert (nephew) dies, age eight" . . . This is how the entry for Gib's death reads in the chronology offered in Sewall's *Life of Emily Dickinson*.

"The little boy we laid away" . . . L907, ED to Louisa and Frances Norcross, 1884

"'Open the Door, open the Door' they are waiting" . . . L873, ED to Elizabeth Holland, 1883

"The Death of the Loved" . . . L801, ED to Elizabeth Holland, 1883

"Memory is a strange Bell –" . . . L792, ED to Elizabeth Holland, 1882

"The Vision of Immortal Life" . . . L868, ED to Susan Dickinson, 1883

"Glee intuitive and lasting" . . . L472, ED to Mary Higginson, 1876

"For each extatic instant" . . . F109, For each extatic instant

"You speak of 'disillusion'" . . . L860, ED to Maria Whitney, 1883

"Blessed are the poor in spirit" . . . Matthew 5:3–4

"Blessed are they that play" . . . L690, ED to Louisa and Frances Norcross, 1881

"Winter under cultivation" . . . F1720, Winter under cultivation

"When thou goest through the Waters" . . . L221, ED to Susan Davis Phelps, 1860

"'Come unto me.' Beloved Commandment" . . . L595, ED to Adelaide Hills, 1879

"unaccustomed wine" . . . F126, I bring an unaccustomed wine

"cup of cold water" . . . Matthew 10:42

"Inasmuch as ye have done" . . . Matthew 25:40

"You are a great poet" . . . L444a, Helen Hunt Jackson to ED, 1875. Helen Hunt Jackson had communicated with Thomas Niles, of Roberts Brothers in Boston, about Emily's verses, leading him to begin soliciting her. His letters requesting poems and manuscripts (as well as hers to him, asking that he return the ones she'd sent him) are printed in Johnson's edition as L749b, L813a, L813b, and L814a. Niles would go on to publish Emily's "Success is counted sweetest" in his 1879 volume *A Masque of Poets*. At the time of its publication, Emily's poem was printed anonymously, but critics soon wondered if it might not belong to Ralph Waldo Emerson.

"It is a cruel wrong" . . . L937a, Helen Hunt Jackson to ED, 1884

"The Savior's only signature" . . . L1004, ED to Mabel Loomis Todd, 1885

"Last – Least – / The Cross' – Request –" . . . F541, The test of love is death

"penurious" . . . L261, ED to Thomas Wentworth Higginson, 1862. That she did not publish was clearly her own choice, as opportunities were not wanting.

"He has obligation" . . . F1362, Lift it – with the feathers

"For unto whomsoever much has been given" . . . Luke 12:48

"Publication – is the Auction" . . . F788, Publication is the auction

"I wish I might say one liquid word" . . . L859, ED to Charles H. Clark, 1883

"Mine be the Ministry" . . . F491, The world feels dusty

PORTRAIT

"Could you believe me – without?" . . . L268, ED to Thomas Wentworth Higginson, 1862

"A step like a pattering child's" . . . L342a, Thomas Wentworth Higginson to Mary Higginson, 1870

"eccentric poetess" . . . The phrase is taken from a note Higginson wrote his sisters on December 9, 1873, and is quoted in Johnson's note to L405, the letter Emily wrote to Higginson after his visit.

"She came to me with two day lilies" . . . L342a, Thomas Wentworth Higginson to Mary Higginson, 1870

"Oh why do the insane so cling" . . . Thomas Wentworth Higginson to his sisters, quoted in Johnson's note to L405.

"The tiniest ones are the mightiest –" . . . L564, ED to Jonathan Jenkins, 1878

"The Bobolink is gone – the Rowdy of the Meadow –" . . . F1620, The bobolink is gone – the rowdy of the meadow

"Unless we become as Rogues" . . . L715, ED to Dr. Holland, 1881

"in a state of mind very near frenzy" . . . L125, ED to Austin Dickinson, 1853

"There were high pews painted white" . . . Martha Dickinson Bianchi, *The Life and Letters of Emily Dickinson*, 88–89

"The morning exercises" . . . L125, ED to Austin Dickinson, 1853

"I know of no choicer ecstasy" . . . L389, ED to Louisa and Frances Norcross, 1873

"Mrs. S gets bigger" . . . L339, ED to Louisa and Frances Norcross, 1870

"The truth I do not dare to know" . . . F1750, Consulting summer's clock

"Our Pastor says we are a 'Worm'" . . . L193, ED to Samuel Bowles, 1858

"What a privilege it is to be so insignificant" . . . L194, ED to Susan Dickinson, 1858. The spelling of the contraction "was'nt" is Emily's.

"I fell to reading" . . . ED to Joseph Lyman, Letter 3, *The Lyman Letters*, ed. Richard B. Sewall (Amherst: University of Massachusetts Press, 1965), 73.

"If prayers had any answers to them" . . . L133, ED to Dr. and Elizabeth Holland, 1853

"I hope God will forgive me" . . . L172, ED to Susan Gilbert (Dickinson), 1854

"although Emily took liberties" . . . Martha Dickinson Bianchi, *Emily Dickinson Face to Face*, 55

"I believe the love of God" . . . L230, ED to Louisa and Frances Norcross, 1861

The manuscript and this image of F1620, The bobolink is gone, belong to Amherst College Archives and Special Collections.

"the Sky" . . . L521, ED to Elizabeth Holland, 1877

"Bobolinks around the throne" . . . F82, We should not mind so small a flower

"The crucifix requires no glove" . . . L539, ED to Maria Whitney, 1878

GRASPED BY GOD

"I heard, as if I had no Ear" . . . F996, I heard as if I had no ear

"Grasped by God" . . . Prose Fragment 76 in *Letters of Emily Dickinson*. The photograph of the manuscript is reprinted with permission of Amherst College Archives and Special Collections, who owns the original. The three words also appear as part of poem F1542, Drowning is not so pitiful, with a slight swap of *by* for *of*. The small scrap of language invites the question: were these words the stem of the poem in which they appear? In the poem, as in "I heard as if I had no Ear," Emily recounts a tri-part experience: this time, the drowning man surfaces three times before, at last, he is "grasped of God."

"*Feu . . . Certitude, certitude*" . . . Blaise Pascal, "*Pensées Retranchées,*" *Pensées*, #711

"Blessed are they that have not" . . . John 20:29 ·

"*En un instant*" . . . Paul Claudel, "Ma Conversion," in *Contacts et circonstances, Œuvres en Prose* (Paris: Gallimard La Pléiade, 1940), 1009–10. The passage reads, "*En un instant mon cœur fut touché et je crus. Je crus, d'une telle force d'adhésion, d'un tel soulèvement de tout mon être, d'une conviction si puissante, d'une telle certitude ne laissant place à aucune espèce de doute, que, depuis, tous les livres, tous les raisonnements, tous les hasards d'une vie agitée, n'ont pu ébranler ma foi, ni, à vrai dire, la toucher.*"

"Conversion of the Mind" . . . F627, I think I was enchanted

"caught up to the third heaven" . . . 2 Corinthians 12:2

"a thorn in the flesh" . . . 2 Corinthians 12:7

REVELATION

"To pile like Thunder to it's close" . . . F1353, To pile like thunder to it's close. The apostrophe in "it's" is Emily's.

"Bees are Black – with Gilt Surcingles –" . . . F1426, Bees are black with gilt surcingles

"Whose fingers comb the Sky –" . . . F334, Of all the sounds despatched abroad

"I bequeath myself to the dirt" . . . Walt Whitman, *Leaves of Grass* (1855), in *Complete Poetry and Collected Prose* (New York: Library of America, 1982), 88.

"I am glad you are in the open Air –" . . . L866, ED to Elizabeth Holland, 1883

"Through the Dark Sod – as Education –" . . . F559, Through the dark sod as education

"'Consider the Lilies'" . . . L904, ED to Alice Tuckerman, 1884

"The heavens declare the glory of God" . . . Psalm 19:1

"Their line is gone out" . . . Psalm 19:4

"Consider the lilies of the field" . . . Matthew 6:28–30

"liquid Commandment" . . . L897, ED to Catherine Sweetser, 1884

"Were all it's advice" . . . L897, ED to Catherine Sweetser, 1884. The apostrophe in "it's" is Emily's.

"sacrament of summer days" . . . F122, These are the days when birds come back

"Our man has mown today" . . . L190, ED to Catherine Sweetser, 1858

"certain Slant of light" . . . F320, There's a certain slant of light

"Nicodemus' Mystery" . . . F90, An altered look about the hills. The apostrophe in "it's" is Emily's.

"Nature and God – I neither knew" . . . F803, Nature and God I neither knew

"The Star's Etruscan Argument" . . . F1574, The moon upon her fluent route

"benediction / And badinage" . . . F1778, High from the earth I heard a bird

"with no disrespect to Genesis" . . . L552, ED to Mrs. Thomas P. Field, 1878

"I was thinking, today" . . . L280, ED to Thomas Wentworth Higginson, 1863

"In the name of the Bee –" . . . F23, In the name of the bee

BEAUTY

"The Bird her punctual music brings" . . . F1556, The bird her punctual music brings. The apostrophe in "it's" is Emily's.

"the punctuality / Of the New England Farmer –" . . . F1520, The robin is a Gabriel

"In humble circumstances –" . . . F1520, The robin is a Gabriel

"Transport's Working Classes –" . . . F1520, The robin is a Gabriel

"I seem to myself a robin" . . . L39, ED to Abiah Root, 1850. She also aligns herself with the robin in F872, Deprived of other banquet, and L86, ED to Jane Humphrey, 1852.

"Durham Breast" . . . F1572, Come show thy Durham breast. No other bird can compete with the robin for its favored spot in Emily's writings, though many others also had poetic love lavished upon them. The bobolink appears in ten poems, the jay and sparrow both in eight, the oriole in four, the wren in three, and the hummingbird in just one.

"The Robin's my Criterion for Tune –" . . . F256, The robin's my criterion for tune

"I raise only robins on my farm" . . . L454, ED to Eugenia Hall, 1876

"They are writing *now*" . . . L890, ED to Elizabeth Holland, 1884. The letter goes on to note that they are writing not poems, but letters—interesting at a moment when Emily herself would have written chiefly letters, too.

"Wherefore sing" . . . L269, ED to Elizabeth Holland, 1862

the thickest years of her writing . . . R.W. Franklin attributes 227 poems to 1862, 295 poems to 1863, 98 to 1864, and 229 to 1865.

"Beauty crowds me till I die" . . . F1687, Beauty crowds me till I die

"The Definition of Beauty is" . . . F797, The definition of beauty is

"Estranged from Beauty – none can be –" . . . F1515, Estranged from beauty none can be

"Beauty – be not caused – It Is –" . . . F654, Beauty be not caused – It is

"Before Abraham was" . . . John 8:58

"I am the way" . . . John 14:6

"To bend the eye" . . . F538, Must be a wo

"There is a syllableless Sea" . . . F1689, To tell the beauty would decrease

"I had felt some uncertainty" . . . L920, ED to Cornelia Sweetser, 1884

"How vast is the chastisement of Beauty" . . . L965, ED to unknown, 1885

"troubadours" . . . F79, New feet within my garden go; F12, I had a guinea golden; F1520, The Robin is a Gabriel. An early draft of this last poem opens with the line, "The Robin is a Troubadour."

"Paragon of Chivalry" . . . F1306, Recollect the face of me

"Angels have that modest way" . . . F1600, Forever honored be the tree

"Gabriels" . . . . F1520, The robin is a Gabriel. Also F1600, Forever honored be the tree

"Like Trains of Cars on Tracks of Plush" . . . F1213, Like trains of cars on tracks of plush

"Breathe in Ear more modern" . . . F50, It did not surprise me

"I told my Soul to sing –" . . . F423, The first day's night had come

"I will not let thee go" . . . L1035 to Sarah Tuckerman, 1886; L1042 to Thomas Wentworth Higginson, 1886

ACKNOWLEDGMENTS

"Gratitude is not the mention of a tenderness" . . . L273, ED to Louisa and Frances Norcross, 1862. Also reprinted as F1120, a stanza that Emily sent to Sue.

"the Creek turns Sea –" . . . L559, ED to Judge Lord, 1878

For a discussion guide and additional
resources visit www.kristinlemay.org

ABOUT PARACLETE PRESS

WHO WE ARE

Paraclete Press is a publisher of books, recordings, and DVDs on Christian spirituality. Our publishing represents a full expression of Christian belief and practice—from Catholic to Evangelical, from Protestant to Orthodox.

We are the publishing arm of the Community of Jesus, an ecumenical monastic community in the Benedictine tradition. As such, we are uniquely positioned in the marketplace without connection to a large corporation and with informal relationships to many branches and denominations of faith.

WHAT WE ARE DOING

Books Paraclete publishes books that show the richness and depth of what it means to be Christian. Although Benedictine spirituality is at the heart of all that we do, we publish books that reflect the Christian experience across many cultures, time periods, and houses of worship. We publish books that nourish the vibrant life of the church and its people—books about spiritual practice, formation, history, ideas, and customs.

We have several different series, including the best-selling Paraclete Essentials and Paraclete Giants series of classic texts in contemporary English; A Voice from the Monastery—men and women monastics writing about living a spiritual life today; award-winning poetry; best-selling gift books for children on the occasions of baptism and first communion; and the Active Prayer Series that brings creativity and liveliness to any life of prayer.

Recordings From Gregorian chant to contemporary American choral works, our music recordings celebrate sacred choral music through the centuries. Paraclete distributes the recordings of the internationally acclaimed choir Gloriæ Dei Cantores, praised for their "rapt and fathomless spiritual intensity" by *American Record Guide*, and the Gloriæ Dei Cantores Schola, which specializes in the study and performance of Gregorian chant. Paraclete is also the exclusive North American distributor of the recordings of the Monastic Choir of St. Peter's Abbey in Solesmes, France, long considered to be a leading authority on Gregorian chant.

Videos Our videos offer spiritual help, healing, and biblical guidance for life issues: grief and loss, marriage, forgiveness, anger management, facing death, and spiritual formation.

Learn more about us at our website: www.paracletepress.com, or call us toll-free at 1-800-451-5006.

SCAN TO READ MORE

You may also be interested in . . .

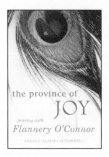

The Province of Joy
Praying with Flannery O'Connor
by Angela Alaimo O'Donnell

"Like a beautiful quilt, *The Province of Joy* is a deeply loving, imaginative work of art and faith."
—Elizabeth A. Johnson

This unique "Book of Hours" is modeled on the spiritual life and prayer practices of one of our most interesting writers.

"Flannery O'Connor's stories help us see grace in the most difficult of circumstances. O'Donnell artfully combines selections from her writings with daily prayers and readings for something wonderful: a prayer book that is old and new, timely and timeless, comforting and provocative."
—James Martin, SJ, author of *Between Heaven and Mirth*

ISBN: 978-1-55725-703-1
$16.99, Paperback

Shirt of Flame
A Year with Saint Thérèse of Lisieux
by Heather King

If you have not read Heather King before, her honesty may shock you. In this remarkable memoir, you will see how a convert with a checkered past spends a year reflecting upon St. Thérèse of Lisieux and discovers the radical faith, true love, and abundant life of a cloistered nineteenth-century French nun.

ISBN: 978-1-55725-808-3
$16.99, French Flap